Eight steps toward recovery

Step One: accepting that this human life will bring suffering
Step Two: seeing how we create extra suffering in our lives
Step Three: embracing impermanence to show us that our
    suffering can end
Step Four: being willing to step onto the path of recovery and
    discover freedom
Step Five: transforming our speech, actions, and livelihood
Step Six: placing positive values at the center of our lives
Step Seven: making every effort to stay on the path of
    recovery
Step Eight: helping others by sharing the benefits we have
    gained

T0273793

Praise for *Eight Step Recovery: Using the Buddha's Teachings to Overcome Addiction*

Winner of the 2015 International Book Awards and the 2014 USA Best Book Awards

"'The Buddha was in recovery'. Taking this bold statement as a starting point, this wonderful book shows how we are all addicted to aspects of life and can all benefit from training our minds and hearts to be free of the tyranny of compulsion. The Mindfulness-Based Addiction Recovery (MBAR) programme draws on a wide range of the Buddha's practical, yet deeply profound, teachings. Over the eight steps you are given a priceless gift – the possibility to gain mastery over your mind and heart and find freedom."

Vidyamala Burch OBE, co-founder and director of Breathworks, author of *Living Well with Pain and Illness* and *Mindfulness for Health*

"Mindfulness is increasingly recognised as offering an important tool for recovery from addiction and other mental disorders. In *Eight Step Recovery*, we are shown how other teachings from the Buddhist tradition can also play an important role in recovery. The eight steps outlined here provide a simple, wise, and practical approach to recovery from a wide range of compulsive patterns of behaviour associated with suffering. They provide a spiritual pathway to recovery for people from any faith tradition, as well as for those who are not religious, and for those who suffer from addiction as well as those who are simply aware of the suffering associated with the human condition. This is a book for everyone!"

Professor Chris Cook, Director of the Project for Spirituality, Theology & Health, Durham University, UK

"Blending Mindfulness Based Addiction Recovery with traditional Buddhist teachings and moving personal stories, Valerie Mason-John and Dr Paramabandhu Groves give us a wise and compassionate approach to recovery from the range of addictions. This comprehensive approach to treatment will be a valuable tool for addicts and addiction professionals alike."

Kevin Griffin, author of *One Breath at a Time: Buddhism and the Twelve Steps*

"Through Buddhist teachings, personal experiences, and case examples, this book provides a wise illustration of the fundamental processes underlying a broad range of addictive behaviors. Mason-John and Groves offer here a practical and compassionate step-by-step guide to freedom from the deep trappings and suffering of addiction."

Sarah Bowen, PhD, Assistant Professor, Department of Psychiatry and Behavioral Sciences, University of Washington, author of *Mindfulness-Based Relapse Prevention for Addictive Behaviors: A Clinician's Guide*

"Instead of searching for commonalities between the twelve steps and the dharma, these authors go straight to the Buddha's teachings and practices as the basis for overcoming the suffering of addiction . . . *Eight Step Recovery* is a useful resource for Buddhists, addicts, and addiction experts alike."

Joan Duncan Oliver, *Tricycle: The Buddhist Review*

"Should become a classic. This book is beautifully written, well thought through and firm but compassionate in its delivery. While it addresses people who clearly experience the serious end of addictions, I found I could apply it effectively to myself and my own range of more moderate addictive and negative tendencies. Its Buddhist mindset and structuring was clear and upfront, yet its usefulness and applicability to non-Buddhists, half-Buddhists or just anyone came through strongly. I found it repaid working-and-living through, rather than just 'reading'. It deserves to join a classic cluster of books whose careful reading in effect delivers a DIY course at home for the reader. I found this book helped me with a number of things: negative thinking, ill-will, attitudes to sex and to alcohol, self-compassion, self-acceptance, self-appreciation, to name but a few. I learned that to treat difficult aspects of myself as 'addictions' seemed, curiously, to be very effective and liberating. A fine piece of work, this book is *not* just for 'addicts'. It also unpacks some aspects of Buddhist thought really clearly. Big thanks to both authors."

Tony Mitton, award-winning author of *Wayland*

Eight Step Recovery

Using the Buddha's Teachings to Overcome Addiction

Valerie Mason-John
Dr Paramabandhu Groves

ⓦ

Published by
Windhorse Publications
38 Newmarket Road
Cambridge
CB5 8DT
UK

info@windhorsepublications.com
windhorsepublications.com

Cover design by Katarzyna Manecka
Photograph Vimalasara © Ángel Catena
Photograph Paramabandhu © Onur Pinar

Typeset and designed by Ben Cracknell Studios

British Library Cataloguing in Publication Data:
A catalogue record for this book is available from the British Library.

ISBN: 978 1 911407 12 6

About the authors

Valerie (Vimalasara) Mason-John has worked as an international correspondent covering Aboriginal deaths in custody, and interviewed Sinn Fein prisoners and ex-rebels from the Sierra Leone war. Their work in the field of conflict transitioned into working with gangs, the incarcerated, bullies, and challenging behavior. Valerie is equipped to work in many modalities. A teacher in the Triratna Buddhist Community, a mindfulness trainer, and a founding facilitator of Dr. Gabor Maté's Compassionate Inquiry, they have also trained in Internal Family Systems, Embodied Somatics, Breathworks, and Shamanism. Their eleven books include *First Aid Kit for the Mind: Breaking the Cycle of Habitual Behaviors, Detox Your Heart: Meditations for Emotional Trauma, Eight Step Recovery: Using the Buddha's Teachings to Overcome Addiction*, and more recently *I'm Still Your Negro: An Homage to James Baldwin*. They work as an international public speaker and trainer in the field of mindfulness for trauma and addiction, and interview high-profile Buddhist and spiritual teachers and leaders for the Wisdom for Life platform. Valerie/Vimalasara has a private counseling/healing practice and lives in Canada with their partner.

Paramabandhu Groves is a psychiatrist for the National Health Service (NHS) in the UK, and has specialized in the field of addiction for twenty years. He is the clinical director of Breathing Space, which is the health and well-being wing of the London Buddhist Centre, and he teaches mindfulness-based approaches to help with depression, addiction, and stress. He developed the Mindfulness-Based Relapse Prevention course for addiction, renamed the Mindfulness-Based Addiction Recovery (MBAR) course, which has successfully run in both the UK and Canada. He is the author of *Practical Buddhism: Mindfulness and Skilful Living in the Modern Era*, and has published academic papers and contributed to several books in the field of addiction. He is an ordained member of the Triratna Buddhist Community.

Acknowledgments

This book would not have been possible without Windhorse Publications' confidence and belief in our vision. Thank you so much to Priyananda for trusting in a vision that was just a rough outline on the page when we approached him. We also have much gratitude toward our developmental editor Vishvapani Blomfield for his keen eye and knowledge of the teachings of the Buddha. We are appreciative of Hilary Jones who did our first copy-edit so we could hand over a clean copy to our publishers. To Dhatvisvari who did our final copy-edit with her diligent eye. Windhorse Publications have been a committed advocate for our book and we have appreciated their tremendous support. We are very grateful to Michelle Bernard for guiding the book through the production stage, and Hannah Atkinson for her work particularly in the marketing and online promotion. Thank you especially to both Priyananda and Michelle who have been with the book right from the start – thank you – and to Giulietta for joining the team. Our readers, Amala, Dayasiddhi, Carolyn Dickenson, Jacky Smola, Julie Lloyd, Liz McGrath, Manjusiha, Marta Meengs, Navachitta, Ruth Atkinson, Ron Frances, Terry Klotz, Upakarin, and Vijayadipa, were so generous in giving up their time to read early drafts and offering their critical helpful feedback.

Thank you so much to Bodhipaksa for his website Fake Buddhist Quotes, which put us on the right track. We are grateful for the input from Jodi Loudfoot, Lynn Fraser, and Roseanna. We would also like to thank the people who have been part of the free 21-day meditation download that accompanies this book, which you will find on our website http://thebuddhistcentre.com/eightsteps: Advayaprabha, Ana Hernandez, Dharmasakya, Dhiraprabha, Candradasa,

Kate Munger, founder of Threshold Choir, Helen Greenspan, Jayakara, Laura Fannon, Nina Wise, Saraka, Sugati, Phap Ho, The Alaska None, Sanghasiha, Karunachitta, Thich Nhat Hanh, Vandanajyoti, and Yeshe Chodron (Laurie Lesk). Thanks to Jinamitra for recording all our reflections in the book, and to Subhadra and Andrew Riches for their skilled editing of the audio files. Behind every writer there are those people who support the creative process, so we would like to acknowledge the kind support of Cheryl Kehoe and the Samaggavasa Community, and the Vancouver Triratna Recovery Monday Team. Thanks also to all our friends who support and believe in our work.

Publisher's acknowledgments

Windhorse Publications wishes to gratefully acknowledge a grant from the Future Dharma Fund and the Triratna European Chairs' Assembly Fund towards the production of this book.

Accessing the guided meditations

This book has been produced with accompanying guided meditations and reflections by the authors, and they are marked in the text with an icon 🛐. These audio files are available in the following ways:

- For the *print* edition and the *non-enhanced ebook* editions, they are available as free downloads, either streamed directly from the Web or downloaded in MP3 format. Please go to bit.ly/eightsteprecovery or windhorsepublications.com/eight-step-recovery-audio

- For the *enhanced ebook* edition, they are embedded in your file, and can be played by simply clicking on the icon.

Terms of use

Also by Valerie Mason-John

First Aid Kit for the Mind: Breaking the Cycle of Habitual Behaviours
Detox Your Heart: Meditations for Healing Emotional Trauma
The Great Black North: Contemporary African Canadian Poetry
Broken Voices: "Untouchable" Women Speak Out
Borrowed Body
Brown Girl in the Ring
Talking Black
Making Black Waves

Also by Dr. Paramabandhu Groves

Practical Buddhism: Mindfulness and
Skilful Living in the Modern Era
Mindful Emotion: A Short Course in Kindness
(with Dr. Jed Shamel)

Authors' note

Apart from the authors' names – Valerie and Paramabandhu – all other names attached to personal stories are fictitious in order to protect the confidentiality of individuals.

Dedication

May those who have suffered be happy!
For the happiness of all beings
For the benefit of all beings
With body, speech, and mindfulness
We dedicate this book.

Adapted from *Puja: The Triratna Book of Buddhist Devotional Texts*, Windhorse Publications, Cambridge 2017.

Contents

List of figures

Preface to the second printing

Eight Step Recovery Meetings

Since we launched Eight Step Recovery we have had many requests on how to run an Eight Step Recovery Meeting. These Eight Step Recovery Meetings have been pioneered in India, the UK, the US, Canada, Mexico, and Finland. Many people have benefited from these meetings and we hope you will too.

The meeting formats, given below, have all been tried and tested. We suggest several formats, but we request that you always include the Welcome, Meeting Guidelines, the Preamble, Moral Inventory, and reciting the five training principles (in negative and positive form) in call and response, and the eight steps in unison. We also recommend that you end with Transference of Merit and the three-minute breathing space (AGE).

It is helpful to print the Welcome, Meeting Guidelines, Preamble, Moral Inventory, Eight Steps, and the AGE and Transference of Merit on cards or laminated paper so that different people can read them out aloud. Make sure you have someone signed up to chair each meeting. Also ensure you have enough printed paper copies of the eight steps and the Transference of Merit for everyone. Some groups create booklets for people.

The chair's role is to begin the meeting and end the meeting on time, and also ask for dana. Some of you will know this as the seventh tradition. Dana is an expression of generosity. Making a donation supports the group to continue holding meetings, and helps to pass on the teachings you have been given.

The chair opens the meeting with the Welcome.

Meeting format

Welcome

Welcome. My name is _____ and I will now lead the three-minute breathing space AGE):

- Become aware of your body; aware of sensations in the body; aware of thoughts; aware of emotions.
- Gather your breath on the upper lip, the chest, or in the abdomen, and let the contact of the breath soothe your thoughts.
- Expand the breath throughout the whole body. Let me hear everyone take a deep breath and expand it throughout the body.

We invite you to briefly introduce yourself and say why you are here this evening. Please take up to a maximum of thirty seconds; thank you. It is also okay for you not to say anything.

(After introductions, ask if there are any newcomers, and please welcome them.)

Will somebody now read the Meeting Guidelines?

Meeting Guidelines

I would like to remind all of us of our suggested meeting guidelines:

- If there is more than one person, there are enough people for a meeting.
- The only requirement to attend this meeting is the desire to live your life by the five precepts, which are training principles to help train the mind, and a desire to be free of your addictions and/or compulsive behaviors.
- Please respect people's personal sharing – let what you hear stay here.
- Be kind to yourself, and in turn be kind to others.
- Enjoy your recovery.

Will somebody please read the Preamble?

Preamble

This Eight Step Recovery Meeting explores recovery through the lens of the Buddhist teachings, and Buddhism through the lens of recovery. If you are attending twelve-step meetings, this can be your expression of your eleventh step and if you are not in a Twelve Step Program, it can be another way to approach your recovery. This is an extra meeting to complement your recovery, whatever that looks like.

For the next one and a half hours or two hours we are temporarily going for refuge to the Three Jewels. What we mean by that is, as best we can, we are placing the Buddha (the Awakened mind), the Dharma (the teachings of the Buddha), and the sangha (the spiritual community that has recovered and woken up to the truth) at the center of our thoughts. Those of us in recovery know too well that our addiction has often been at the center of our thoughts.

Will somebody please read the Moral Inventory?

So we begin with our moral inventory. We are turning our thoughts over to the Three Jewels. To the Buddha, the Awakened mind, which has gained liberation from suffering. To the Dharma, the teachings that point to the truth. And to the sangha, the spiritual communities, which have gained liberation. We will now recite the training principles to help train the mind in call and response. I will say a line and you repeat it.

1. I undertake to abstain from harming life. With deeds of loving-kindness I purify my body.
2. I undertake to abstain from taking the not-given. With open-handed generosity I purify my body.
3. I undertake to abstain from sexual misconduct. With stillness, simplicity, and contentment I purify my body.
4. I undertake to abstain from false speech. With truthful communication I purify my speech.
5. I undertake to abstain from taking intoxicants. With mindfulness clear and radiant I purify my mind.

We will now say the Eight Steps together.

Eight Steps
Step One: Accepting that this human life will bring suffering.
Step Two: Seeing how we create extra suffering in our lives.
Step Three: Embracing impermanence to show us that our suffering can end.
Step Four: Being willing to step onto the path of recovery and discover freedom.
Step Five: Transforming our speech, actions, and livelihood.
Step Six: Placing positive values at the center of our lives.
Step Seven: Making every effort to stay on the path of recovery.
Step Eight: Helping others by sharing the benefits we have gained.

Below are several formats that can take place at your meeting. Please decide which meeting format you will use before you begin your meeting.

1. Step Meeting
2. Book Study Meetings
3. Speaker Meetings

Once this part of the meeting is over, please always end with the following:

The chair will lead the three-minute breathing space (AGE):
AGE
- Become aware of your body; aware of sensations in the body; aware of thoughts; aware of emotions.
- Gather your breath on the upper lip, the chest, or in the abdomen, and let the contact of the breath soothe your thoughts.
- Expand the breath throughout the whole body. Let me hear everyone take a deep breath and expand it throughout the body.

Let's all say the Transference of Merit together.

Transference of Merit and Self Surrender
May the merit gained
in my acting thus
go to the alleviation of the suffering
of all beings.
My personality
throughout my existences,
my possessions,
and my merit in all three ways
I give up without regard
to myself
for the benefit of all beings.

> Just as the earth
> and other elements
> are serviceable in many ways
> to the infinite number of beings
> inhabiting limitless space,
> so may I become
> that which maintains all beings
> situated throughout space
> so long as all have not attained
> to peace.

Please ask at this point for dana (voluntary financial contribution) – nobody is paid. Dana is an act of generosity, showing an appreciation of the Buddhist teachings. However, there is no suggested fee, and nobody is turned away. There is no price to attend a meeting. And nobody should be made to feel uncomfortable if they don't put into the pot. This must come from each individual's generosity of spirit. Some people may give dana by offering to open up and put out chairs each week, and tidy up after. Being of service as dana is as valuable and generous as giving money.

Just as recovery is a process, so is the act of generosity. Dana will pay for your meeting space, for materials, books, non-alcoholic beverages, and anything else you need. If you have a surplus, you might wish to give money to a participant who wants to attend a recovery retreat.

At a future date we will also be introducing a donation facility on an appropriate website for Eight Step Recovery work in underprivileged communities, which will help some of the poorest communities in the world to deal with addiction, as well as helping to support people to go on recovery retreats.

Format 1: Step Meeting

(If you only have an hour – or there are a lot of people – we suggest you work through the steps weekly in the following way.) You could perhaps read a short passage from the step you are reflecting on before people answer the prompt question. Some groups go through one step a month, others one step a week, and once they have completed eight steps they just begin all over again.

Prompt questions for short meeting

> Today we will focus on Step One: Accepting that this human life will bring suffering. What does it mean for you to accept that this human life will bring about suffering, in the context of your dis-ease?
>
> Today we will focus on Step Two: Seeing how we create extra suffering in our lives. How do I create extra suffering in my life?
>
> Today we will focus on Step Three: Embracing impermanence to show us that our suffering can end. What do I need to let go of in my life today?
>
> Today we will focus on Step Four: Being willing to step onto the path of recovery and discover freedom. How willing am I to step onto the path of recovery today? or What is one aspect of freedom I have discovered since being on the path of recovery?
>
> Today we will focus on Step Five: Transforming our speech, actions, and livelihood. How can I begin transforming or continue to transform my speech, or actions, or livelihood? Just choose one to focus on.
>
> Today we will focus on Step Six: Placing positive values at the center of our lives. What are some of the things that tend to occupy my thoughts? What is the impact of having these thoughts at the center of my life?

> Today we will focus on Step Seven: Making every effort to stay on the path of recovery. How can I make more effort to stay on the path of recovery?
>
> Today we will focus on Step Eight: Helping others by sharing the benefits we have gained. What could I do this week to help share the benefits I have gained?

Another way of holding a short meeting is asking somebody to select a text that they would like to focus on from one of the steps, and read for fifteen minutes and then ask people to share on the reading.

End with the AGE and Transference of Merit and Self Surrender.

Format 2: Book Study Meeting

(This is for longer meetings of ninety minutes to two hours.)

> For the next few weeks we will be exploring Step One. We will discuss every exercise, one exercise a week, and when a meditation or reflection comes up, we do the practice and discuss it afterwards. We will work through each step in this way, until we get to the end of the book, and then begin again. We suggest that, if you have the technology, you play the meditation or reflection out loud. They are hosted as a free download on the website – the link can be found at the end of the book.

Participants begin from the beginning of the book. They read a section for fifteen to twenty minutes, and then discuss the text. When a reflection or meditation comes up, either listen to it from the download or somebody leads it, and then discuss. Mark the page you finish on at each meeting so you can begin from the correct page at the next meeting.

There are several ways of holding this meeting. You can work through the book chronologically, beginning with the foreword. Once the book is completed you may choose to begin the book all over again. Or you may choose to study another book that is related specifically to Buddhist Recovery. For example, you could study Kevin Griffin's *One Breath at a Time* or *A Burning Desire*, Noah Levine's *Refuge Recovery*, or Valerie Mason-John's *Detox Your Heart: Meditations on Emotional Trauma*.[1]

End with the AGE and Transference of Merit and Self Surrender.

Format 3: Speaker Meeting

In some meetings you may like to introduce a speaker by asking someone to tell their story of recovery, abstinence, sobriety, and their connection to the Buddhist teachings. Some groups like to invite people to their meetings and ask them to give a fifteen-minute talk on a topic concerning the Eight Steps. Sometimes groups choose the chair to speak on a topic concerning the Eight Steps. After the fifteen-minute talk, people are then asked to share their reflections, thoughts, and own journey with the steps.

End with the AGE and Transference of Merit and Self Surrender.

Should groups be closed?

Some groups may choose to be closed while working through the book and others may choose to be open. Some groups may choose to have the group just for a specific addiction, gender, or sexuality. Even if it is just for a particular addiction, such as alcohol, we do not say you cannot mention other addictions in the group. This is because everything is interconnected, and the only requirement to attend a meeting is to live your life in line with the five training principles, and a desire to be free of your addictions and/or your compulsive behaviors.

You can be creative with the formats, although every meeting needs to begin with the Welcome, Meeting Guidelines, the Preamble, and Moral Inventory and the Eight Steps, and then end with the AGE and Transference of Merit and Self Surrender.

Remember there are also meditations attached to the book, so for some meetings you could choose to listen to a meditation and then discuss how the meditation was for you. All the meditations in the book can be downloaded for free from bit.ly/eightsteprecovery or windhorsepublications.com/eight-steprecovery-audio (see p.xi). There are additional meditations on our website: insighttimer/vimalasara.

How to run meetings

We request that all meetings are free of any food and only serve soft beverages like tea, coffee, or water. If you want to mark somebody's abstinent birthday, this can be done by the practice of rejoicing in merits, whereby you open the meeting up for fifteen minutes, and invite anybody to rejoice or celebrate in the good deeds or qualities of the person's whose abstinent birthday it is. We request that there is time for others to share about their hopes and struggles in the meeting too. So, while the rejoicing is to help inspire and motivate others, it needs to take up only fifteen minutes of the meeting. Cakes and cookies are not required. Rejoicing and celebrating someone's achievements is enough. In this way we learn to celebrate without a substance.

Many of you may know how to meditate, although many of you will not. Therefore we request you read the three-minute breathing space or remember it verbatim, so that everyone can feel comfortable in leading it. There is a logic to the three-minute breathing space, which is why it is important to stick to the script and not take up more than three minutes. We begin and end with the three-minute breathing space to allow us to pause and gather ourselves. This helps us to arrive at the meeting and to connect with how we are at the end of the meeting before going on with our day. It also helps us to get into the habit of stopping and checking in with ourselves. We recommend that the AGE practice is no longer than three minutes, although shorter is fine.

Meetings are peer led. Each group will decide, for example, on someone taking responsibility for making the Welcome and asking people to read the Preamble and lead the AGE, for a month or two. Make sure responsibility is shared.

You may want to close your meeting – this is the group's decision. You may want to set up Eight Step Meetings for specific addictions, or more generally for substance abuse. This again is the decision of the people who set up the group.

Abstinence and harm reduction

Some people will come to a meeting and ask: "Is Buddhist Recovery an abstinence-based program or harm reduction program?" Beware of this question. The teachings of the Dharma do not tell people what to do. The teachings advise us to try for ourselves and see what happens. We clearly state in the Meeting Guidelines that the only requirement to attend a meeting is to live your life more in line with the five training principles to help train the mind, and a desire to be free of your addictions and/or compulsive behaviors. Therefore we start from where we are at in our recovery. The precepts are principles to train the mind. They clearly state that we undertake to abstain from specific behaviors, actions, and habits. So it is hoped that all of us in recovery are moving in the direction of letting go of harming ourselves and others, from taking the not-given, from sexual misconduct, from false speech and taking intoxicants. How you do this is up to you. We recommend avoiding telling people what to do. For example, saying it is okay to have a drink may be unproblematic for one person, but could be a matter of life and death for another. So please observe the above when asked this question. We are not professionals. We are a group of people in recovery sharing our wisdom.

Foreword by Jon Kabat-Zinn

It is always good and helpful to hear the basics of the Dharma expressed through the voices of authentic practitioners, and especially ones who know the depths of human suffering first hand, as these authors do – and who equally know the very real potential, as well as the daily challenges involved, for us humans to free ourselves from such suffering, especially when it is engendered and sustained through craving of one kind or another, as is virtually always the case if one looks deeply enough.

The human and economic costs of craving and of addictions of all kinds worldwide are staggering. Yet the statistics barely scratch the surface of the suffering that drives people to addiction in the first place and keeps them there once ensnared. In the face of this multidimensional global epidemic that destroys lives, families, and large segments of communities and nations, any effective inroads are not only welcome, but absolutely necessary. As Chan Master Venerable Ben Huan of Hongfa Temple, Shenzhen, China, age 97 at the time, said to me during a 2004 conversation about bringing mindfulness in the form of Mindfulness-Based Stress Reduction (MBSR) into the mainstream of medicine and health care,

> There are an infinite number of ways in which people
> suffer. Therefore, there have to be an infinite number of
> ways in which the Dharma is made available to people.

The program offered in Eight Step Recovery is one of those ways, one that is credible, creative, and inviting. The authors, on the basis of their own experience, have chosen to shape their path explicitly around Buddhist teachings, while following a framework based in large measure on a more mainstream mindfulness-based intervention, what they are calling

Mindfulness-Based Addiction Recovery (MBAR).

This revised edition includes a great deal of helpful new material to support those who are drawn to replicate this program in their communities. It offers mindfulness/heartfulness meditation practices and their applications to the cravings and addictions that are common to all human beings and that are particularly valuable to any of us who are in the grip of their most toxic, imprisoning, and life-destroying clutches. Liberation through one's own efforts to cultivate intimacy and kindness with the workings of one's own self-imprisoning mind and behaviors is indeed possible, as the authors point out, echoing the teaching of the Buddha's third noble truth. Indeed, the entire program is presented in the context of the four noble truths, explicitly bringing the liberative heart of Buddhist meditation practices and teachings to bear on the mind that is imprisoned in its own nightmarish and self-destructive habits by cultivating other, healthier, usually unknown and undreamed of aspects of that very same mind and heart. These teachings and the container of the MBAR program are offered as both a refuge and a practical curriculum for this hardest of all journeys back to the well-being that is our birthright as human beings, and which is, paradoxically, already here and already ours for the developing. The basic message from the authors is that reclaiming your life and what is deepest and best in yourself is not only possible but actually workable if you are willing to engage in a certain kind of interior work on yourself, and to give yourself over to this intrinsically kind and trustworthy invitation to heal your own life and heart and relationships.

May this MBAR program prove to be just the door you need to open, and if so, then enter, enter, enter, and give yourself over day by day, thought by thought, moment by moment to this reliable and profound form of nurturance and healing.

Jon Kabat-Zinn
January 2, 2017
Northampton, Massachusetts

Foreword by Gabor Maté

"Suffering is universal," the authors of this book point out. "It's not a terrible mistake that we are suffering, nor a personal failure. Pain happens to us and it happens to everyone."

The challenge for human beings is not how to avoid suffering, but how to face the pain that is inherent in our lives, and how not to create more suffering by our desperate attempt to avoid pain. Addiction is, perhaps, the most desperate measure we employ to escape suffering. It does not work, as so many of us have found. "Every addiction starts with pain and ends with pain," Eckhart Tolle has written.

My definition of addiction, close to that of the authors, is any behavior, substance-related or not, that brings temporary pleasure or relief, a behavior one craves but is unable to stop despite negative consequences. As the Buddha pointed out thousands of years ago, almost any human pleasure can become addictive:

> Some ascetics and Brahmins ... remain addicted to
> attending such shows as dancing, singing, music,
> displays, recitations, hand-music, cymbals and drums,
> fairy shows; ... combats of elephants, buffaloes, bulls,
> rams; ... maneuvers, military parades; ... disputation and
> debate, rubbing the body with shampoos and cosmetics,
> bracelets, headbands, fancy sticks ... unedifying
> conversation about kings, robbers, ministers, armies,
> dangers, wars, food, drink, clothes ... heroes, speculation
> about land and sea, talk of being and non-being...[1]

The point is not that any of these behaviors are in themselves necessarily addictive, but that it is our relationship to them that defines the addiction. One could dance or sing, for example, as an act of creation and even divine worship – or, as one of the authors, Valerie, writes: "When something traumatic happened in my life I would go out dancing all night, even without intoxicants." Addiction happens when an activity is used as a means to escape from the distress of experiencing oneself.

And why should people wish to flee from themselves? We do so when we have suffered as children, and when, being alone and in despair, we could not see how to be with our pain and how to learn from it. The healing of addiction is all about how to learn from pain. "Whatever you do, don't shut off your pain," Sogyal Rinpoche writes in *The Tibetan Book of Living and Dying*.

> However desperate you become, accept your pain as it
> is, because it is in fact trying to hand you a precious gift:
> the chance of discovering, through spiritual practice,
> what lies behind sorrow.[2]

What lies behind sorrow is liberation and joy. A powerful spiritual practice to get us there is the mindfulness taught by the Buddha and revitalized by many great teachers since. Mindfulness reveals that we are not our thoughts, not our bodies, not our emotions, that we can notice and compassionately observe our feelings, thoughts, and bodies without being controlled by them. The key is awareness, as taught in this book, based on Buddhist principles but not requiring any Buddhist affiliation or identification.

The eight steps taught here may also be seen as eight principles to live by. We begin by accepting that whatever we have suffered – and some do suffer more than others – our pain is not ours alone, not personal, but simply a way life may show up while we are in this world. The other steps lead us away from the path of creating more suffering for ourselves and, gradually, onto the path of compassion for others.

It takes practice. In this volume Vimalasara (Valerie) and Paramabandhu gently introduce us to the practice of breathing and self-awareness, beginning with small increments, until breathing and awareness become the anchors for us being grounded in all the eight steps.

Foreword by Gabor Maté

There is no one fail-safe way out of addiction. Nothing works for everyone. Challenged by addiction to substances or to behaviors that generate more pain, we need to find the right path for ourselves. Twelve steps, five steps, no steps, eight steps: what is right is what works. The eight steps here recommended may be the primary path for many, but they can also be a powerful support to anyone, no matter what the addiction and no matter what path they are on.

Mindful awareness, conscious breathing, being present in our body, compassion for ourselves and toward others: addicted or not – and most of us are, in some way – these qualities and practices can serve us all.

May we all find peace.

Gabor Maté MD
Author of *In the Realm of Hungry Ghosts:
Close Encounters with Addiction*

Introduction

Human nature has an inbuilt tendency toward addiction. For some people this tendency can lead to the destruction of their lives, through their addictive and obsessive–compulsive behaviors. However, we can all struggle with the nature of the mind that tends toward addiction. We could say that we are all in recovery.

Thinking itself can have an addictive quality to it. Thinking that tells us stories, thinking that can make us angry, thinking that can literally intoxicate us and impair the mind. Accidents and even fatalities can be caused when we are under the influence of this type of thinking. In Canada, distracted driving and aggressive driving are among the top five most common causes of car accidents.

We also live in a world where many of us self-medicate in response to our hardships. We turn to food, drugs, alcohol, pharmaceuticals, sex, relationships, work, consumerism, the Internet, video games, and so much more to help promote happiness in our lives.

Even those of us who do not think of ourselves as having an addiction might be regarded as addicted to life: to physical wellness, to youthfulness. We do not want to age, become sick, or die. In fact, many of us consciously or unconsciously do our utmost to prevent this. And why not? It is natural to want youthfulness, health, and longevity. However, such attachment will inevitably cause us suffering, so that the very way we seek to reduce our suffering just adds to it. This in turn can lead to trying to manage it with more addictive behavior. It's not surprising, then, that addiction is so widespread.

You could say that recovery is widespread too. Many of us who have been dominated by addiction became addicted while trying to recover from a painful experience. We found that self-medicating took the sting out of the pain.

Many people who walk through the doors of a church, a mosque, a synagogue, or a Buddhist temple are looking for solace or recovery. And many who haven't turned to a spiritual tradition have found peace in creative pursuits, campaigns, and recreational activities. The Buddha's teachings can offer us an understanding of how the mind works. They are tools for working with a mind vulnerable to addiction. They can help us to overcome addictive and obsessive behaviors by cultivating a calm and clear mind without anger and resentments. The Buddha's teachings can offer us a path to recovery.

A definition of addiction and of recovery

For the purposes of this book, what we mean by addiction is any mental or bodily habit that has a compulsive quality to it and causes us to suffer. This is a broad definition. It includes what we might normally think of as addictions, such as dependence on alcohol or pathological gambling. However, this definition also encompasses other behaviors such as binge eating or compulsive Internet use, which aren't always considered to be true addictions. A key element is feeling unable to control an activity, even though it is causing us harm. For example, in the case of alcohol, if we have one glass of wine, we are unable to stop drinking until we have finished the bottle. Or with sexual activity, we can't stop chasing sexual encounters, even though this behavior threatens other aspects of our lives. The reason for our broad definition is that the Buddha's teachings presented in this book can be helpful to us whether our addiction is to heroin or an obsessive pattern of thinking that prevents us from leading a more fulfilling life. We may need additional assistance, such as medication to help us safely stop drinking if we are dependent on alcohol. However, in terms of learning to create a satisfying life free from our addictive tendencies, the same principles – the eight steps of this book – apply.

By recovery, we mean finding a path away from the trouble caused by our addictive tendencies. We see this as more than merely stopping the addictive behavior – hard as that can be. It is untangling the compulsive drives of our addiction to discover a richer and more fulfilling way of living.

Our personal stories

This book has arisen from the coming together of two very different journeys. The paths of our lives have led both of us (Valerie and Paramabandhu) to use the Buddha's teachings to help people overcome addiction. Together we share our personal experiences, stories of addiction, and our knowledge of the Buddhist teachings, which we believe can help anyone who is ready for change on the difficult road of recovery from addiction. How we got here is something of a contrast!

Valerie's story

When I was 28, I accidentally began my process of recovery from addiction. Unknown to me, meditation and the Buddhist teachings were about to transform my life. A friend invited me to sit with her meditation teacher from India because she believed it would help me with my stress levels. She was right. I walked into my friend's house tense and hyper, and two hours later I was flying out the door. My body felt light, my voice had softened and I could hardly feel the pedals on my bike as I cycled home. I had not known bliss or peace like this before. "This is great," I thought. "Cost me nothing, I didn't drink, swallow, or sniff anything and I'm as high as a kite. I want some more of that."

Needless to say, addict that I was, I became addicted. I soon learned you could go on a weekend or week-long meditation retreat. I went on as many retreats as possible just so I could have the feeling of tripping, of getting out of my body and my head, the experience of all my senses being heightened. I became ungrounded just as if I had taken a hallucinogenic drug. I was fortunate that I was not one of those beginners who experience the arising of past trauma while meditating. I thought I had found a new drug. However, once the retreat was over, I would, of course, experience the inevitable comedown. I would find my way to the nearest supermarket, buy and consume an entire gallon tub of Häagen-Dazs ice cream, and throw it up.

I cleaned up in the meditation rooms. I was a failed anorectic. I began eating more than my regime had allowed me, which was six cream crackers a day. The only way I knew to keep control of my food intake was by purging. I lost control over food and soon was eating food enough for five people in a day. I became a compulsive eater, obsessed with where I was going to get my next serving of food. I was a sugar and white-flour addict. Once I began eating this food I could not stop, and when I came to the end of what I was eating, I had to get more. It was as if somebody was driving my body toward the food. I went into a trance state and my only focus was on the food. In the midst of a binge I often lost awareness of all my senses, and my balance was completely thrown off-kilter. I went into a hypnotic surreal space, which was seductive. I even experienced real moments of happiness and contentment in the early days of bulimia nervosa. I also enjoyed the buzz of bingeing. Once I had reached a most uncomfortable limit in my body, I threw up and began all over again. I often threw up to experience the sensation of my whole body tingling. Bingeing and purging became my secret drug.

I could not walk past a food shop without entering it. I could not be in a room with food without eating and purging several times. You could not leave me alone with food and expect to come back to it. It would be eaten and I would concoct the most monstrous story to cover my secret. At the peak of my disease I was purging over forty times a day, sometimes after just one cookie, and sometimes after I had eaten two loaves of bread and a family tub of Kentucky Fried Chicken, and drunk as much fluid as possible. Once I almost killed myself when food lodged in my windpipe while I was trying to throw up. I jumped up and down, terrified, stuck my fingers down my throat, and suddenly I was relieved. I collapsed beside the toilet. Half an hour later when I came through, I went on another binge, and threw up down the toilet again. My front teeth crumbled from the acid in my stomach, my hair stopped growing, and my throat was continually hoarse. I told lies about missing food in friends' houses. I broke every promise to myself to stop, and lay in bed many days wishing for a magic pill that could give me respite from the hell of my addiction.

I'm telling you all this because people often say: "What, you call bulimia an addiction?" My response was: "Yes. It was a matter of life or death. It's one of the worst addictions anybody could possibly have." It was my secret. Unlike someone with alcohol, drug, sex, shopping, and other addictions, I could not say: "Well that's it. I will be abstinent from food for the rest of my life." I needed to eat to survive. I had to find a relationship with food that was not going to kill me. I had to identify which foods were my drugs or alcohol, foods like sugar and white flour.

So, finally, what changed? It was that meditation and the teachings of the Buddha came into my life. I remember thinking after coming back from my third retreat: "I must be kidding myself if I think the teachings are not having an effect." For the first time in my life, I experienced a temporary reprieve. I would go on retreat and miraculously not crave for more food and keep my meals down. My thoughts were not obsessed with food. While on retreat, I wanted the experience of the meditation high more than I wanted to eat and throw up. But I relapsed as soon as I returned home. I hated leaving the retreat and tried to maintain the blissful feelings by eating and purging. Then one day I said to myself: "Why don't I chant those precepts I've been taught on a retreat? Maybe they will help." There was always a part of me that wanted to let go of this addiction, but it was just a whisper in my heart. This whisper of recovery had not become louder because it was drowned out by thoughts of my addiction. The practice of morality woke me up. My whisper began to get louder, and thoughts of my addiction began to slowly quiet down. I was inspired by the five traditional precepts to help train the mind:

I undertake to abstain from harming life.
I undertake to abstain from taking the not-given.
I undertake to abstain from sexual misconduct.
I undertake to abstain from false speech.
I undertake to abstain from taking intoxicants.

I was not living in accordance with any of the precepts, but these teachings gave me the possibility of changing my life. They were not commandments or some order from an almighty being above, and I would not go to hell if I broke them. They were guidelines to live my life, and I began to see that, when I did not apply the precepts to my daily activities, unhappiness arose, and, when I worked at applying them to my life, more happiness arose. I began to recite them daily in the privacy of my home, and slowly I began to see a difference. I was starting to have some periods of abstinence in my life.

The practice of loving-kindness meditation also taught me to love myself. When I walked through the doors of a meditation temple, I had so much negative chatter and resentment whirring around in my head. It was sometimes hard to meditate, and so I began chanting mantras, sacred syllables that radiate the qualities of mythical beings in Buddhism. I chanted *om mani padme hum*, and imagined being held by the thousand arms of Avalokitesvara, a mythical being who radiates compassion to all beings. When I chanted his mantra I felt nourished, and my voices of self-hatred and resentment began to quiet. On my own I took up the practice of chanting several mantras to help transform my life, some of which we will share in this book.

Meditation was crucial for me to learn to love and like my friends better, to forgive those people who hurt me, and even to open up my heart to people I didn't know. I learned all of this by sitting on a cushion and cultivating unconditional loving-kindness toward all these people. Through meditation I had begun to think differently. I had cultivated positive thinking in my life. The Buddha's teaching of the four noble truths was one of the most important teachings for me in my personal recovery. When I first heard them, I understood them at the time to literally mean this:

> There is suffering,
> A path that will lead to more suffering,
> An end of suffering,
> And a path to lead me away from suffering.

I could see so clearly how I was on the path that led to more suffering, and, when I heard what I needed to do in order to be on the path that took me away from suffering, I felt inspired. I felt there was hope for me to find my way out of addiction. I knew the only way I could do this was to set up the conditions to help me transform my body, speech, and mind. Finally, the teaching that hit me right between the eyes was the idea of turning my life over to the inspiration of the Buddha (awakening my mind), to the teachings of the Buddha, and to the spiritual community, and placing all three ideals at the center of my life. This is what is called going for refuge to the Three Jewels: the Buddha, the Dharma, and the sangha. I was not Buddhist, and yet the thought of going for refuge resonated for me. I could see so clearly that I was going for refuge to the food that was at the center of my life. All my decisions were based around how I could get my next binge and vomit up everything I had eaten in secret.

I didn't want food at the center of my life any more, and I didn't want the partying either. I began to see that I had been running to food to protect me from all sorts of uncomfortable and challenging experiences. I had sought refuge in food as if it were my mother, lover, and friend. It came first in my life. But it was a false refuge because in the long term I just spiraled into deeper suffering. If I was to have abstinence and sobriety of mind, a recovery that could be maintained, I needed to choose different things to put at the center of my life. I chose the ideal of waking up to reality (the Buddha); the teachings of the Buddha (the Dharma); and the spiritual community (the sangha). Notice I was not putting people at the center of my life, but the ideal of understanding the working of my own mind, the Buddhist teachings, and the idea of creating community around me that wanted to change, develop, and grow.

I'm also not saying that you have to place these three ideals at the center of your life to overcome addiction. I am saying that you have to find positive and healthy things to put at the center of your life if you want recovery. And that may include healthy relationships that help you to change, develop, and grow.

Admittedly, it took several years to maintain recovery. Most stimulants in my life seemed to naturally fall away, but I held on to bulimia, like a dog with a slipper in its mouth. Food was the one thing that was not going to be taken away from me. It was the one thing that had not abandoned me. Yes, I had periods of abstinence, but I always ended up relapsing. And once I was able to abstain from purging, I had to deal with the compulsive eating. I had to begin to find sobriety of thoughts and feelings.

It was winter 1998. I had completed six months of specialist treatment for my eating disorder, and I remember clearly thinking: "Well, I've done five years of therapy, and now specialized treatment. If this doesn't work, I'm doomed." I panicked. Shortly after this I went to Rome to visit friends at Christmas, and once again I relapsed. Too much Prosecco and too much good food. So I purged to deal with my consumption.

After a hedonistic holiday, I returned home distressed. That first night I lay in bed reflecting on my life ahead of me. Three days later I was about to go into rehearsal for my new one-woman show. I knew there was absolutely no way I could get through three weeks of rehearsal and a three-week run, bingeing and purging every day. I was terrified. The publicity for this event had already gone out, so I couldn't cancel. What was I going to do? I agonized, tossed and turned in my bed, and told myself there was no way I could go through with the show. "Yes you can," an inner voice whispered, and I shouted out loud: "How?" The voice just said: "Stop bingeing and throwing up." I heard it crystal clear. The next day I woke up and that was it. I had found something that I wanted much more than my bulimia. I wanted to do this show.

I was abstinent for eighteen months, while cultivating some sobriety of mind, and then I lapsed for a couple of days. Notice I say lapsed and not relapsed. Fortunately I had enough recovery to know that I wanted my abstinence and sobriety more than the hell of my addiction. I remember clearly knowing I had a choice: to pick myself up from this small slip, or relapse and spiral back down into my addiction. It was hard, but I knew I did not want to relive the hell of my disease, and that I had to commit to a different way of living. It was at this point that I chose to walk away from my addictions and move toward healthier things in my life. I began to set up the conditions to help me in my decision.

I began cultivating five new senses: the five spiritual faculties. Sharpening my faculties of faith, energy, mindfulness, concentration, and wisdom has been the backbone of my sobriety. Staying abstinent was the easy part. Not bingeing and throwing up was tough, but my fear of living as an anorectic/ bulimic kept me abstinent.

However, cultivating a sober mind was much harder. I still had addictive behaviors. My energy of craving just latched on to other things, like sexual relationships and going to the gym obsessively. In fact, you could say my first addiction was to be in control of my life at the age of four. I was living with my fourth family, and there were many more to come. My second addiction was sniffing shoe conditioner, and my third shoplifting, but at the bottom of it all my biggest addiction was the craving to be loved and noticed. It just manifested through different disguises.

The practice of meditation was the container that held me throughout my radical changes. That was what gave me sobriety. Abstaining from purging and compulsively eating was only the first stage. Without abstinence I had no chance of healthy sobriety. Living my life more in line with the five precepts brought about sobriety of mind and a new happiness in my life. The practice of loving-kindness and mindfulness meditations restored me to sanity.

The momentum of wanting to continue to change emerged at the center of my life, and so most of my decisions were about change and transformation. I came to one of the twelve-step recovery programs ten years after my journey of recovery began. I moved to a new country, with no Buddhist community to support me. A close friend introduced me to the twelve-step program, which I have much gratitude for. I experienced being in a room of people that had suffered and were still suffering from a disease similar to mine. Working the twelve-step program has given me a fresh perspective on my own recovery and deepened my spiritual practice. There are many things that can support our recovery. I wholeheartedly believe that meditation, chanting mantras, a practice of mindfulness, reciting the five training principles, and an understanding of some of the core Buddhist teachings can help anyone overcome addiction. It saved my life. I will continue to tell my story to help save other people's lives. What I have to offer is my recovery.

Paramabandhu's story

I started working in addiction in 1992 as a psychiatrist in training. At the time it seemed to be just by chance. Only later was I able to see the patterns that led me there. For as long as I can remember, I have had a strong desire to find meaning in my life. I wasn't unhappy in my childhood and no big tragedies befell me, yet growing up I yearned for something more satisfying and fulfilling in my life. I had a loose sense that I wanted to help people and, since I liked biology, I decided to study medicine.

At university I was exposed to a greater range of ideas than I had come across in my rural home life. In particular, I was affected by some of my close friends who, taking inspiration from existential thinkers, sought meaning through creativity. The basic message seemed to be that life was inherently meaningless, but that one could find meaning through being creative. As students of the liberal arts, my friends were pursuing creativity through writing poetry or novels. My time was taken up studying anatomy, physiology, and biochemistry, which I experienced as a dry slog to get through.

Instead of creating art, I thought that perhaps the way forward for me was to be creative with myself, in the sort of person I was. This idea gathered momentum as I met more fellow students with an interest in personal development. I found a whole peer group of medical students who were interested in such areas as psychotherapy, complementary medicine, yoga, and meditation. One friend was especially interested in Buddhist meditation. I had had some contact with Buddhism in Sri Lanka, but had not been that impressed by its philosophy as I had understood it. Nevertheless, after many long debates with my friend, I found my way to an introductory meditation class at the London Buddhist Centre.

Unlike Valerie, my initial experience of meditation was not great. I was disappointed to find that I wasn't a born meditator. Whenever I sat to meditate, my mind seemed to prefer to plan or go to sleep. However, the ideas in Buddhism spoke to me. I liked the pragmatic emphasis on testing out the Buddha's teachings in your own experience, rather than following them with blind belief. I liked the vision that Buddhism presented of an unfolding path leading to greater and greater freedom. As I came to know Buddhism more deeply, I also liked the stress given to altruism: helping to alleviate the suffering of all beings. In fact, as I learned, finding my own freedom and helping others were two facets of one experience that culminated in the twin qualities of wisdom and compassion, which characterized the Awakened mind of the Buddha.

As time went on, I committed myself more fully to the study and practice of Buddhism, while in parallel I completed my medical studies, qualified as a doctor, and then started specializing in psychiatry. Given the interest I had gained from Buddhism in the study of the mind, psychiatry was an obvious choice. After I had completed my basic training in psychiatry, I needed to choose which area of psychiatry to specialize in and apply for training in that specialism. However, deciding what branch to go into was a quandary. I had been drawn to psychotherapy for a long time, so I put off applying for specialty training by taking another basic training-grade post, one half of which was in psychotherapy. The other half of the post was in substance misuse.

I found that I enjoyed working with the drug users I met in this job. Part of my work was prescribing methadone but, alongside this, I was helping people to change their lives. Most of the people who made a successful break from illicit drug use found new strands that made their lives more satisfying. This could be taking up a new hobby such as learning to play drums, helping out in a home for stray dogs, or reconnecting with old non-using friends or family. Although I didn't have to overcome dependence on heroin, in some ways we were all in the same boat. We were all trying to find something in our lives that provided sufficient meaning to help us go on each day, and to let go of unhelpful habits. I decided to specialize in addiction psychiatry.

By now, I was already teaching meditation and Buddhism at the London Buddhist Centre, and began to feel that Buddhism might have something to offer people in recovery from addiction. A colleague and I published a paper on Buddhism and addiction, outlining some preliminary ideas.[1] However, the ideas we discussed in that paper lay mostly dormant until a decade later, when the practice of using mindfulness as a therapeutic approach became more widespread in the UK.

Mindfulness is deliberately paying attention to our moment-by-moment experience, with an attitude of friendliness and curiosity. It is a key part of the Buddha's teaching, so I had already been practicing and teaching mindfulness for some years. Jon Kabat-Zinn was the first person to popularize mindfulness as a therapeutic approach. In his stress clinic in Massachusetts, started in the late 1970s, he showed that a course of mindfulness could help people with chronic pain and with anxiety. We referred to his work in our paper on Buddhism and addiction, and wondered if mindfulness might also be helpful in addiction. However, at the time we didn't take the idea any further, and, although mindfulness was gaining rapid ground in the US, it had not caught on across the Atlantic.

The use of mindfulness to help with mental and physical health problems only became popular in the UK with the work of Mark Williams and colleagues, who developed Mindfulness-Based Cognitive Therapy (MBCT) for depression.[2] Drawing closely on Kabat-Zinn's work, their studies indicated that mindfulness could help prevent relapse into recurrent depression. I started teaching MBCT at the London Buddhist Centre, and quickly saw that this could be adapted to prevent relapse into addiction. Soon I was teaching Mindfulness-Based Relapse Prevention (MBRP), as I called it, both at the Buddhist Centre and in my NHS work.

Coincidentally, around the same time, Alan Marlatt – a key figure in the research and development of relapse prevention in addiction – produced a similar MBRP course with colleagues in Seattle. Clearly the time was ripe for using mindfulness to help with addiction. Although it is still early days in the use of mindfulness in addiction, preliminary studies are promising and suggest that it can be effective.

Having started to teach mindfulness to help with addiction, I began to question: could there be more than mindfulness in the Buddha's teachings to help people suffering with addiction? This question was the seed that led to the ideas in this book.

Valerie's own experience of overcoming addiction, described above, and our practice of teaching Mindfulness-Based Relapse Prevention (MBRP) suggested that there might be more riches in Buddhism that we could draw on. Out of our quest to make more of the Buddha's teachings comes Eight-Step Recovery, which Valerie and I have explored and put together. Before we begin to describe the eight steps, we need to look at who the Buddha was.

Who was the Buddha?

The Buddha was a human being, not a god, who lived in northern India about 2,500 years ago. The title "Buddha" means "One who is Awake." The man who became the Buddha was called Gautama. He was born into a wealthy family. Although materially he had a life of luxury, as a young man he was deeply troubled by the prospect that one day he would get sick, grow old, and die. He realized that the comfort of the palace he lived in and the abundant wealth that he would inherit could not prevent the deterioration of his body. They could not keep him secure and happy.

The legend says that Gautama went on a series of outings from the palace, during which he successively saw a sick person, an old person, a dead person, and then a wanderer or holy man –

these are known as the four sights. The first three sights brought him face to face with the frailty of the body. However, it was the fourth sight – seeing a wanderer with a begging bowl – that gave him hope. And so he renounced everything he owned, left his wife and child, and "went forth" from the palace into a homeless wandering life in a search to end suffering.

The Buddha was in recovery

Initially, Gautama took up meditation. He sought out the foremost teachers of his day and quickly mastered their teachings. He experienced highly refined states of consciousness, but this did not provide him with the solution he was looking for.

Next he tried extreme self-discipline that included abstaining from all forms of indulgence: the practice of asceticism. His self-mortification included eating just one grain of rice a day, and sometimes walking around with one arm in the air for weeks. In his search for an end to suffering, Gautama became like an addict to asceticism. Like today's addicts, he had learned how to master pain, or so he thought. He grew as thin as a skeleton, and did not budge from his addiction. Still he did not find an end to suffering. Until one day he realized he was getting nowhere.

It is said that Gautama, emaciated, was sitting on a riverbank, and remembered an incident from his childhood. He had been sitting in the shade of a rose-apple tree, watching his father plow the field – perhaps a ritual at the start of the season. Spontaneously, the young Gautama entered into an intensely pleasurable concentrated state of mind. Recalling this event turned his whole heart and mind around, and he realized why his practices of self-mortification were getting him nowhere. For the first time he could see clearly how extreme, dangerous, and useless they were. He saw that both extremes of worldly sensual pleasures and painful self-mortification would continue to cause suffering. The pleasure that had arisen under the rose-apple tree was not forced, like the meditation he had learned after going forth, nor did it lead to being caught up in the body or craving, in the way that indulgence in ordinary sensual pleasures did.

In fact, it was the path of moderation he needed to discover, the path that was not full of self-indulgence or self-mortification. The Buddha called this path the Middle Way. He realized that it was through the practice of meditation that he would find an end to suffering, but meditation that was not forced and that allowed natural pleasure to arise in the mind. He vowed to sit concentrated, mindfully, until he attained Enlightenment and became Awake to the reality of the human condition.

Letting go of his obsessive behavior was not easy. There are many versions of the story that follows, but all refer to how the Buddha's mind was seized by strong emotions like craving, doubt, and anxiety. One legend says that, when the Buddha committed to sit, be still, and meditate beneath the bodhi tree, every demon one could think of arose in his mind. It is said that Mara, the lord of misfortune, destruction, sin, and death, arose in his mind.

However, he experienced this with great calm, without wavering from his goal. He had nightmares, and he was tempted with images from his past. He came face-to-face with conceit, arrogance, and pride. He was challenged by ill will, sensual desire, doubt, restlessness, self-righteousness, and ignorance. Things became even worse when Mara tried to entice the Buddha with his three daughters, called Craving, Boredom, and Passion. Yet the Buddha did not waver from his stillness. You could liken this to the Buddha experiencing a detoxification on the deepest level and coming right up against his raw mind.

The legend goes on to say that Mara ordered every evil spirit he could think of to attack the Buddha, in the hope of deterring him from his goal. However, the Buddha was unperturbed. He remained calm and observed the evil spirits as if he were watching something harmless. The Buddha transformed the evil spirits into lotus blossoms.

Finally, Mara threatened him with the taunt that Gautama did not have the right to an Awakened mind, the right to see things as they really are. The Buddha Gautama touched the earth and said: "Let the earth be my witness." Instead of pushing Mara out of his mind, he embraced Mara by saying: "You are my mother and father. You are my liberation. From the beginningless past to the endless future, you and I are one."

It's believed that it was at this moment that Gautama became a Buddha, Awakened. Gautama had reached the end of his path of suffering. He had gained recovery from the human condition – the existential troubles of human existence such as aging and death. He finally understood the workings of his mind, and was freed from the mental bonds that had caused him suffering. He saw that the idea of a fixed self was part of the illusion of the mind. He could see clearly that, when he identified with his perceptions, his thoughts, feelings, and consciousness, he was deluding himself, creating unnecessary suffering in his life. He also saw that everything that arises is dependent upon conditions, that nothing exists independently, and that we are all interconnected. With these realizations he saw how we as human beings create our misery and our joy, but he also saw that there was an end to suffering. This is what is called the Buddha's Enlightenment.

The Buddha thought nobody would understand him, since he recognized that the truths were subtle, even counterintuitive, and hard to fathom. However, he soon realized he must teach what he knew. For the remaining forty-five years of his life, he taught men and women from all walks of life and helped them to find the freedom he had discovered. The Buddha offered his recovery to the world. His teachings can release us from the sting of suffering, so we do not need to self-medicate or push away the reality of life. The Buddha's example prepares us for the tough road of recovery. There will be many things that will challenge us along the way. As we start to leave our addiction behind and step onto the path of recovery, we are likely to meet our demons. Yet if we cultivate a spacious mind, even though we may relapse many times, we can learn to embrace our demons and find recovery.

The Buddha's teaching

It is believed that the Buddha's first teaching to his disciples referred to addiction. He says:

There is addiction to indulgence of sense-pleasures,
which is low, coarse, the way of ordinary people,
unworthy, and unprofitable; and there is addiction
to self-mortification, which is painful, unworthy,
and unprofitable. Avoiding both these extremes, the
Tathagata (The Perfect One) has realized the Middle
Path; it gives vision, gives knowledge, and leads to calm,
to insight, to enlightenment and to Nibbana.[3]

The Buddha understood the way the human mind works: we
tend to get caught up in addictive or compulsive habits as we
pursue pleasure or try to avoid pain. The starting point for
setting ourselves free is to understand the nature of what it
is to be human in this world; we must understand the human
condition. Like the Buddha, we need to understand how our
minds and hearts work, and how we create the suffering that
we find ourselves in. The tragedy of addiction is that people
turn to a substance or a distraction to attain freedom from
their suffering, but end up in a vicious cycle of creating more
suffering and craving. The core Buddhist teaching of the four
noble truths sets this out clearly:

- There is suffering: birth, aging, sickness, and death
  are all suffering. Suffering is also caused when we are
  separated from people we love, and when we come
  into contact with people we don't like. When we are in
  contact with the unpleasant or parted from the pleasant,
  there is suffering. When we don't get what we want,
  there is suffering: this is the frustration of desire. When
  something becomes mine, or ours, this too is suffering
  (because we may lose it or fear that we may lose it).
- Suffering is caused by craving. Craving is like a
  path that leads to more suffering, keeping us in the
  vicious cycle of suffering. For example, we can crave
  sensual pleasure or self-annihilation, or even thirst for
  happiness or blissful states of mind. Yet, in the pursuit
  of the objects of our craving, we set ourselves up for
  suffering. Thirsting and craving for things we cannot
  have causes suffering.

- The end of craving will also bring the end of our suffering. That means relinquishing all addictions and letting go of craving. That's liberation.
- There is a path that leads us away from suffering: the noble eightfold path (leading to freedom from suffering) – understanding, motivation, speech, action, livelihood, effort, mindfulness, and concentration. The eightfold path was one of a number of different formulations of the way to freedom that the Buddha taught.

Even though they show the way to freedom, at first sight the truths may seem pessimistic. Each of us had a different response to this teaching when we first heard it.

Paramabandhu

I first came across Buddhism in Sri Lanka. Through my student eyes, pre-civil-war Sri Lanka seemed idyllic: lush beautiful countryside, palm-fringed sandy beaches, clear warm seas, and friendly people. And I was falling in love with another student who was traveling with us. We often saw monks in saffron robes and, curious to find out something about Buddhism, I picked up a tourist leaflet on the subject. The leaflet explained the four noble truths of the Buddha. First noble truth: all life is suffering. "Well no," I thought, "my life is pretty much perfect." Intoxicated with my youthful life, I put the leaflet down and didn't give much more thought to Buddhism.

It was not until a few years later, when I learned more about Buddhism, that I understood the Buddha was not saying that life is only suffering. The Buddha acknowledged that life contains both pain and pleasure. He drew attention to our suffering, since pain can often motivate us to change. The suffering that I experienced was subtle, such as the tightness I felt when caught up in anxious planning, trying to get my own way. Although the discomfort was subtle, it had a powerful effect, driving me almost breathlessly from one activity to the next in the pursuit of pleasure and other rewards. And though I often obtained the rewards I was seeking, it meant that I was unable to fully enjoy them, and the pursuit kept my experience of myself narrow and superficial.

Valerie

When I first heard the four noble truths, tears came to my eyes. They resonated within me and presented me with the opportunity to work with my life differently. The truths and meditation also changed my life profoundly. They shook me awake. They were the most exciting things I had learned in all my years of education.

The four noble truths turned everything around in my psyche. They made sense of my life. The truths taught me that I was not much different from anyone else. I was no longer alone with my labels that I had become so attached to, that had become my fixed false self. I realized that, although I had experienced my fair share of suffering because of the conditions I was born into, I had also piled a whole lot more suffering into my life through the choices I had made. The truths presented the possibility of freedom from that suffering: freedom from my addictions and the vicious cycle of bulimia nervosa. For the first time in my life, I could see a way out of my suffering. I could step onto the eightfold path.

I remember as a young child being mesmerized by the pet gerbil who used to run round and round frenetically on the inside of a wheel, and when it fell off onto the floor of the cage, it would jump right back on again. And I would wonder, why did it keep getting back on the wheel if it knew it was going to fall off? Several years ago, I realized I was just like the gerbil running frenetically around in the cycle of suffering, falling off and getting straight back on without even pausing or thinking. Finally I learned to slow the wheel down, step off, and get onto the path of recovery.

Eight steps toward recovery

We have taken the principles of the four noble truths and expanded them to help with recovery from addiction. The first three steps relate closely to the first three noble truths. All eight steps together make a path that leads away from the suffering of addiction, which is equivalent to the fourth noble truth – the path leading from suffering to freedom. These are the eight steps:

> Step One: accepting that this human life will bring suffering
> Step Two: seeing how we create extra suffering in our lives
> Step Three: embracing impermanence to show us that our suffering can end

Step Four: being willing to step onto the path of recovery and discover freedom

Step Five: transforming our speech, actions, and livelihood

Step Six: placing positive values at the center of our lives

Step Seven: making every effort to stay on the path of recovery

Step Eight: helping others by sharing the benefits we have gained

The first three steps involve paying close attention to our experience – to our thoughts, feelings, and emotions – and to our bodily sensations. We can think of this as a voyage of discovery, as we explore in moment-by-moment detail how our minds and hearts work.

Paying deliberate attention to the fine detail of our experience, as it unfolds in the present, is called mindfulness. We try to inquire into exactly what is happening with an attitude of friendliness and curiosity. We try to stay open to whatever we might find, not making assumptions about what our experience is like. Often we hold on to an idea of our experience – for example: "This pain is unbearable" – which, when we face it calmly, may turn out to be quite different. Through mindfulness we begin to see and experience the nature of our suffering and how we cause ourselves more suffering, especially through addiction. We also start to see the possibility of letting go of some of our suffering.

Having a clearer understanding of how our minds work, in the fourth step we introduce kindness – one of the qualities of mindfulness – more fully. We aim to bring more kindness to our experience so that we can explore the pros and cons of both addictive behavior and life without addiction. The purpose of this step is to help us boost our decision to let go of addiction. With a clear intention to overcome our addiction, we will need to come to terms with our past actions and transform our current bodily actions, our speech, and our livelihood in ways that promote our happiness – this is the fifth step.

The sixth step looks at what values can help us stay oriented toward recovery. We speak of this as a "positive refuge." We begin to explore what will take the place of the addiction(s) that our lives have been centered around. We ask ourselves: "What healthier alternatives could we put at the center of our lives?" This is hard, because it may mean letting go of people who have journeyed with us up until this point. If we want to stay on the path of recovery or return to it when we have a slip, we will need to make some effort. We explore the sort of effort that is helpful to recovery in the seventh step.

Finally, in the eighth step, we are concerned with helping others. We share open-handedly with others what we have learned or gained. As well as benefiting others, this consolidates our own recovery.

Who is this book for?

These eight steps are aimed at anyone who is struggling with an addiction or compulsive behavior. As well as those with drug, alcohol, and gambling addictions, the book is for people who experience compulsive or addictive aspects to eating, sex, or other behaviors. Although we recognize that recovering from addiction can be a matter of life or death for some people, this book is also for people who do not think of themselves as having an addiction, but who have habits that are harmful in their lives. We hope the book will be of value to professionals working in the field of addiction, as well as to those caring for someone with an addiction, or in relationship with a person struggling with addiction.

We can't avoid suffering if we open our eyes to it. Suffering is all around us. However, freedom from suffering is in front of our eyes too. Some of us, who realize our difficult human predicament, reach a crisis and turn to a spiritual path, faith, or religion to deal with the shock. Others turn to an addiction to find meaning in life. Fortunately, addiction itself and the suffering it causes can lead people through the doors of a Buddhist temple, a church, a mosque, a synagogue, and many other places that offer some type of solace.

Sometimes, though, our suffering can seem too overwhelming, or the possibility of freedom from it can be so painfully close that we refuse to see it. We may know there are places we can go for help, but we choose to stay in our suffering. Many people caught up in addiction are afraid of recovery. They are afraid of the institutions that could help them.

One such organization that has helped people with addiction has been the twelve-step program of Alcoholics Anonymous, and many other programs in this fellowship. It has saved many lives, helped many families, and outlined twelve steps and twelve traditions to the path of freedom. If the steps are followed diligently, there are twelve promises ranging from having a new freedom and happiness, to having no fear of people or fear of financial insecurity. However, twelve-step programs are not for everyone, and some have turned away, desperate for another way of recovery.

These eight steps can be used by people who have not responded to the twelve-step approach, as well as by those who are in twelve-step recovery. For example, they can also be used by people in a twelve-step program who are perhaps trying to understand their eleventh step more fully. This step is: "[We] sought through prayer and meditation to improve our conscious contact with God as we understood him, praying only for knowledge of God's will for us and the power to carry that out."

In the twelve-step fellowship, God can be interpreted as the God of your understanding, "Good Orderly Direction," or "Higher Power." Although the Buddhist tradition has no place for God as a creator divinity as understood by the theistic traditions, there is nevertheless a clear and definite understanding of a suprapersonal dimension, an "other power," in Buddhism. This dimension is available to every human being, and for those interested we are including the suprapersonal in the eight steps, providing the groundwork for people to readily connect with it, beginning with the breath. However, the eight steps can equally be practiced without reference to or belief in a higher power or suprapersonal dimension.

Our book draws on the teachings of the Buddha, but the steps can be used by someone from any religious or spiritual tradition or from none. In the spirit of the Buddha's advice to some of his disciples, we encourage you to test out the teachings here in your own experience and utilize those you find helpful.

How to use this book

To be able to write a book and explain our eight steps, we need to put them in an order. The order has a certain logical structure that can be helpful to follow. While we recommend working through the book sequentially, we realize that, in the messiness of our everyday lives, some of us may prefer to move back and forth between different steps and stages. Depending on what is happening in our lives, the challenges and opportunities we are facing, and how inspired we are feeling, we may respond to and want to practice different steps. Moreover, we are likely to need to revisit different steps again and again as our understanding deepens and as we ourselves change.

In each step there are exercises to practice. It may seem like an exercise is breaking your flow, but we want you to slow down and reflect before moving on to the next idea. We also encourage you to pause after each step, and we introduce a three-minute breathing space (AGE) to help you do this.

The book can be used alongside other help, whether professional or peer. In particular, if you are dependent on a substance, it may be dangerous to stop taking it abruptly without some medication, so we recommend that you seek medical advice if this applies to you.

The book can be used in a facilitated or self-facilitating group context where each step can be discussed among those present.

Recovery can be hard and is often thought of as a lifelong journey. We would encourage you to seek out whatever you may find helps you – we offer the eight steps as aids and support to accompany you on your journey.

A great ally on the path of recovery is our breath. We carry our breath around with us all of the time. Connecting to our breath can help us to pause and slow down, which makes recovery possible. The breath underpins all eight steps. We will be learning to slow our lives down by working with our breath and short meditations in the book. In Tibet, the word for meditation is *gom*, which means "to become familiar with one's self." That is what this book will help us to do. Through short meditations, meditative exercises, and reflections, we will begin to understand the nature of our thoughts, feelings, actions, and mind. Using the breath is one of the most common ways to help us calm the mind. So let's connect to the breath before we begin exploring the eight steps of recovery.

If meditation brings up anxiety, we have lots of other tools to help you slow down. The tools section at the end of the book has additional exercises, as well as further resources, such as led meditations that you can also find online.

Three-minute breathing space, AGE

The breathing space is a way to put a pause in what you are doing. It can help you notice and break your unhelpful, automatic habits. It's also a chance to slow down for a few moments. Having paused and caught up with yourself, you can decide what to do next. There are three stages to it: **Awareness**, **Gathering**, and **Expanding** (hence AGE). A typical length of time for the breathing space is three minutes – one minute per stage – and so it's sometimes called the three-minute breathing space. However, you can make it longer or shorter depending on the circumstances.

Once you have read the instructions, put this book down, and take three minutes to practice the breathing space.

1. Bring **Awareness** to whatever is happening right now. (Assume a gently upright posture.) Become aware of your thoughts: what are you thinking right now? Allow your thoughts to be there, without pushing them away.

   What are you feeling right now? Let your feelings be there too. Acknowledge them as they are, even if they are difficult.

   Become aware of sensations in your body, especially any strong physical sensations. As best you can, just allow them to be there and bring an attitude of friendly curiosity toward them.

2. Then, **Gather** your attention on the breath, becoming aware of the breath coming in and going out of your nostrils and the movement of your chest and belly. Focus on the physical sensation of the breath. When you breathe in, it may feel cool, and when you breathe out, it may feel warm. Physical sensations of the breath can be tickling, throbbing, pulsating, hot, a dull ache, or sharp pain. If you feel something in your belly, nostril, or upper lip, no matter how slight, this is sensation.

3. Finally, **Expand** your awareness to include the whole body. As best you can, feel the physical sensations in the whole of your body. If you wish, to sense the body as a whole, you could imagine the breath going in and out of the pores in your skin, as if your whole body was breathing. If you notice any areas of tension or tightness, you could direct your attention there. You could imagine directing your breath to these areas, breathing into and exploring the sensations with the breath.

Step One

....

Accepting that this human life will bring suffering

> Life is difficult. This is a great truth, one of the greatest
> truths. It is a great truth because once we truly see this
> truth, we transcend it. Once we truly know that life is
> difficult – once we truly understand and accept it – then
> life is no longer difficult. Because once it is accepted, the
> fact that life is difficult no longer matters.[1]

Step One highlights the teaching of the first noble truth. That
there is suffering. Everything will one day come to an end. That
delicious dessert will satiate us for a moment and in the next
moment we will want more. Good news will excite us, and
sooner or later we will be feeling flat. Step One may seem all
doom and gloom, as if life is hopeless. That is how the first noble
truth can appear to some people. However, the Buddha is just
highlighting that nothing will give us everlasting satisfaction.
He isn't saying there is no joy or reason to continue living our
lives. So what we are saying is that there will be dissatisfaction,
frustrations, unmet needs, and desires in life.

Although suffering is inevitable, many people are not in
touch with their suffering or don't want to know about it. Some
people live a life of sex, rock 'n' roll, or work morning, noon,
and night and are not in touch with the pain that is lurking deep
inside them. And why would they want to be? They have found
a way to live, and keep a lid on all their pain, until one day they
are unable to control their life with external stimulants. Others
are unable to hide from their pain.

The Buddha said that birth, aging, sickness, and death
will bring about suffering. And of course he was right. As

soon as we are born we are old enough to die. As soon as we are born we will begin to age, and inevitably will become sick. How many of us ignore or brush aside these basic facts of life? How many of us turn to alcohol, food, drugs, sex, work, or another coping mechanism when we are faced with an illness, with the death of a loved one? How many of us fear our death or the death of a loved one? Or fear aging, sickness, and the inevitable suffering in life? We cannot escape this reality.

Three types of suffering

The Buddha identified three sorts of suffering: physical, psychological, and existential.

Physical suffering

This is direct suffering of the body: a headache, stomachache, toothache, a wound to the physical body. As human beings with a body, we cannot help feeling physical pain. However, how we respond or react to the pain will exacerbate or diminish our suffering. Some of us have developed addictions because of pain and physical suffering. Others have become meditators and/or Buddhists because of physical pain. Through meditation we discover that pain is always changing; that physical pain does not remain at a constant intensity. We learn that responding to it with a calm mind really has an impact. It may not take away the pain, but it gives us a creative way to work with it.

We have learned that responding to physical pain with an agitated mind can increase the intensity of pain, rendering us at risk of becoming addicted to inappropriate use of painkillers or dependent on alcohol.

We're not saying that we should never take painkillers, because, as we know, a painkiller can help to restore the calm we need in our minds to work with the physical discomfort. We can work with pain by becoming aware of what is going on when we are in physical pain.

Have you ever been under the hands of a masseuse giving a deep-tissue massage? If they catch a knot, it is excruciatingly painful. We become agitated, wishing we had a painkiller, and the masseuse gently says: "Take a deep breath. Breathe in and out slowly." Hey, presto – the pain feels much more bearable.

Physical pain is real. We cannot get rid of all physical pain, but we can let go of mental, emotional, and psychological pain, which so easily develops in the wake of physical pain.

Psychological suffering

This is our stinking thinking, the stories we tell ourselves. Have you ever told yourself you know something is not going to happen? You have angst about it, convince yourself there is absolutely no way it will happen. And, lo and behold, it does happen.

Have you ever told yourself that somebody didn't turn up to meet you because they don't care about you? Later, you learned that a mini-crisis occurred in their life that had prevented them from arriving.

Have you ever told yourself that you didn't get the promotion because "there is something wrong with me" or "I'm not good enough"? Later, you found out that the job was given to someone with much more experience. This is psychological suffering.

Then there are our expectations. For as long as we have expectations we will suffer. As soon as something does not live up to our expectations, we will be disappointed.

There are more subtle forms of psychological suffering that many of us experience daily. When we are clinging to a happy experience, there can be a background disquiet because somewhere deep down we know this pleasurable moment will not last. Have you ever held on to a memory of a meeting with a friend, and, the next time you met, felt disappointed because it did not live up to the memory? This too is psychological suffering.

It is so typical for our lives to seem to be going well, then something changes. A partner leaves us, or the washing machine breaks down. A friend cancels a meeting, or our cat dies. We are fearful of change. We get a new phone, but we are anxious about it being stolen. We worry that our partner might leave us or find someone they are more attracted to. The good things in our life are tinged with an awareness that they won't last forever.

Of course suffering can lessen, especially psychological suffering. We create the dramas in our lives. In a life of addiction, there will be great highs and great lows, continually swinging from craving to hatred. It's not possible for suffering to lessen while we are in the throes of an addiction. We have to stop moving away from our suffering, and do what the celebrated American author, teacher, and Buddhist nun in the Shambhala Buddhist tradition, Pema Chödrön, suggests:

> Lean into the sharp points and fully experience them.
> The essence of bravery is being without self-deception.
> Wisdom is inherent in (understanding) emotions.[2]

Look at it, accepting that it is there; don't identify with it; and let it go. It's possible for suffering to become part of the subtle ebb and flow of the mind, rather than the overwhelming emotions that we get hooked by and need to self-medicate or act out. When we become aware of the subtleties of suffering and trust, suffering will arise and cease. If we don't go into panic or fear, it will not overwhelm us with strong emotions.

Existential suffering

At a deeper level, the unstable, changing nature of all experience means that we cannot find lasting satisfaction in anything, because nothing will stay the same. Everything around us – people, places, objects – is in flux. This creates a sense of dis-ease. We can't completely relax into this changing world – at least to the extent that we try to fix it or lean on it for security. Sometimes we can feel that if we could just get to the end of our to-do list, everything would be OK. We would sort everything out, get on top of our lives, and arrive at the perfect state. Unfortunately we never get there: there is always more change. Nothing and nobody can give us permanent, lasting satisfaction and happiness. This is true for everyone, not just those of us with an addiction. There is no one we can turn to who can provide us with complete security. Whenever we seek out permanence or perfection, even though we may do it unconsciously, we will have an undercurrent of dissatisfaction.

We might experience existential suffering as a nagging sense of disquiet or insecurity, lingering in the background of our awareness. Alternatively, we might feel it more strongly, for example, as an overwhelming lack of meaning in life, perhaps when confronting aging, sickness, and death.

Physical suffering will always occur; we can't prevent it from ever happening to us. But mental and existential suffering can cease. We are what we think. We multiply our pain. When we let go of expectations, happiness will begin to naturally arise. When we can accept this, our suffering will lessen.

The Buddha was asked: what is the difference between how an ordinary person and a wise person respond to pain? He replied with the analogy of the two darts. All of us experience pain – whether that is physical pain like catching your finger in the door or mental pain such as when someone rejects you. This is the first dart, which we could call primary suffering. An ordinary person then gets caught up in trying to push away or avoid the pain: in blaming themselves or others, or feeling self-pity. This has the effect of making matters worse and constitutes the second dart, which we can call secondary suffering. A wise person just has the first dart. They don't get stuck in avoidance or obsessing about the pain. Instead they mindfully accept it for what it is, without making it worse with secondary suffering.

Face your pain with the breath

In this meditation we follow the breath as an anchor for the meditation. Then, whenever we notice that we are experiencing bodily pain or difficult emotions, as best we can we try to face the pain just as it is and let go of any stories we are telling ourselves about the pain.

Begin by settling into a comfortable posture, bringing your attention onto your breath and following your breath as it moves in and out of the body. Then, whenever you notice a painful sensation, as best you can, recognize the difference between the raw primary painful sensations and the responses of aversion toward it. If the pain is emotional, notice the difference between the raw emotion and the thoughts about it – the stories or narrative we tell ourselves about it. As best you can, allow the primary painful sensations to be there. Breathe into the sensations. If the pain is mainly emotional, there will be physical sensations associated with the emotion – breathe into these bodily sensations, with a sense of friendliness and curiosity. As best you can, let go of the stories about the pain; open to and feel into the raw sensations. If the sensations are very strong, breathe onto the edge of the area where the sensations feel intense. If it's helpful, say to yourself: "It's okay, it's already here, let me feel it."

Suffering and addiction

Valerie

When I first came into contact with Buddhism, I was addicted to feeling high. The first whiff of pain was my trigger to make myself feel high. When something traumatic happened in my life I would go out dancing all night, even without intoxicants. The dancing made me feel momentarily better. I was not aware that I was still suffering. I had many coping strategies to deal with all my pain. I would never have admitted to being depressed. But when I look back on my life I can see how I was self-medicating. The binge–vomit cycle of bulimia was most definitely a form of depression. And when I needed a break from the cycle, I would take a stimulant.

I was told I had the perfect body, and was often asked if I was a model. I had achieved the ultimate goal of controlling my body. I thought that if I could control my body, this would control my world. But once I went below 100 pounds I was perceived by the world as sick, and when I went over 130 pounds I perceived myself to be obese. I could not cope with my body changing. I refused to face the truth of my suffering. I would rather die a miserable death than accept change. I could not see that throughout my twenty years of anorexia, bulimia, and hedonism, I was playing a deluded game of sensations, swinging from craving to aversion, without even a pause in between. My career would be going seemingly well as a successful journalist, and then something would happen, and I would be in protest against the change.

My nostrils collapsed from snorting so much cocaine, and yet I still continued to use. My front teeth crumbled away from the acid of purging, and yet I still continued to binge and purge. I did not want to be reminded of change, and certainly did not want to put down the coping mechanisms that had protected me from the pain of my trauma as a child and adolescent. But once I had the courage to reflect on the Buddha's teaching on suffering, it was as if I'd had brain surgery. My coping mechanism just began to slip away. I began to glimpse spaciousness and could see the insanity of my addictions. I could see how I had been torturing myself through self-induced mental suffering. I could see how I had created the suffering I was experiencing in life. I wanted something different. I wanted to move toward spaciousness. I wanted more positive emotion.

Sooner or later, addictive behaviors are likely to lead us into trouble. For example, we wake up with a bad hangover, or in bed with someone we have no memory of meeting. Secretive bingeing and vomiting will destroy our only set of natural teeth. Working in the office or at home over sixty hours a week may lead to isolation. One day we may return home only to find the creditors have seized our house due to our gambling or credit-card sprees. No matter what the addiction, it can lead to depression, isolation, the breakup of a relationship, loss of family, living on the streets. When we are addicted, we heap upon ourselves unnecessary suffering, and often associated with this are feelings of shame.

Part of the truth of suffering is simply that sometimes painful things will happen. Part of the delusion of suffering is that we can avoid our own suffering, perhaps just holding it off at arm's length. Our addictions are part of the delusion and ignorance that we as humans cultivate, causing our lives to become a whirlwind of chaos. We think that we are managing our emotions, that we can remain constantly high. We think that we can defeat the law of gravity, even though we know that what goes up must come back down. When we are high, we will plummet from the euphoric state induced by stimulants back down into the depths of despair.

Cocaine may give us a high, keep us out dancing all night, even help us have creative ideas and keep us awake to achieve all the things we need to do, but it can also lead to depression and psychosis. Alcohol may make us more sociable, humorous, and likeable, but it can also make us more argumentative and even violent. Gambling may earn us a living, but it can also make us bankrupt. It may also be fun, but a livelihood that has an overwhelming amount of stress attached to it will create much tension and resentments in life. Similarly, using avoidance strategies like staying at work all day and night may feed the family, but inevitably it will have an impact on personal relationships.

Addictions are a dis-ease, an illness of the heart, body, and mind. Even without any addictive behavior, we all experience illness and dis-ease at times. We catch a cold or strain our back or are affected by more serious sickness, or emotional distress. It's built into the nature of being human. The workings of our bodies are incredible, but eventually our bodies must wear out, break down, or go wrong.

However, the truth of suffering goes deeper than this. Nothing stays the same and everything is in flux. All things are impermanent – the Buddha's fundamental insight. If we try to fix things and keep them the same, we will suffer.

Reflection: counting the costs of addiction

Take ten minutes to stop and reflect on your life and how addiction affects it. Find a quiet place to sit and settle yourself in a chair or on the ground. If you are comfortable doing so, close your eyes, or keep them slightly open, directed downwards. Feel the ground beneath your feet and anywhere else your body touches the ground. Allow the ground to support your weight. If you are sitting in a chair, feel the support of the chair. Notice that you are breathing and follow the sensations of the breath as it enters and leaves the body.

Now recollect your addiction.

How does it help your life?

What do you gain from this behavior? Perhaps recall what first led you into this behavior. If you notice any judgments or qualifications about your reflections, just acknowledge them and try to let them go.

How does your addiction cause you suffering?

What are the costs of this behavior? Again, if you notice any judgments or qualifications, as best you can, acknowledge them and let them go.

Now allow the reflections to drop away. Notice the breathing again and follow the sensations as the breath fills and empties the chest and belly. Notice how you are feeling. If you are left with the thought that you want to move away from any discomfort, remember it is just a thought and not you. Take a breath and pause. There is no need to identify with the thought. Just let it arise and cease. And there will be a new thought telling you something different.

When you are ready, open your eyes. If you wish, write down your reflections.

Everyone has pain

In an affluent society, we have so many things to distract us that we are often unaware of the pain we are carrying around. We don't realize that the sudden angry outburst we had, the conflicts that seem to keep on arising in our lives, and our intense dislikes or cravings are all connected to pain.

When we slow down, and let go of our addictions and avoidance strategies, we can quickly discover how busy our minds are. Our minds are like a tumble dryer, often with the same old stuff going round and round. We rerun and rehearse arguments, we fantasize about the future, we make up shopping lists, we go over past difficult events. We plan what we are going to have for dinner. We meet someone we fancy, and before we know it we have married them, and in the next breath killed them off in our heads. We can get completely caught up in any number of mental troubles or physical pains.

We may even think that we are the only ones with this type of noise going on inside our heads. The world is full of calm-looking people. It can seem that everyone else is having a better life than we are. We think that, unlike us, they must all be sorted, happy, and have focused minds. We might feel a pang of anguish or jealousy, perhaps berate ourselves, and even feel self-pity.

Chances are, once we have slowed down, people will look at us and think we are living perfectly calm and happy lives. The reality is that the majority of people have minds that are just as busy as ours. We can't tell what is going on in someone else's mind, and we have become very skilled at masking what is actually going on in our own lives.

Most of the time we are preoccupied by the thoughts and feelings that assail us. Sometimes, this is painful. And when it is, it's hard not to be caught up in it. Occasionally we look at other people, and often they look fine; they don't seem to have the pain and suffering we experience.

In fact, everyone has pain. Not all of the time, but definitely sometimes. This is a basic fact of life.

The four reminders

The Buddha's teaching is a prompt to face this reality and take responsibility for our own lives. There are four reminders to nudge us to do this. They are a poignant, gritty message to help us remember that change is a bittersweet reality.

If we do not wake up to the four reminders, we can spend our lives chasing after pleasure in the guise of our addictions, or reaching out for something external to numb our pain. If we wake up to the four reminders, we can begin to accept calmly that this human life will bring suffering, and start to shape our lives in ways that bring greater fulfillment.

The first reminder is that this life is precious. What this means is that we are fortunate to have a human birth; we have the capacity to live a rich and fulfilling life. If we are born into a family of alcoholics or a family of hate, we still have the potential to change our lives, and not continue the family's vicious cycle. We can break the family history and pathology. We don't know how long we will have on this planet, but we do know that we are living right now in this moment. And this present moment is an opportunity to change and to let go of our addictions. Do we want to waste any more of our precious time? What changes would we like to make in our lives?

The second reminder is that death is inevitable, that everything is impermanent. It has been said that the teachings of the Buddha can be summarized in one sentence: everything changes. Everything that arises will cease, and without warning our death will greet us. Our body one day will be a cupful of ashes, or a corpse in a coffin, or an abandoned piece of rotting flesh. One day we will have to renounce everything we have ever loved, owned, or been addicted to. We do not need to create drama in our lives; reality will bring its own stock of drama. Life is complex in itself. The addictions we use (so we believe) to keep us sane, and our fear of change and ultimately death, will only enhance that complexity. The fact that we will die is not a tragedy. Our addictions, and our denial, create the tragedies in our lives. Can we contemplate our death calmly? Can we use the fact of our death to make the most of our precious lives?

The third reminder is that actions have consequences. It's as plain and as simple as that. We act, and positive or negative consequences follow. Just as our bodies move in the world, our shadows follow us. Just as we are born, death follows. We cannot escape this law of cause and effect. It is with us in every breath that we take. We may drink one glass to drown our sorrows and, before we know it, that action has led to the consequence of finishing a whole bottle. And when we wake up, our heads are thick with a hangover, and so the consequences continue.

By paying attention to the consequences of our actions, we can discover whether our actions are helpful or unhelpful; whether they promote harmony in our own and others' lives, or whether they lead to our unhappiness. Are we aware of the consequences of our actions? Are we willing to take responsibility for our actions? Are we willing to admit to ourselves and face up to the consequences of our actions?

The fourth reminder is that suffering and dissatisfaction are part of everyday life. It is the painfulness of existence, which we discussed above in the three types of suffering. It is a reminder to help wake us up to the reality that our birth is precious, that we will not live forever, and our actions will have consequences. The fourth reminder nudges us out of living a life of complacency. What is the pain in our lives that we hide from or try to avoid? How much time do we think we have to complete everything we want to do?

If we can form a relationship with these reminders and welcome them into our lives, they will help us to face our pain, and not avoid it with our addictions or coping mechanisms. We will have the courage to face ourselves in the mirror and witness the truth of our lives. We will see that everyone suffers. That pain is pain. Money may be able to buy us a few more years of life, or a few more years of life for a loved one. It may even be able to buy cosmetic surgery to superficially slow down external aging. But, in the end, money cannot prevent sickness, aging, and death. We all will suffer in the end.

The four reminders can put suffering in context by helping us to recall that suffering is universal and that our brief lives are a precious opportunity. Reflecting on the four reminders can help us to make the most of our lives and to connect with other people as we remember that we are all in the same boat: we will all experience suffering and death.

Four reminders reflection

Having read these reminders, pause for a moment, put the book down, lie down if you are in bed reading, or just relax in your seat, even if you are traveling on public transport. Allow yourself to reflect on one of these reminders for ten minutes. After the reflection, let it germinate for the whole day, and then reflect on another reminder the following day. Take your time with each. You may want to reflect on each one for a week. We are just giving pointers. The four reminders are strong medicine, and difficult issues may arise; they may even feel overwhelming. It may be helpful to find somebody to talk to, rather than go it alone.

- Reflect on why your life is precious. Ask yourself: "What inspires me to live?"
- Reflect on the fact that death is unavoidable, and on how you want to live your life. Ask yourself: "How am I being in this life? What am I doing with my life?"
- Reflect that actions have consequences, and on some of the consequences of your actions. Ask yourself: "What actions have been a gain to my life? What actions have been a cost in my life?"
- Reflect on the ocean of inevitable suffering, the waves of sickness, aging, and death that one day will come even to you. Ask yourself: "What am I feeling right now?"

What is meant by the truth of suffering?

Suffering is universal. None of us can escape this life without a share of pain, discomfort, and grief. It's not a terrible mistake that we are suffering, nor a personal failure. Pain happens to us and it happens to everyone. We do create our own suffering – mostly through not understanding how we do it or seeing an alternative – but so does everyone.

Suffering tends to isolate us. We feel alone and helpless in our pain, often feeling that no one else understands the extent of our suffering or has experienced anything like this. Recognizing that suffering is universal changes its quality. It connects us to humanity and opens the door to changing our relationship to suffering and learning to alleviate its excesses.

Suffering can come from our personal response to the mental or physical pain we experience. Therefore suffering is often our stinking thinking that can turn into emotions like resentment, anger, hatred, or jealousy.

How we practice this step

Let's be clear: we are not recommending suffering as a good thing. Self-martyrdom has no place in recovery from addiction. So if you have a headache, we are not saying: "Don't take a painkiller." Or if you break a leg, we are not suggesting that you don't get it fixed, or that you deliberately stay in a violent relationship to experience the pain of it.

Our overall purpose in recovery is to overcome and move beyond suffering. However, in order to do that effectively, we need to look at our suffering in a clear-sighted way. We need to really get to know our suffering and how we cause ourselves to suffer. There is pain in our lives, some of which is inevitable or cannot be changed, and there is our response to pain, which often makes our suffering worse.

We will explore more fully in Step Two how our responses to pain create more suffering in our lives, and how we can change our responses so that we suffer less. In order to do so, we will need to face our pain and get to know it – but in a new way. That is the work of Step One.

We need to fearlessly take stock of the pain in our lives, to look at it unflinchingly and without judging it. This may feel like a big task. Facing our pain and suffering is the last thing we want to do. Indeed, it doesn't seem like a remotely sensible thing to do. However, if we focus on our suffering, we may be surprised at what will arise. It requires a degree of courage, and should be done slowly and gently. We can start by noticing the smaller discomforts, and learning from these, before tackling bigger areas of pain.

Mindful attention to our suffering

Mindfulness is deliberately paying attention to our moment-by-moment experience as it unfolds. We do this in a non-judgmental way, with an attitude of friendliness and curiosity. Mindfulness is a key part of the Buddha's teachings, used increasingly to help with a range of health issues, including chronic pain, depression, and addiction.

The Buddha's last words are said to have been: "With vigilance strive to succeed." This statement reminds us that we must pay attention to every moment, one moment at a time. Those of us living with addictions know how hard this is to do. We also know that, when we don't pay attention to each moment, it is so easy to spiral back into overwhelming addictive behavior.

We learn to pay attention to our minds and our bodies through connecting to the breath. The three-minute breathing space, AGE, which we introduced earlier, is one way to help us begin to notice what we are thinking and feeling. We become aware of what we are covering up and what is really happening in our lives. Sitting meditation is one way we can begin to bring awareness to our experience as we go about our daily lives. This is why we include meditation as an important tool for recovery in this book. The practice of loving-kindness and mindfulness meditations can restore a mind to sanity. As well as the shorter versions we describe as we go through the steps, you will find fuller versions of these two meditations in the tools section at the end of the book.

Many of us find it very difficult to stop, and being asked to sit and meditate for ten or more minutes could be the end of reading this book. There are simple ways to try and bring the pause into our lives. If we practice AGE for three minutes in our day there will be benefits. It is something we can do while at work, stopping for three minutes. However, if you would like to explore a sitting meditation with a dedicated amount of time, you could begin with ten minutes.

Mindfulness of Breathing – ten-minute version

This meditation can be a good way to start to give mindful attention to your experience and to learn to pay attention to your suffering. As you become more comfortable meditating, you can do the longer version of the Mindfulness of Breathing, which is in the tools section at the end of the book.

Meditation can be done sitting in a chair, on cushions, or on a meditation stool. Try to be as comfortable as possible. The lower body should be stable, supported by the ground and your chair or cushions. At the same time the upper body should be upright, but without straining. Meditation can also be done lying down, especially if you have chronic pain, although that brings a greater risk of falling asleep.

First, scan your body. As best you can, allow your body to relax with alertness whether sitting or lying down. Pay attention to your body. Allow yourself to feel your body in contact with the clothes you are wearing, in contact with the seat you are sitting in or the surface you are lying on. Bit by bit, scan through your whole body. Begin with your left foot, moving up through your left leg before doing the same with your right leg. Bring your attention into the groin area, and the buttocks. Become aware of your torso, and your stomach rising up and down. If you are sitting up, feel the natural curve of the spine rising out of the pelvis, and if you are lying down, feel your spine being supported by the ground. Become aware of where each hand is resting on your body, and then move up each arm, and into each shoulder. Become aware of your neck, throat, the back of your head, the top of your head, and face. Now notice that you are breathing; feel the chest and perhaps the belly expanding and contracting. Without trying to change your breath in any way, allow yourself to follow the movement of the breath in and out of the body. Become interested in just what the breath is like: whether it is deep or shallow, long or short, smooth or irregular.

Sooner or later your mind will wander off, away from the breath. That's just what minds do. When you notice your mind has wandered off, you can use this as an opportunity to notice where your mind has gone. Note what has taken up your attention. If you have been caught up in something that is uncomfortable or painful, just note that discomfort is present.

Once you have noted where your mind has gone, gently bring your attention back to the breathing.

Do this again and again: each time your mind wanders off, note where it has gone, then return again to the breath. When you are ready, bring the meditation to a close. Pause a little before getting up and perhaps stretch your body before continuing with your day.

If you noticed you had to keep on bringing your mind back, that you were really distracted, and you spent the whole ten minutes having to bring your mind back to the breath: well done. You have been meditating!

When we sit in meditation and we try to stay with our breath, we start to notice when painful sensations of body or mind are present. We can also notice that we are rerunning an argument with our partner or that our belly is clenched with fear about our debts. We catch in their infancy the little triggers that can slide into our mind unawares, build up and run away into a seemingly unstoppable force demanding a fix or a binge to assuage them. We learn to notice early on that we felt hurt by a comment from a friend or that insecurity over our job is gnawing away and building tension in our body. We also begin to see how we relate to our suffering. As the mind wanders away from the object of meditation, we see how it turns to blaming or pity, or we find that we have distracted ourselves from some discomfort by getting lost in our head.

Change begins with ourselves. If we are attentive to ourselves, we will begin to notice the triggers that lead us into addiction and we will then have a choice to pick up or not. When we are in the throes of addiction, it can seem that we have no choice. This is because we are like the gerbil running around and around inside of the wheel, never allowing ourselves to pause.

You may say: "This is all too overwhelming. I can't sit still for more than five minutes, and, if I do, I can hear all sorts of crazy thoughts in my head." This is excellent. Sitting still for five minutes a day is a great start. Don't undermine it. And the fact you can hear all the insane thinking means that you have finally paused, and allowed some of your suffering to arise. We do not have to act out our thoughts; we do not have to cling to our thoughts; we can just observe them arising and ceasing without desire or hatred. When a strong thought seems to grip you, just say to yourself: "Let it go, let it go."

If we can let go, let the thought arise and cease, the feeling of being overwhelmed will be able to subside and there will be no need to turn to our addictive behavior. There will be no overwhelming thoughts to numb. It is an opportunity to pay attention to ourselves, give ourselves some affection, appreciate ourselves, and, ultimately, learn to accept ourselves.

Recap

In Step One, we accept that this human life will bring suffering. We learn to face our pain. We do this by noticing our pain with mindfulness. We begin to notice our pain with a calm mind. We learn to stop, pause, and slow down. We occupy the breath and the body and become aware of what is going on in the mind. We also reflect on our precious life, that death is inevitable, actions have consequences, and unsatisfactoriness is part of everyday life.

This is a gentle reminder for us to pause at the end of Step One, and take a three-minute breathing space.

 Three-minute breathing space, AGE

Awareness of thoughts, feelings, and body.
Gather the breath, notice the breath, become aware of the breath.
Expand the breath throughout the whole body – connect to the whole body.

Step Two

....

Seeing how we create extra suffering in our lives

The Buddha taught that one of the main ways we create suffering is through craving, and aversion, which is the flip side of craving. This is the second noble truth.

Craving is the urge to have a different experience from the one we are having now. It is the intense desire for a particular experience. It is the overwhelming sensations that arise in the body and manifest as an obsessive urge for things like food, drugs, sex, or any other experience. When we crave something, we are holding on to the desire for the pleasurable aspects of an experience, while denying or ignoring its painful and unpleasant aspects. Craving is inextricably linked to suffering. We can be abstinent and still crave the experience we have abstained from, which is why it is important for us to cultivate sobriety of mind: a mind that is free of craving, calm, and clear-sighted.

Aversion is wanting to push away an experience that we are having, especially a painful experience. It is the intense dislike of something and the avoidance of unpleasant and painful experiences. Aversion is also the separation of ourselves from the rest of the world.

Craving can take many forms: craving to have and control things; craving sensual pleasure; and craving fame. Aversion may be directed toward unpleasant sensations, whether physical pain or mental discomfort, such as fear, anger, or jealousy. Craving and aversion often arise as responses to pain, but, in seeking to escape our pain, we bring ourselves more suffering.

It is helpful to distinguish between unpleasant experiences that have already arisen, and the further discomfort we may cause by our response to them. We can call the former "pain," and the results that follow from our response to pain "suffering." The suffering we create is summed up succinctly by the American meditation teacher Shinzen Young, who says: "Suffering equals pain multiplied by resistance."[1] Therefore, the more we resist pain, the greater the suffering we create in our lives.

Given that pain and suffering are inevitable, at some point we need to develop different ways of responding to them.

For now, just notice how you respond when something painful happens in your life. Maybe there is something happening right now. Perhaps your shoulder is aching or you are thinking about a conflict you are in with a colleague or a neighbor. Or you could bring to mind a recent painful experience, such as a toothache, a big bill arriving in the mail, or being let down by a friend. Notice what your reaction is. Does your mind want to blame the other person or life in general? Do you want to hide away from the pain or make it vanish, perhaps with a drink, a snack, or watching TV? Do you feel self-pity, or find yourself thinking that things like this always happen to you? Do you notice any thoughts like "Life is not fair"? Is there a thought deep down that this should not be happening to you? Whatever the response, try to be curious; try to be willing to let it be there, just for now (since it is already here).

The common ways we deal with suffering

There are four common ways of dealing with suffering, which we may notice if we pay attention to how we react to painful experiences: we avoid or deny it; we blame other people; we blame ourselves; or we fall into self-pity.

Avoiding

Most of us want to get rid of our suffering: our fears, anxieties, anger, and jealousies, and all the painful thoughts that go with these emotions. So we may try to push them away and avoid them, or attempt a quick fix to make them go away. And why not? In the short term it can work. Sometimes it

Fig. 1: The vicious cycle of addiction

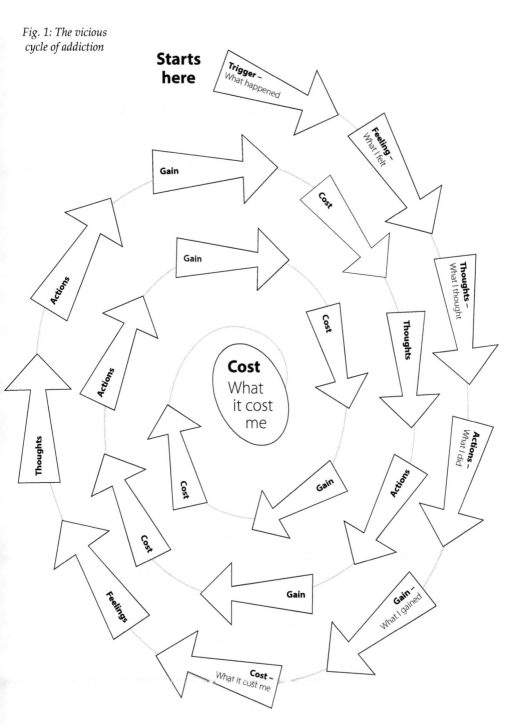

Once we have been triggered and are on the cycle, the trigger becomes irrelevant because we are in the feelings and thoughts, to the extent that we will go around and around, where in the end we will only be aware of the cost.

can be helpful to distract ourselves from our difficulties, especially if it is done consciously. We might decide that, just for now, we will watch a movie or read a novel to take our minds off something difficult.

The problem is that pushing away painful thoughts and emotions usually makes them stronger if we never allow ourselves to face the pain. It's like trying not to think of a pink elephant – the more we try not to think of one, the more pink elephants show up in our minds.

Addiction is one way to avoid suffering. When something difficult shows up, we have a drink, eat some chocolate, reach for something external like sex or gambling, or take a substance. Many of us try to brutally eradicate our thoughts and feelings with our choice of self-medication. And guess what? The feelings and thoughts just bounce back again once the medication has worn off.

One of the clients we have worked with was a compulsive eater. Her overeating began at age nine when her father died. People brought food every day for a month to comfort her and her mother. Thirty years later she was still eating away her feelings. She was still suffering the loss of her father. The only intimacy in her life was the food.

As our addiction grows, this behavior becomes more and more the default for any sort of discomfort. It becomes a vicious cycle, since the more we use the addiction to deal with difficulties, the less able we are to handle suffering in other ways, and so the more we resort to the addictive solution. It is like a nightmare in which the harder we try to escape our difficulties, the worse they become.

The vicious cycle can often look like the diagram in Figure 1.

- The trigger: something happens, which we experience through one or more of our senses.
- The feeling: the trigger produces feelings in us – often of upset or hurt.
- The thought: this is where we can interpret our feelings as the result of having been violated, abused, or whatever is our habitual take on what happens to

us. This is where we tell ourselves the story, and we lose clarity as we get more and more caught up in our story.

- The action: we pick up a drink, a pharmaceutical pill, a stimulant; we may even act with verbal aggression or physical violence. Whatever action we take, there will be an impact.
- The gain: we may gain several things: feeling calmer for a while, or avoidance of our hurt and pain.
- The cost: our actions can often lead us into all sorts of trouble, and leave us feeling more angry or ashamed – so much so that we sink even more into our addiction. This is where the cycle is perpetuated. The trigger becomes irrelevant. We are back at feeling pain, back into the toxic thinking, back into numbing our pain by our choice of action, once the small gain of feeling momentarily better has worn off, and back into the cost of feeling angry and awful. The cycle is so toxic that we get to the point where our thoughts, actions, and gains become so irrelevant that we are thick into the huge cost of our decisions without awareness.

And so the cycle continues.

Avoidance of pain doesn't just happen through ingesting something; we can equally lose ourselves through burying our heads in work, mindless television, or surfing the Internet. One of our patients described how she was unable to part with articles that she had compulsively cut out of newspapers and magazines and stored in boxes. The act of cutting out stories and saving them had a mind-altering effect that took her away from any painful feelings. Some people find a way to phase out or go numb when suffering appears. Sometimes this can go on at quite a subtle level. We may find ourselves with discomfort in meditation that we thought we had acknowledged, only to later realize we had been tensing up around it, gritting our teeth until the end of a period of meditation.

Blaming others

Blaming others is a popular strategy for dealing with pain. For example, we can't find something at home. An unpleasant feeling of frustration, upset, or anger arises, and we automatically move away from these feelings. Our mind jumps to blaming anyone who might have moved what we're looking for, or even kicking the cat out of the way. This type of behavior can be very seductive. It can make us feel like the problem is no longer our fault and we get off squeaky clean, often with the full moral conviction that goes with righteous indignation. Blaming masks the uncomfortable feelings because, when we blame, we often feel in control of the situation and powerful.

So when we are rejected by a friend, or our partner leaves us, we blame them and make it their fault. That way we don't have to look at ourselves, but in the end we can fall into the hole of self-pity. A parent dies, and it was because the medical profession didn't do enough to keep them alive. We go into battle with the health-care system, which can drag on for years. Blame doesn't allow us to grieve. We have not fully accepted the demise of our loved one. The sister failed to call when her nephew was in trouble with the police, and from then on her brother holds her at a frosty distance, which somehow displaces the discomfort about his son being in trouble. Or our boss at work is seen to be against us. We think that's why we never get promoted, and we get sick with stress.

Of course, sometimes people do hurtful things, make mistakes, or are negligent. However, holding on to blame, without looking at our contribution and our response, keeps us stuck and unable to move on. It is as if we keep stoking a fire burning painfully within us.

Blaming ourselves

The other side – blaming ourselves – keeps us stuck just as much as blaming others. It's not that we recognize our mistake, but that we won't let it go and keep tormenting ourselves with it. The child blames herself for not standing up to protect her mother against a violent father, and continues to hold on to that blame as an adult. A son commits suicide and the father blames himself for something he said the last time they spoke. It is as though, by taking on all the blame, we have it under our control, as though there might be a magical way of changing the past. Blaming ourselves can also divert us from facing a pain beyond our control or, by getting there first, help us avoid the frightening prospect of other people blaming us.

Self-blame can keep us in addiction or lead us back to it. For example, one client we worked with was rear-ended in a car. He suffered whiplash. It wasn't his fault. However, a day later he proceeded to beat himself up with phrases like: "I hate myself; how stupid of me – I should have pulled away faster." This self-flagellation went on so much that he relapsed into his addiction. He couldn't cope with all his negative and self-belittling thoughts.

We might experience the consequences of our self-blame when we try to get up in the morning. We may not be able to get out of bed because we have binged on our stimulant, or have gambled away so much money that we can't bear to face the reality of our misdeeds.

Self-pity

Self-pity is another way we can keep ourselves stuck. For example, a friend cancels a meeting. We feel sad, and then fall into self-pity (perhaps thinking: "No one likes me").

Self-hatred can be an aspect of self-pity. It's as if we fall into a pit from which there is no way out. Although it's a painful place to be, it can also be alluring because it can mean that there is nothing we have to do about it; we are helpless. We fall ill and sink into self-pity. This lets us off the hook of taking action about our illness and working with our mental responses to it. Or we stay in a destructive relationship. It's unpleasant, we are full of self-pity, but we fail to do anything about it.

We can even become addicted to self-pity and self-hatred. Every time something painful arises in our lives, we can flee to the place of self-pity because it's familiar, and we do not have to face up to what is happening in our lives.

Addiction can run alongside or alternate with any of the latter three responses. Our drinking is blamed on other people. We feel self-pity at the mess our lives are in from all the gambling debts. Or we blame ourselves for our lack of moral fiber in being unable to stop bingeing – which in turn just leads to more bingeing. The ex-wife is blamed for alienating the son from his father, which induces feelings of self-pity at the loss of contact with the son. Drinking is used to cope with the sorrow, and its effect on the new girlfriend leads to self-recrimination, which is blocked out with more drinking.

Blame may make us feel better, but it can also keep us angry. Blame can be the Band-Aid to keep our pain at bay. But that Band-Aid will not stick forever. We have a choice: we can remain angry for the rest of our lives, hold on to resentments and ill will; or we can begin to let go of our addiction, let go of blaming and create a space where we can feel our sorrow and let it go. Where there is sorrow there will be joy if we are patient, if we allow the law of cause and effect to take its natural time.

Craving as the cause of suffering

The Buddha said that craving is the chief cause of suffering. Craving is the default response to pain or pleasure. We have a visceral urge to move away from pain (that is, aversion) and to seek pleasure, or at least the alleviation of discomfort. This is a completely natural and understandable response. Our bodies and minds shrink from pain and the drive for pleasure is like an inbuilt thirst that cannot be tempered. The result is that most of us are searching for something outside of ourselves to make us happy, to complete us.

When we are addicted, we can often think: "If I have a drink, a line of coke, a meal, a quick fix of something, this will make me happy." And for a moment it does. Once the brief moment of happiness has passed, however, we are likely to become dissatisfied and so it's back to pain, again. We want the feeling of happiness never to end. It has been said that heroin is so addictive because, when people take it, all their troubles disappear. Every issue or problem just melts into the background. This appears to give users a reprieve, until they come down off the drug and feel absolutely rotten. So we go round and round, a cycle of craving, running after pleasure or being chased by pain.

The cycle of craving may come into being from an initial thought, such as: "I want a drink." This thought can arise and cease, and cause us no more suffering at all. However, sometimes craving arises and manifests as thoughts that become a story or a rationalization. This story is often intoxicating. Craving and thinking feed each other. As each becomes stronger, we become more likely to act on our thoughts, and are in danger of using or relapsing. Beware of this stinking thinking.

We can think of wanting a drink, but not act on it. We may then fight against this thought. But when we fight it, we have not let go of the thought. We have identified with it, by listening to it and believing it, and this stinking thinking eats away at our resistance. We may think we have dealt with the thought because we did not act on it that same day. But beware. When our guard is down, we can be taken by surprise. Two days later we may well be reaching for that drink or that drug we thought we had control of. Our minds will play games with us.

A relapse may be caused by a strong identification with a thought, or a trigger that occurred through one of the senses two months ago. We may have mistakenly taken a sip of a drink, had a small slip with food, hung out with people who were taking drugs, had a small flutter with gambling, or glimpsed a piece of porn, and told ourselves that it didn't make us relapse. We were fine the next day. Then one or two months later, we find ourselves in a relapse and can't understand why.

We have to learn to let these thoughts arise and cease, without identifying with them, acting on them, or fighting them. Have the courage to sit with the discomfort of a thought about indulging in our addiction, without fear, trusting the thought will arise and cease on its own. Fear is often the anticipation of the danger of a relapse for many people with addictions. When we anticipate a relapse we are at risk, which is why it is important to be calm when the waves of craving arise and cease.

What makes craving such a problem?

To want pleasure and avoid pain is a natural human response. We might have a drink to help us relax, or feel more creative or more confident. If we could just have one glass of wine once a year when work was especially stressful or to celebrate an anniversary, that might not be a problem. However, if our relationship with alcohol is such that one glass leads to consuming the whole bottle, or if wine becomes our way of dealing with any difficult feeling and the only way to find pleasure, then we are on the path to creating more suffering. We get fixated on a particular way of managing pleasure and pain. We might believe that we can only be creative under the influence of a stimulant, and then our using can end up controlling our lives.

We all have strategies to help us feel OK about ourselves, or to deal with difficulties, that can end up running us. We might pursue wealth, power, fame, sex, or approval. The more we become fixated on our strategies, the more they take over our lives.

This attachment to a particular coping style means that we are less flexible in meeting what shows up in our lives. In the grip of our craving, we don't see what is actually going on. If our only tool is a hammer, then all objects appear like a nail. If sex is our way of coping with difficulties, then all situations will be colored by how they can be opportunities for obtaining sex.

Types of craving

According to the Buddha, there are three main types of craving. They are seductive and take our lives crashing onto the rocks. There is craving for sensual pleasure, craving for existence, and craving for non-existence. Every time we push away or flee from suffering, we create more suffering in our lives. This is what we must understand if we are to realize Step Two in recovery.

Craving for sensual pleasure

Experiencing pleasure and pain comes with having a body, with its five senses. Enjoying the pleasure of our senses, such as that of a warm bath, an uplifting piece of music, or a beautiful view, can bring us a feeling of ease and be beneficial. However, we can get so caught up in chasing pleasure that it creates difficulties. We can easily be lured by the craving of indulgence in all the senses in the pursuit of pleasure.

So many of us consciously or unconsciously seek to excite our senses. We can be on our way to an appointment. We walk along the road, and out of the corner of our eye we are distracted by something. We see a shop. The window display is full of candy, cakes, or clothes. Our eyes are excited. We may even salivate without realizing it. Before we know it, we are inside the shop buying something we saw in the window. In seconds, our desire has been retriggered. We have a feeling of excitement, we tell ourselves we want it, and we act out and buy it. The irony is that, once we have bought the item and we are walking out of the shop, the feeling of pleasure is already waning. These are the stages of the vicious cycle that we spoke about earlier.

If we are struggling with an addiction, we may have the strong desire and determination to stop using. Yet, if we are not aware of what is going on in the mind, we can be picking up in seconds as soon as we are retriggered. The trigger for someone with an addiction can be seeing someone else drinking, eating, or gambling. We become excited at the sight of their drug of choice. We may even experience a rush of pleasure in the body. Then, instantaneously, we are thinking: "I want it. I want what they have." Before we know it, we are in a cycle of thinking, perhaps obsessively, of using, of how to get it, and next thing we know, we are in a relapse.

Noticing your triggers

It can be helpful to notice what triggers put you in danger of relapsing or acting on your addiction. Triggers might include painful mental states such as anxiety or anger, or social situations such as a birthday celebration. We call these high-risk situations, as they are often associated with strong craving. If you can identify your triggers, and especially if you can catch them early on, you have a better chance of avoiding the cycle of craving and getting caught up in your addiction. You may be able to find a more effective way to respond to the triggers.

Take this opportunity to look at the things that trigger your desires. See what is happening in your mind:

- Name your trigger.
- Name what you feel when you see the trigger.
- Name what you think.
- Name what you do.

You could also try this when you have picked up or distracted yourself with something external. Backtrack, and see what was going on in your mind. See if you can identify the point at which the thoughts become about using and picking up your choice of fix.

Craving for existence

Craving for existence is clinging to what we already have, like the dog who will not let go of the slipper. We fear losing what we have, and we are therefore in denial of impermanence. It is as if, by holding on tightly to what we have, we believe we can escape the inevitability of change. It is natural that we do not want to lose our loved ones or our prized possessions, but one day we will have to let go of absolutely everything. Unless we can find a wise way of coming into relationship with impermanence – something we will explore more in the next step – our fear of change will fuel craving and clinging, together with the suffering that goes with them.

Craving for existence also refers to pursuing a different state of being. It is natural to want to alleviate our suffering and to improve our lives so that we experience happiness. Unfortunately, our desire to make things better can fuel craving for a different experience – often a quick fix to escape from our suffering – which can keep us in the cycle of addiction. It is what we call misguided loving-kindness toward ourselves.

The act of turning to addictions for recovery from pain or difficult situations is deluded self-help. We are looking in the wrong place for happiness. This misguided kindness toward ourselves perpetuates a cycle of pain. In trying to become happier, we reach for things that bring temporary happiness. And then the chase begins. Chasing for that great high, that great experience we once had. The compelling urge to become wealthy, successful, to have everything we don't have, is also part of the craving for existence that leads to more suffering.

Why can't we desire these things? Well, of course we can. The issue is that, in desiring something, we begin to chase, crave, and cling to what we want. Instead of holding our desires and goals in a light way, we hold on to them tightly and end up being driven by them.

All of which creates suffering.

Craving for non-existence

When we are struggling with difficult emotions, such as fear, depression, or jealousy, we may crave being in a completely different state, as described above. Alternatively, we may just want it all to end: we may crave non-existence. Use of alcohol or heroin, for example, may be a way to dim our consciousness and dissolve our worries. People with addiction have a higher rate of suicide than the general population, and the allure of craving for non-existence may lead us to want to end our lives, to bring an end to our suffering.

However, there is hope. We do not need to be victims of craving. When we are, we risk becoming addicted and piling more suffering into our lives. Craving only has power over us for as long as we act on it and chase after the objects of our desire.

Craving is energy, admittedly an uncomfortable energy, that wants to latch on to something so we can feel better. Often we panic when craving arises, especially if we are in recovery. We may think: "I should not be feeling this. I am in recovery." Relax. It is inevitable that craving will still arise. What we are trying to do in recovery is meet the sensations of craving with a calm mind so that we don't move into fear and become overwhelmed by it, spiraling into a relapse.

Craving and high-risk situations

Here are some questions to ask yourself about your craving:

- What does the energy of craving feel like in my body?
- What do I crave right now?
- Why am I reaching for it?
- What would happen if I did not act on my craving?
- What are my high-risk situations?

Make a list.

Become aware of your feelings when these high-risk situations arise.

Become aware of your thoughts and emotions.

See if you can identify the point at which your thoughts turn to using and picking up your choice of fix.

When you slow down, you'll notice what is going on. This can give you the opportunity to make a different choice next time you are in a high-risk situation.

We learn to trust that craving too will pass. If we remain calm when craving arises, and we don't get caught up in it, it will cease. What often happens when we are determined to recover from our addictions, but find ourselves relapsing, is that we panic when the craving for our fix arises. In our panic we may lose all sense of awareness and pick up.

When craving arises, we stop what we are doing and take a few deep breaths. We become aware of our thoughts and say to ourselves: "Let them go. Let them go. Let them go." Or just name it "craving," accept that the sensation of craving has arisen, and don't act on it. We trust that craving will cease if we don't act on it. Instead of acting out of craving or identifying with the thoughts of craving, we can take this opportunity to have a three-minute breathing space, AGE.

The hungry ghosts: an image of craving

Fig 2: Hungry ghosts

In Buddhism, the hungry ghosts (see Figure 2) are depicted as having extended bellies, with tiny mouths and necks so thin that it is almost impossible for food to pass through. Any food they manage to ingest turns to fire or filth, causing pain and loathing. The hungry ghosts are an image of intense craving. In this state, what we consume is just not enough. Nothing will satisfy us, and our craving is insatiable.

A modern interpretation of the hungry ghost is the state of addiction.[2] When we are trapped by addiction, we may have voracious craving, and have lost all capacity to do anything besides picking up and using, distracting ourselves whenever a whiff of suffering arises. We may be driven by greed, envy, jealousy, obsessions, and the addiction itself. We may never feel satisfied.

Caught up like this, we are unable to step off the path of suffering. We are unable to imagine life without our quick fix, despite the fact that our chosen self-medication doesn't seem to work anymore, and our highs are heavily weighed down by frequent lows. We may be still chasing after that great high that occurred the first time we used twenty or more years ago, or just trying to cope with the consequences of our addiction. As for the hungry ghosts whose food turns to fire or filth, our addictive behavior may bring us more pain and leave us feeling ashamed.

Of course, not all addictions manifest in such an extreme way. Many of us have low-level acceptable addictions. We are able to function in the world and can think of life without a fix, but we may still be addicted.

In a sense we can all identify with the hungry ghosts, because we live in a culture where nothing is enough. Many of us crave to have more than we own. We want a bigger place to live in, a better job, more holidays, the latest technological gadget, the latest everything. Even if we don't define ourselves as addicts, many of us use acceptable suppressants like food, the sociable drink, pharmaceuticals, sex, shopping, relationships, to deal with the emptiness in our lives. This all comes at a cost. Yes, of course, as we mentioned earlier, we may gain momentary happiness and contentment, but there can also be a cost to ourselves, our families, and our work.

Eight Step Recovery

This path that leads to more suffering can end with us losing everything, including our families and homes. We can end up living on the streets, in prison, in and out of rehab, isolated, or dead from our dis-ease of mind. We may think this is extreme and only happens to the alcoholic and the drug addict. But even the compulsive overeater can end up dead from the addiction. Many have died from illnesses related to obesity. Some gamblers have committed suicide because they could not face the pain of their debts.

There are high-functioning people living with addictions who somehow keep it all together. Their families have not given up on them or thrown them out. Some make it into old age and finally grow out of the addiction. However, there are casualties of their addictive behavior. Many people with addictions were brought up in such homes. The hungry-ghost syndrome is perpetuated from family to family and generation to generation.

How we practice this step

Turning toward difficult experience

In Step One, we introduced the idea of mindfulness as a way to begin to notice our suffering. In Step Two, we begin to identify our triggers. If we can catch the triggers early on, we have a better chance of responding in a different way and not acting on our craving. In this step, we take mindfulness further by learning to stay with our pain and suffering as it arises.

Every time we pick up and act on our addictions, we create more suffering. We often think that if we indulge in our addictive behavior, it will make things better. Momentarily it can, and then the suffering comes back. We have just increased our suffering by moving toward our addiction. By contrast, if we can stay with our difficulties, rather than trying to make them go away with our addiction, we are on the path to recovery.

Learning to be with difficult experiences, such as the loss of a loved one, the death of a child, a relationship breakup, or a terminal illness, is a practice of compassionate patience. These can all bring about emptiness in our lives, the meaningless, the unknown, and the questions of what life is about. How many of us are patient enough, prepared to sit still and reflect on these questions? It is easier to reach for something to put in our mouths or in front of our eyes, to distract ourselves from the fact that life is fleeting and out of our control. Distractions and mood-altering substances point us in the direction of the path of suffering, and the denial of impermanence leads to more suffering.

So how can we help ourselves to sit with the discomfort? This is a tough question. To sit with painful experience, rather than try to immediately get rid of it, goes against the grain. Our instincts may tell us to get away from pain as quickly as possible.

From our experience, we know that self-medicating to anesthetize ourselves from suffering is not the answer. One day we will have to face the suffering, so we have a choice: to face it now, and begin to lessen the suffering, or avoid it and multiply the suffering for years and years.

First of all, we need to recognize that avoiding all pain, whether through addiction or some other behavior, is not going to work. Pain is an inevitable part of life. It's so tempting to try to push it away. It's so easy to feel that there must be a way to avoid all pain, if only we were smart enough. The temporary relief that we may get from drugs, alcohol, or eating can convince us that a pain-free life is possible. We need to feel in our bones that avoiding pain doesn't work. Or, at the very least, we need to take that seriously as a working hypothesis if we are going to make some real changes in our lives.

Bruce's story

Enjoying the peace of walking at the beach, I stood for a time watching the waves. Deeply relaxed, I was startled by a dog that came up from behind me barking and snarling. I've had post-traumatic stress disorder and can have a high startle reflex. I politely asked the owner to get the dog under control, explaining that it scared me, which was not well received. As I walked away, I had the residue of the scare and our exchange of harsh words in my mind. Seconds later, I had the idea to order pizza that evening. Through non-dual mindful inquiry I had been learning to recognize the ghost image that flashes through the mind just before we have the compulsion to act. So I had been mindfully watching my mind and saw that, just before I had the idea of getting pizza, I had a flash of me opening the door to the delivery person, the rich, cheesy aroma of the pizza, and the feeling of comfort and safety that flooded over me.

What I really wanted was to feel safe, to settle after being scared. I have an inappropriate pairing equating pizza with safety and comfort. Through mindful inquiry, I've begun to unravel the Velcroed ball of emotions, thoughts, memories, and sensations that have led to compulsive behavior. As they peel away, I'm able to be present with what is coming up without feeling I need pizza to help me cope. It's not a willpower issue. When the inappropriate pairing is seen through, it drops. There is still momentum in the mind and these thoughts will come up. Once I look directly at them, however, they lose their compulsive power. I was able to stay with the discomfort of my scare and enjoyed the rest of my walk before going home to a healthy, home-cooked meal.

When we try to avoid our pain, to avoid all the difficult feelings and thoughts that beset our minds, it is like pushing down a beach ball in a swimming pool and trying to keep it under water. It takes a lot of effort, and sooner or later the ball will bounce back up to the surface. Tell someone not to do something, and what are they doing when you turn your head? As soon as we try not to think about it, we are thinking about it. The very attempt not to have our painful experience only adds to it: we create tension in the effort to hold it out and we become overfocused on it, leaving little room in our lives for anything different.

The key to freedom from the trap of suffering is to realize that we are responsible for multiplying our suffering. We are the maestros of our own suffering. We can determine how much suffering we create for ourselves and how much we want to get lost on the path that leads to more suffering. It is possible to be happy without our addictions. It is possible to feel simplicity, contentment, and stillness in our lives if we are willing to sit with our minds and become aware of what is going on inside them.

Yes, there will always be external factors that cause us suffering, but we do not have to multiply it with our internal mental reactions. We can enable ourselves to have choice.

Often the people we have worked with have felt helpless, overwhelmed, and doomed, as if some external force had condemned them to destruction.

Valerie

When I was in the throes of my addiction, I thought that somebody had jumped inside me and pushed me into the shop to buy the food. I felt I had no choice, as if I was completely out of control. And to an extent I was.

I was not able to see that letting myself be driven by my feelings of fear guaranteed that I would live a life of suffering. I could not see that fear was an obstacle of the mind, which was preventing my recovery. I had found a way to deal with my feelings at a big cost. The cost was remaining a bulimic anorectic for over twenty years and being unable to let go of my addiction.

Learning to be with our experience is not easy. It can feel counterintuitive, like the last thing one should sensibly do. Hearing our thoughts can be even scarier. It can help to recognize that we are not our thoughts, and that we don't have to act out our thoughts. We don't have to believe our thoughts. We don't have to identify with our thoughts. If we can trust that our thoughts will arise and cease without us identifying with them, we will begin to find freedom from our thinking.

For example, a thought arises: "I am a failure." If we take the thought at face value and believe it, we may soon be caught up in thinking about all the reasons why we are failures, or in trying to push the thought away, which will only make it more persistent. However, if we just watch the thought and let it be there, just as a thought, we may discover that some space opens up around it. In this space we can begin to do something different. This space between the thought arising and us grasping onto it (through ruminating on it or fighting it) is where the power to change lies. It's the place where we can let go of the thought and not identify with it. It's the place where we become separate from our thoughts, and create space around them. We can see that thoughts just pop into our heads – we are not our thoughts. As we learn to watch our thoughts come and go, we can decide which ones we may want to act on, and which ones to let go of.

When we are controlled by our thoughts, we make interpretations, believing our thoughts to be true. Based on those interpretations, we make decisions, which can have detrimental outcomes for our recovery. However, if we are able to let go of our thinking and see the facts of the situation more clearly, our decisions and the outcomes may be different.

For example:

- There is the trigger: someone has left a can of beer in the fridge.

We move into interpretations – stories about the beer in the fridge:

- Interpretation: "The beer is speaking to me" or "This is a sign I can't keep abstinent" or "Someone is trying to sabotage my recovery."

Based on the interpretations and stories we tell ourselves, we make a decision:

- Decision: we drink the beer.
- Outcome: we relapse.

However, if we stuck to the facts:

- There is the trigger: someone has left a can of beer in the fridge.

If we are able to pause, we can connect to the facts without making interpretations:

- Fact: there is a can of beer in the fridge.

Clearly seeing the facts, we can make a calmer decision:

- Decision: shut the fridge door.
- Outcome: we don't drink the beer – and don't relapse.

When we are able to see the facts more clearly and not move into interpretations, we can remain calm, take a breath and pause, and create the gap to act differently, rather than go into automatic-pilot mode. When a trigger like this occurs, the three-minute breathing space, AGE, can be a very helpful exercise. It can help us to see the true facts more clearly and not listen to our interpretations as if they were the true facts of a situation.

Which of these thoughts have you made fact?

We can easily take the thoughts that appear in our minds for granted. We assume that they are true and believe that we must act on them. With mindfulness, we are trying to relate to our thoughts differently – not take them so seriously or buy into the stories they are telling us. To create this space around your thoughts, it can be helpful to write them down or to be able to recognize your "favorites" – the ones that regularly appear in your mind and that you get caught up in.

Listed opposite are a variety of thoughts that can pop into our heads. Read each thought and indicate how frequently, if at all, it occurred to you over the last week. Circle the appropriate answer on the sheet in the following way: 1 = "not at all"; 2 = "sometimes"; 3 = "moderately often"; 4 = "often"; and 5 = "all the time."

Then indicate how strongly, if at all, you tend to believe that thought when it occurs. On the right-hand side of the page, circle the appropriate answer in the following way: 1 = "not at all"; 2 = "somewhat"; 3 = "moderately"; 4 = "very much"; and 5 = "'totally."

If you wish, substitute the phrase "my addiction" with "smoking" / "drinking" / "(over)eating" / "drug use" / "gambling" / "(compulsive) sex," etc., as appropriate.

After going through this list, you might like to asterisk the ones that are your personal "hot hits": the ones that occur especially often or take you in. When they appear in your mind again, perhaps you can take a breath, even smile, and remind yourself they are just your "favorite" thoughts. In addition, having marked the frequency and strength of belief in these thoughts for the last week, you could mark the list of thoughts again (perhaps with an X) for a time when you were more deeply entrenched in your addiction. You could see if any of them have changed in intensity of belief or frequency of appearing in your mind. If there has been a change, it gives you an opportunity to see how your thoughts – which at times can feel completely true and require acting on – are just thoughts, not absolute truths.

Frequency	Thoughts	Degree of belief
1　2　3　4　5	1. Life without my addiction would be boring.	1　2　3　4　5
1　2　3　4　5	2. My addiction is the only way to increase my creativity and productivity.	1　2　3　4　5
1　2　3　4　5	3. I can't function without it.	1　2　3　4　5
1　2　3　4　5	4. This is the only way to cope with the pain in my life.	1　2　3　4　5
1　2　3　4　5	5. I'm not ready to stop my addiction.	1　2　3　4　5
1　2　3　4　5	6. The cravings/urges make me do it.	1　2　3　4　5
1　2　3　4　5	7. My life won't get any better even if I stop my addiction.	1　2　3　4　5
1　2　3　4　5	8. It's the only way to deal with my anger.	1　2　3　4　5
1　2　3　4　5	9. Life would be depressing if I stopped.	1　2　3　4　5
1　2　3　4　5	10. I don't deserve to recover from my addiction.	1　2　3　4　5
1　2　3　4　5	11. I'm not a strong enough person to stop.	1　2　3　4　5
1　2　3　4　5	12. I could not be social without my addiction.	1　2　3　4　5
1　2　3　4　5	13. Addiction is not a problem for me.	1　2　3　4　5
1　2　3　4　5	14. The cravings/urges won't go away unless I use (my addictive behavior).	1　2　3　4　5
1　2　3　4　5	15. My addiction is caused by someone else (e.g., partner, family member).	1　2　3　4　5
1　2　3　4　5	16. If someone has an addiction, it's all genetic.	1　2　3　4　5
1　2　3　4　5	17. I can't relax without my addiction.	1　2　3　4　5
1　2　3　4　5	18. Having this addiction means I am fundamentally a bad person.	1　2　3　4　5
1　2　3　4　5	19. I can't control my anxiety without my addiction.	1　2　3　4　5
1　2　3　4　5	20. I can't make my life fun without my addiction.	1　2　3　4　5

Darren's story

Halfway through a Mindfulness-Based Relapse Prevention course, Darren reported a shift in his experience. Some friends had given him a dog to look after overnight. Unknown to him, the dog had a terminal illness. As the evening went on, Darren became aware that the dog was dying. He was upset by the dog's plight, which led to feelings of anger in him. Why should he feel bad over a dog dying? He felt stupid for being upset. It wasn't even his dog.

Anger was one of Darren's main triggers for drinking. But this time, instead of reaching for the bottle, he put aside his judgments and allowed himself to feel upset. He cried – not something he would previously have let himself do. To his surprise, the feelings of anger passed and, as he related to the group with a sense of achievement, he didn't drink.

Darren helped himself in two main ways. First, he did not take his judgments at face value – he recognized that, just because a thought appears in his mind, it is not necessarily true or helpful to treat it as though it were true. Second, he was willing to turn toward the feelings of upset.

One of the ways we can turn toward difficult feelings and emotions is to pay attention to bodily sensations. If we can stay with the bodily sensations, it helps us to let go of being caught up in the thoughts and stories around our feelings. We can begin to see this more clearly in the exercise above.

As we pay attention to our sensations – with an attitude of curiosity and kindness – we may find they keep changing, and the seemingly unbearable experience dissolves into an ever-changing flux of sensations. We can practice this approach in mindfulness meditation (see p.68). Even when the cause of our distress is physical pain, it can be helpful to pay attention to bodily sensations in this way.

Working with physical pain

Having a body means that we will inevitably have some physical pain. It's the body's way of telling us that something is wrong. There may be a straightforward way of alleviating the pain. For example, if we have strained a muscle, we could take a simple analgesic. Or, for more serious pain, we may need to seek medical advice. However, there are times when we are still going to be left with pain. Either the doctor can do no more for our pain, or we are in circumstances where we cannot immediately get relief.

If we can respond to the painful sensation by turning toward it, we can make the experience of physical pain easier to manage. If we surrender to the pain, it can be extraordinary to witness how the pain changes – how at times it throbs, at times it aches, and at other times it is thumping throughout the whole body. It is easy to get caught up in our ideas of what the pain is, and to believe it is just one unpleasant mass of pain, which we then label in our minds with a thought such as "This is totally unbearable" – which makes our experience worse. We may respond to the sensations of pain with aversion and ill will, perhaps becoming angry that they are there. This is likely to make us tense up around the pain, and again exacerbate our suffering.

However, as we learn to pay attention in more detail, we may discover that there is a whole range of physical sensations. The more we can stay with the raw sensations, the more we can let go of the unhelpful thoughts and other mental responses, such as ill will, that add to our suffering.

Kabat-Zinn, who pioneered using mindfulness to help with health problems, initially worked mostly with people who had severe chronic pain. His studies showed that people following his course had significant reductions in pain.[3]

The good news is that we can free ourselves of mental and emotional pain and, if we do that, our experience of physical pain will be different.

Mindfulness of Breathing – ten-minute meditation on turning toward difficulties

Begin by bringing your attention to the contact with the ground. Allow a sense of being supported by the ground. Now bring attention to your contact with the cushions or chair, and allow them to take your weight. Bring awareness to the top half of the body, the torso, perhaps rocking it back and forth slightly to find a point of balance. Similarly, rock the head slightly to find a point of balance. Take awareness to the shoulders and arms and relax. Allow your hands to rest supported in your lap or a blanket. Now notice that you are breathing; feel the chest and perhaps the belly expanding and contracting.

Without trying to change your breath in any way, allow yourself to follow the movements of the breath in and out of the body. As best you can, take interest in just what the breath is like: whether it is deep or shallow, long or short, smooth or irregular.

From time to time your mind will wander off. That's fine; just notice where your mind has gone, then return to the breath. If you find that your mind keeps getting caught up in the same thing, or you are experiencing something painful or difficult, then choose to turn toward it. Turn toward it by noticing which part of the body is most affected by what is going on. Perhaps there is tension in the shoulders or churning in the belly or maybe there are painful sensations in the back.

Using the breath to guide your attention, "breathe into" the difficult sensations. As best you can, notice just what the sensations are like – where they are, whether they are dull or sharp, how long they last. As best you can, bring a quality of friendliness, curiosity, and acceptance to whatever is happening. Allow and open to whatever is there. If you find it helpful, say to yourself: "It's okay, whatever it is, it is already here, let me feel it." When you have spent some time with the difficult experience or notice that it has changed, return to just following the breath.

When you are ready, gently bring the meditation to a close.

Staying with difficult experience – avoiding misunderstandings

It is important to become aware of our mental and emotional responses to what happens in our lives – what we sometimes call our mental–emotional support system (MESS).[4] The things that hinder us or sabotage us can be part of the MESS that gets in the way of our recovery. We need to work at making our MESS healthier, stronger, and more resilient. We do this by learning not to blame ourselves or beat ourselves up every time we make a mistake, have a slip or a relapse. This is a trap our minds can make for us, which only adds more suffering. We learn to become aware of what is going on in our minds and let go of it. This means realizing that we are not our thoughts or our habits.

Sometimes we need to allow ourselves to break down so we can choose different bricks to build ourselves back up. Breaking down can be part of staying with a difficult experience and part of letting go of old hurts. Becoming aware of our MESS, the obstacles that get in the way of recovery, is a healthier way of breaking down.

Our addictions can also bring us to a place of breaking down. This is sometimes called hitting rock bottom. Reaching this place can wake us up and make us take action. However, all too often, once we have recovered, we forget that awful experience and revert to our old behaviors. Awareness of our mini-breakdowns is important because they can shake us up and make us want to change our lives. Breaking down does not have to mean reaching a catastrophe.

Do we need to hit rock bottom to start our recovery?

The lightbulb may have already flashed on. We may feel inspired by what we have read, and feel ready to make changes in our lives. So what are we waiting for? Rock bottom? The place where we feel so desperate that we have to do something or we will physically, emotionally, or mentally die from our addiction? We need to beware of waiting for this kind of experience, because we will be broken and will have little strength and few emotional resources to work at our recovery once we are out of the crisis.

When some of us hit that broken place of rock bottom, we are motivated to get out of the hell of addiction. But once we have risen from the destruction of our addictions and are back functioning in the world, we can easily forget where we were and return to our old habits. Many people hit rock bottom over and over again and still do not recover. And for those who do get recovery, rock bottom is very different from what it looked like five years earlier.

Yes! It seems we do have to suffer to make great changes in our lives, but we don't need a life-or-death emergency in order to change. There are other painful places we can reach before crashing to this lowest point. We must also beware if we are still able to function in the world, keeping our lives and work together. We can delude ourselves and think: "I haven't lost my job, my home, or my family, so why bother changing? I don't owe anything. I haven't stolen to pay for my addiction." This thinking can keep us in our addictions. Our lowest point may not be a matter of life or death, but there will be other places of suffering in our lives if we are honest.

Adi's story

Adi believed that she performed much better in a crisis. Her childhood had been full of high drama. She was the eldest daughter and often left at home to feed her four siblings for weeks at a time. When her mother came home, she often brought abusive men back with her. Adi was drinking and smoking dope offered by her mother's boyfriend at the age of ten. While high, she had to learn to protect herself and her siblings from sexual abuse. She did well at school and managed to finance herself through university. She believed that she performed much better in chaos. So she often created chaos in adult life when she needed to achieve something important.

When Adi came into recovery from living on a cocktail of antidepressants, she told us that the only way for her to get better was to get completely wrecked so she could begin picking up the pieces. She would go on an alcoholic binge, clean up for one week, and go back on the bottle and her antidepressants again. Adi was searching for the lowest point of suffering to cure her, but it never came. Yet she had her children taken away from her, lost her home, and even lived on the streets.

Adi had to accept that the place of suffering she was waiting for was here in this moment and progressing in different ways. She didn't have control over her addiction; it had control over her. Her old coping methods were no longer working. In her recovery she began to see that the binges just made her frail and unwell, and once she was feeling strong again she could cope with going back to her addictive habits.

When she learned to slow down in the Mindfulness-Based Relapse Prevention course, she came into relationship with her chaotic life. She realized that she did not need to create more crisis; she needed to attend to what was going on in her life. She accepted that creating crisis had been her way of avoiding the pain and stress in her life. She began to see clearly that she needed to do something urgently or she would die. Only this time, she was not physically and emotionally frail. She was robust, and could begin to slowly make changes in her life.

A low point of suffering can be a spiritual crisis. It could simply be realizing, like the Buddha, that we will age, get sick, and die. Alternatively, it could be reflecting on the question: "What is the meaning of life?" A reflection like this can bring about a crisis. Of course, a low point or crisis can be triggered by someone dying, by losing everything we have, or by accidentally overdosing, but we do not have to wait for such catastrophic moments to arise. If we look deeply we may be able to see that the reason we are distracting ourselves with our addictions is to move away from an emotional or spiritual crisis.

Slowing down

Often we run our lives at a hectic pace, or simply don't give ourselves the space to notice what we are really experiencing. In order to learn to see how our minds work, what the triggers for our addictions are, how we create more suffering in our lives, and how we start to change those habits, we need to slow down.

Take a few deep breaths now and pause. Find moments in your day when you can slow down the movie of your life. Practice AGE throughout the day. Stop and pause for three minutes.

Slowing down

Another way to slow down is to pay mindful attention to simple routine activities that you perform during the day. When you wake up, you could mindfully clean your teeth, watch yourself squeeze the toothpaste onto your brush, slowly brush your teeth in circular movements, become aware of the taste and spitting out into the sink. When you are in the shower, you could choose to pay attention to the sensations of the water. Instead of just letting your thoughts run off and planning the day, you could keep coming back to how the water feels on your body, noticing the temperature and the sensation of soap or shampoo. You could choose one meal a day to become aware of each mouthful, your chewing, your swallowing, and how full you feel after each bite.

When we next try to move away from that uncomfortable feeling, we could become aware of what we are about to reach for, of when the thought arises and we make the decision to pick up our quick fix. Our thoughts can feel so strong and believable that they can cause a relapse. In the moment that we have a thought telling us to pick up, if we identify with it, this thought will overwhelm us and facilitate a relapse or lapse. Let's see if we can step back, take a breath, pause, and try to tell ourselves a more helpful thought. This will help us make a new decision.

So if we become aware of when we make that decision, we could make a new decision not to pick up our fix. We could lean into the uncomfortable thought. The potency of recovery is in slowing our lives down, being mindful of every moment and everything we are doing. When we speed our lives up so much, we are often not even aware of how we got into a binge. Slowing down sounds simple, but it is not easy. It goes against our belief that, if we distract ourselves from our minds, we will be able to cope with our lives more efficiently.

Reflecting on why we create more suffering in our lives

Why do we keep creating more suffering in our lives? It's a question that everyone could benefit from reflecting upon. We can stop digging that hole we keep falling into. We can put the shovel down at any time, and walk away from the hole. It sounds simple, but we know from experience it's not that easy. If it were easy, we would probably not be reading this book. Our habitual behavior patterns make it hard.

Blame keeps us on the path that leads to more suffering. Many people blame their past. Although our past affects us, it does not have to determine our future. With awareness, we can choose how to respond to what is happening in our lives now. By actively choosing our responses, we take responsibility for our lives. We take our lives into our own hands. When we blame our past, we stop taking responsibility for our actions today. How can we blame our parents for what is happening in our lives ten, twenty, or thirty years later? They are not responsible for the way we choose to live today. Some of us have had tough childhoods, but never became overwhelmed with an addiction, and made different choices in our lives.

Ignorance keeps us on the path that leads to more suffering, because we can deny our addiction or pretend everything is OK.

Habit keeps us on the path that leads to more suffering. As the saying goes, if you always do what you've always done, you'll always get what you always got, and you'll always feel what you always felt.

Delusion keeps us on the path that leads to more suffering. Some people at the beginning of their recovery think they can do all the same things, go to all the same places, and not sink back into their addiction.

Not seeing the bigger picture keeps us on the path that leads to more suffering.

When working with this step, try what we suggest and see for yourself. Taking the risk to try for yourself is the only way you can know. Try it out several times before you throw it out. Here are some questions to help you explore this step. Prepare yourself by practicing the three-minute breathing space, AGE.

Becoming aware of the suffering we create in our lives

Become aware of how you create more suffering in your life. This is not about hating yourself, but simply becoming aware of the way things are, without reacting. Our breath is a helpful ally in this reflection. Watch the breath. Everything in life is like the breath arising and ceasing. Your breath is your best teacher. It will warn you when you are panicking; it will tell you when you are at risk; and you will know when you are calm.

Here are some questions you could ask yourself. Be gentle. The object is not to give yourself a hard time. It is to see suffering clearly in your life and recognize how you create it. Perhaps write your responses down in a journal.

- What does my suffering look like?
- How do I create more suffering in my life?
- What have I gained from creating more suffering in my life?
- What has creating more suffering in my life cost me?
- What do I need to do to lessen the suffering in my life?

You might wish to plan some changes you would like to make in your life.

Give yourself a time frame. State where you would like to be in one year's time.

Then backtrack, and state where you would like to be in nine months, six months, three months, and one month.

Set yourself a goal for each of these time periods.

Visualize your recovery.

If you wish, write yourself a small script and record it several times so you can play it to yourself daily. A script could read like this:

Now that I realize that I create more suffering in my life, I can easily lessen my suffering. I am learning that my thinking can cause me great harm and trigger me to self-medicate. Now that I see this, I am easily letting go of my harmful thinking and actions. I am now allowing myself to sit with the discomfort, trusting that it will change and cease. I don't need to pick up my fix anymore. I am using the power of my breath to calm my thoughts. I am using the power of slowing down to keep me sober and abstinent. I am enjoying my life much more now. I am feeling so much happier. I continue to develop and grow.

Several authors, including Deepak Chopra, David Richo, and Dyan Yacovelli, talk about the importance of cultivating more attention, affection, appreciation, and acceptance in our lives. All of us need to connect to these four basic needs of the heart.

This is particularly important when we are trying to change our habits and engaging in the difficult task of learning to stay with unpleasant experiences. The four basic needs are: kind attention, affection, appreciation, and acceptance. Often we look outside of ourselves for people to notice us and give us attention. Some people become addicted because deep down they want to be noticed; they desperately need affection; they need to be appreciated and accepted. And so they turn to their choice of stimulant to be their friend, their lover, their confidant. However, we all need to look within to be fully nourished. We have to learn to meet these basic needs in ourselves if we are to lessen our suffering.

Recap

In Step Two, we realize that we create more suffering in our lives. Every time we move away from pain, we multiply the suffering in our lives. We need to learn to sit with the pain calmly. We begin to do this by identifying the things that trigger us, and the high-risk situations that may bring about a relapse. We must also remember that our thoughts are not fact. We do not have to believe our thinking. We can create space whenever we feel at risk of reaching for our addiction, or overwhelmed by the intense feelings of craving, by practicing the three-minute breathing space, AGE. In this space we can learn to do something different.

This is a gentle reminder for us to pause at the end of Step Two, and take a three-minute breathing space.

Responding to the four basic needs of the heart

For the next ten minutes, sit or lie down and begin to get in touch with these four needs of the heart.

First bring attention to your breath. As you breathe, imagine your breath carrying kindness, like a beautiful, warm light, filling your body with kindness and well-being.

Kind attention: with this sense of breathing kindness, give yourself some attention. Visualize a photo you like of yourself and take a good look at yourself without judgment. Then notice your physical suffering and let it go. Notice your psychological suffering and let it go. Notice your existential suffering and let it go. In essence, just notice what you are thinking and feeling and let it go. Cultivate more loving-kindness in your life, by just paying more attention to yourself.

Affection: give yourself some affection. Look at yourself with warm eyes. Imagine yourself as a tiny baby, and as yourself today; you are holding that tiny baby and looking at it with warmth. Notice yourself. Squeeze that tiny baby into your being and give yourself a literal or metaphorical hug. Cultivate more compassion in your life by looking at yourself, with all your pain and difficulties, with loving eyes.

Appreciation: give yourself some appreciation. Appreciate yourself right now for having the courage to open this book and begin reading it. Go on to appreciate yourself for having the courage to continue your journey of recovery. Cultivate more sympathetic joy in your life, by telling yourself: "Well done."

Acceptance: give yourself some acceptance. Accept yourself right now in this moment. Let go of the past. And let go of the future. Let go of the judgments, the critical voice. If they arise, just say to yourself: "Let it go." Cultivate more equanimity in your life, by saying: "I am at peace with who I am right now in this moment."

We all need some pauses in our lives. Practice this when you are walking, working, or in the middle of something. If you have been triggered, or are feeling at risk, allow yourself to stop in your tracks and give yourself three minutes to pay attention to yourself, while giving yourself some affection, appreciation, and acceptance.

Three-minute breathing space, AGE

Awareness of thoughts, feelings, and body.

Gather the breath, notice the breath, become aware of the breath.

Expand the breath throughout the whole body – connect to the whole body.

Step Three

....

Embracing impermanence to show us that our suffering can end

In Steps One and Two, we explore suffering in great detail. The good news is, in Step Three, we come to see how there is an end to suffering. The third noble truth tells us that there is an end to the cycle of suffering. When we realize that there is an end to suffering, a new freedom and happiness can emerge in our lives.

This liberating realization can begin to free us from craving. Impermanence is pivotal. If things did not change, there would be no end to suffering. Knowing that everything changes means that suffering must end too. We do not always have to be the person with addictions, compulsive or obsessive behaviors. However, although we might know in principle that everything changes, we can easily forget it or behave as if it weren't true. For example, when we identify with being an alcoholic or an addict, this says that we believe our identity is fixed and unchanging.

In the twelve-step fellowships, we know that it is very important to identify as an addict /alcoholic etc., so that we never forget that we have the disease of addiction. In the Buddhist teachings we believe to have recovery, you must study the self, which is looking at all the identities that have trapped us. We learn these identities are labels, and often stories in the mind. When we realize this we can begin to let go of these identities that have shaped our lives, and see we are much more than the addiction that has enslaved us. We always remember that we are liberating ourselves from the suffering of addiction by staying on the Buddhist path, or by living the Buddhist teachings breath by breath. Because we know that, as Adyashanti says: "Once you

....

think you have got it you have lost it." Recovery from addiction is a lifetime quest.

If we start to pay careful attention to our experience, we will find that nothing stays the same. All around us we can see the changes in the weather and the seasons. Even seemingly solid things like buildings age, and new ones are built. Our bodies too change as we move from childhood into adulthood and old age. Our minds change even faster; our thoughts and feelings come and go. Even that first high we had is never experienced in the same way.

This means we can change. If we embrace impermanence, we can shape our lives in helpful directions and let go of unhelpful habits. Even when things are difficult, we can remember that they will change in time. Permanence is a concept in the mind that has no existence in living reality. When we hold on to the idea of things being permanent we cause ourselves suffering, since sooner or later they will change.

Living with the truth of impermanence can help us to find freedom. This freedom will bring about an end to suffering, which is a welcome relief. It can help us to know that even if our lives are in chaos right now, they will change. Seeing impermanence, we let go of our thoughts that say "It can't change" or "It won't change." We are always changing: this is the law of nature.

The significance of impermanence

When we go about our daily lives, we can assume a degree of stability. We assume that when we sit on a chair it will take our weight. We assume that when we turn the ignition key in the car the engine will start, just as it did last time we drove. When we turn on the shower in the morning, we expect water to appear. We see the bus coming and we anticipate that our body will let us run to catch it.

We assume that people, places, and things will stay pretty much the same and behave in the way that they have in the past. To constantly doubt this would stop us in our tracks. If we felt we had to check the chair each time to see if it really would hold our weight, or expected someone always to be lying to us when we had never known them to lie, we would find it hard to do anything.

So for practical purposes, we rely on our world having some predictability. We learn that we need to leave for work at a certain hour in the morning, or the traffic will be so heavy that we will arrive late. We get to know the quiet times in the supermarket when there won't be a long queue. We find that a certain friend will be a good ear when we are having problems, but it's not a good idea to ask them for help to put up shelves.

However, if we hold too tightly to the expectation that things won't change, we are likely to suffer. At some point the chair will break. Maybe one day our friend won't be listening to us with the usual attention (perhaps they are unwell or have suffered a loss).

Inevitably we will get ill and our bodies won't function as well as they did, and the bloom of our youth will evaporate.

If we continue turning to our addiction, expecting our anxieties and worries to subside, one day we will find it doesn't work anymore. We increase our fix in the hope of it numbing our feelings. It still does not work, and we spiral down in our addiction, sometimes ending up on the streets.

We can recognize the truth of change or we can rail against it or pretend it is not happening. Closing our eyes to impermanence puts us under strain as we fend off any evidence to the contrary.

Getting annoyed at change – unless it leads to some constructive action – causes stress and can make us bitter. Finding a way to live with impermanence can reduce unnecessary suffering and bring a peaceful quality to our lives.

Difficulties are impermanent

Sometimes our lives feel stuck. When we are facing painful times, it can feel as though the pain will never end. This is partly a natural response. Physical and mental pain can trigger a defensive survival mode. For example, if your back suddenly goes into painful spasm, the intense pain can fill the mind so that it is hard to pay attention to anything else. It can feel as though there is nothing but pain in our lives. The same can happen with mental pain, such as when a partner leaves us.

Holly's story

Holly had long enjoyed drinking fine wines with her husband. She would often end up drunk, especially on weekends, but she managed to keep her high-powered job running smoothly. Then, after a short and unexpected illness, her husband died. Her world fell apart. She hit the bottle more than before, and her work started to be affected to the extent that she could no longer do her job. The pain of her losses seemed unbearable and she drank throughout the day to try to cope with it. At this time Holly felt that her suffering would never change and she turned to alcohol to drown out her despair.

In survival mode, our mind is taken up with the pain and seems unable to look beyond it. Yet even these intensely painful experiences will change. In fact, they are changing all the time. If we pay attention to physical pain, we may notice that the sensations wax and wane; they may move about the body. Mental pain often comes in surges. Alongside these sensations there are often thoughts, a whole narrative even, that in the moment seem as if they are permanent. This makes the experience worse and gives it a hopeless quality. We tend to tense up to bear the pain, although the extra tension just adds to the discomfort, as we saw in Step Two.

If we can pay attention to the changing nature of our experience – even when it is very difficult – we are less likely to feel so hopeless. If we can see our thoughts as just thoughts, we may be able to lessen their grip. We can watch the thoughts that say "This is unbearable" or "This is never going to change" as just thoughts that come and go in the mind. Sometimes they may be loud and commanding, sometimes soft and seductive. They are still thoughts, the mind's story about what is happening.

Paying attention in this way, we move from being caught up in the pain and the story about it to being a silent observer of the whole show. The painful sensations and the difficult thoughts are still there, but that's not everything. We are not so caught up in them, and they don't drive our lives in the same old way. Seeing impermanence at times of difficulty can bring us this bigger perspective. Instead of being in the grip of the painful thoughts and feelings, we are able to contain them and move beyond them.

Eight Step Recovery

We can change

Perhaps the most important message of impermanence is that we can change. Not only is everything around us changing, we too are changing. We can cooperate with the process of change by not feeding unhelpful habits and nurturing helpful ones. Each time we feel the impulse to act in a way that won't help us, we have the opportunity to do something different. As the old adage goes, if we keep doing the same thing, we will get the same result.

If we act even a little differently, we can start to make changes in our lives. In their book on stress, Mark Williams (who developed the mindfulness approach to depression: Mindfulness-Based Cognitive Therapy for depression or MBCT) and Danny Penman encourage practicing "habit releasers."[1]

Changing things that we do repeatedly can help us to break habits, bringing more awareness and creativity into our lives. For example, if we have a usual spot where we sit in a meeting, we could choose a different seat. Even though it is a small change, we may find we have a different perspective and feel differently. If we tend to watch TV all evening, we could make a deliberate choice about what we will watch, and try turning the TV off between those programs.

Impermanence doesn't mean that anything is possible. Even though both of us can play a musical instrument, it is highly unlikely that we will become rock stars in this lifetime. Part of the secret is holding what is possible lightly. We can't know where this mysterious life will take us; all we can do is take the next step. So even if we never become rock stars, movie directors, or fashion models, the urge to be those things might point us in a direction. Dusting off the guitar and strumming again might bring in a new dimension of satisfaction. Making time to watch interesting films or pay more attention to the clothes we choose to wear might be a valuable movement in our lives.

Impermanence and addiction

Pete's story

Pete had been drinking heavily for many years. To begin with, it was just on weekends. Gradually, it crept into the weekdays and then he started to need a drink to get him going in the mornings. He used to go out drinking with friends and would return home drunk. Eventually his girlfriend got fed up with his drinking and left him. He was discovered drinking at work and was fired. He had always drunk more than his friends, who began to distance themselves from him. In the end he was just drinking at home, alone. He was getting behind on his rent, and the threat of eviction was looming.

On his way to buy alcohol, he passed out and found himself in the hospital, where the doctor told him that he had liver cirrhosis and that, if he continued to drink, he would not have long to live. Pete went home and was straight back on the bottle. He couldn't see the point in doing anything else. He felt that he had lost everything valuable in his life and his only solace was drink. What was the point in changing now?

It was springtime and, out of his apartment window, Pete noticed a cherry tree coming into bloom across the street. He remembered how he always enjoyed watching it bloom each year: the deep pink buds, then the blush blossom smothering the boughs and finally the petals scattering like confetti and lying in the street. He didn't want this to be the last time he saw the cherry flower. Somehow, seeing the budding cherry filled him with hope. Maybe he didn't have to live out the rest of his life with things going from bad to worse. Perhaps he could make some changes and alter the direction of his life.

Before Pete had his cherry-blossom moment, if you had asked him about change, he might have said "Yes, things change – they get worse!" Another version of this we sometimes hear is, "Whenever I try to improve my life, make an effort, something comes along and knocks me back. There is no point in trying."

There are two sides to impermanence. We experience things coming into being, arising, appearing, and things going, disappearing, ending. Often we have a bias to seeing only one side. So we notice perhaps only the endings. When viewed in this way, impermanence can seem devastating. Step Three asks us to pay attention to both sides.

When life is difficult, especially when we have experienced a number of setbacks, it is easy to fall into a mindset that believes it can never get any better. This is the mind making an assumption of permanence; we believe that we are always going to feel this bad. The urge, then, is to continue with our addictive behavior. We feel that there is no point in doing anything differently, and we believe that the addiction, such as drinking, helps to blot out the uncomfortable feelings. We may get some temporary relief, but in the longer term it just compounds matters, as the addictive behavior itself adds to our problems. To see impermanence at these times can help us to see that change is possible. We can make constructive changes to our lives, and our lives can improve.

This does not mean that past tragedies are erased. We can't change the past, but we can change our interpretations of the past. We can only work with our minds and our lives as they are right now. We can only work with what we are experiencing in each moment. Part of that is changing our relationship to what has happened in the past. That's something we will be exploring more later in the book.

The importance of Step Three is to see that change is possible. If we do not believe that we can change, there will be no reason to try to make any changes, and we are likely to remain stuck.

Jackie's story

Jackie had been using crack cocaine since her teens. She remembered the first time that she had smoked it. She felt confident and invincible. All the troubles of her life vanished. The effect stayed with her for a while, but then wore off. She began to use crack more and more frequently. Each time she would get a lift, but not like that first time. The comedown was more marked and she started to use tranquilizers to help. In her heart she knew that this was not a helpful way of living, but she kept trying to get back to that first high.

A turning point came after a prolonged binge on crack when the comedown was particularly severe. She felt depressed and suicidal. Then she saw that she was never going to get that first high again. It was gone. And she was never going to get to a place where she could always feel high, where none of life's troubles could touch her. She had to learn to live her life and face its difficulties. Seeing that the past had gone, and letting go of wanting to hold on to the past, enabled Jackie to move forward. She had finally accepted change in her life.

How we practice this step

We begin practicing Step Three by paying more attention to the small changes in our lives. We can notice the changes in the weather and the changes of light during the day. We can watch the trees change in the park or perhaps buy some flowers for our home and follow their movement from bud to bloom to fading.

Noticing change

Take ten minutes or more to do this reflection. You can do it while walking, sitting outside, or in your home looking out of an open window. If possible, choose a place that has some plants, such as a garden or a park. If you are outside, notice the sensation of the air as it meets your body. If you wish, slow down your pace. There is no hurry to get anywhere. Notice the quality of the light. Is it bright or dull, sharp or soft? Try to get a feel for the time of day and notice any changes in the light. Is there a breeze, a strong wind, or is it completely still? Notice any changes in the movement of the air – gusts of wind or increased stillness. If there are any clouds, notice their shapes and colors. With its undefinable shape, each cloud is unique; you have never seen one exactly like this one and you will never see another one exactly the same again. If you can, watch how the shape changes. Pay attention to plant life. Notice any signs of new life: new leaves opening, flower buds or new growth sprouting from the ground. Even in winter, you may be able to see the buds of trees waiting for the spring to burst. Notice the mature leaves or flowers in full bloom. Look for any aging or decaying leaves, flowers, or shoots. If there are buildings, notice any signs of recent work: fresh paint or new brick for example. Is any of the paintwork peeling, or are any of the bricks eroding?

As you observe all the changes around you – the weather, the plants, the buildings – notice how you feel. Seeing the changes, do you feel happy, sad, indifferent, fearful, joyful, or what? As best you can, stay open to whatever feelings arise.

Like the clouds and the plants, you are changing moment by moment. See if you can notice any changes from when you began this reflection. Are there different thoughts or feelings?

Does your body feel any different? Can you recall another walk you took in the past? How were you different then from how you are now? How do you feel about changes in yourself? Can you allow change to be present in your life?

Sometimes we forget that, once upon a time, we lived without being under the complete control of our addiction. We can think we have always had an addiction. Yes, for some people addiction began in the womb, for example in fetal alcohol syndrome (FAS), but there was a time when the person did not drink. Many people with FAS choose not to drink because they do not want to live with the consequences of drinking.

Remember, we are always changing. When we recover we are not the same people we were before we had an addiction. We have grown into someone different; this can be scary.

Mirror-like wisdom

Find a picture of yourself as a child, look at it deeply, and then look in a mirror and see how you have changed.

Sometimes we forget how small and vulnerable we once were. This small child is always with us. Begin to nurture her or him and take care of this little one. Perhaps when you see small children in the streets, you can have the thought: "I was small like that once." This thought can help to open up your heart to self-love.

Now look at a picture of yourself before your addiction began. Look at every detail of yourself in the picture. Now look at yourself in the mirror, and look at every detail of yourself today.

Mohammed's story

Mohammed was too scared to recover because he knew he had damaged his brain through drinking. He did not want to face the change and so kept on relapsing, because of his fears. When he was finally able to let go of his addiction, he found it incredibly hard to accept that his brain did not work in the same way. Once, he had had what he called a scientific brain, one that remembered every calculus and theory. Now he was fortunate if he could remember someone's name after meeting them.

Slowly, Mohammed began to accept the change, to let go of his old identity as a scientist, and to pursue other interests. Although he had changed, he could see that his life was not over. In letting go of his old identity, he was able to face his fears of having damaged his brain, stop beating himself up with unhelpful thinking, and step onto the road of recovery.

We can watch our moods and thoughts coming and going. Sometimes we get completely caught up in a particular set of thoughts, a story about our lives. Later it is not there, or we get caught up in another narrative. Our minds are like a great pageant, or a parade with floats and marching bands. Perhaps the band is marching to the tune of "You are a loser, your life is going nowhere." Or maybe there is a glamorous woman on the float with a banner that reads "Just one fix and your worries will go." When we get caught up in our thoughts and feelings, it is as if we join the parade or leap up onto the float. Instead, we can train ourselves to watch our minds like a bystander following the whole spectacle from the pavement. Since everything changes, even the most compelling thoughts and emotions will pass.

When desire for our addictive behavior arrives, if we just notice it, rather than acting on it, we can watch the craving arise, grow, peak, and then wane. We might feel the first itch, then see how it fills our minds and perhaps creates mounting tension in our bodies. We might notice the persuasive thoughts: "I really need some chocolate to cope with this" or "Just one drink wouldn't hurt." If we can stay with the desire, following our minds and bodies, we will notice as it comes and goes. This is sometimes called urge surfing. Like a surfer riding the waves, we watch our experiences and ride the waves of our minds.

Bringing kindness to craving

When craving is triggered, there is an emotion that has made you feel uncomfortable. Fear, sadness, and anxiety are a few, and even emotions like excitement, happiness, and pleasure can make you feel uncomfortable. The uncomfortable emotion impacts you on a subtle physical level. The body can have unpleasant sensations, and you want to move away from feeling this discomfort. If you are aware of the emotions you are feeling, or even if you realize they have been triggered, stop what you are doing, practice the three-minute breathing space, AGE, and then say to yourself:

This is a moment of craving
Craving is energy arising and ceasing
I don't have to identify with this energy
I trust the sensation of craving will pass.

Take time out with your breath. Occupy your breath. Your breath is the key to change. Feel the breath filling your lungs, feel your chest and belly expand, and then feel the breath passing back out again as the chest subsides with the out-breath. Perhaps give yourself a metaphorical hug.

In bringing attention to impermanence, we are trying to get a bigger picture. The great sweep of change over time can give us a perspective on our lives that can keep us from getting stuck in our immediate difficulties.

To do this, we need a balanced perspective that includes both arising and falling away. If we start to feel bleak when we contemplate impermanence, it usually means we are paying attention to only one side. We might feel that there is no point because we will lose anything good that we might gain. This needs to be balanced by attending to new (welcome) things coming into being or new possibilities opening up, even if they are small.

We can try to catch the bias that would have us only notice the unpleasant and ignore or discount the pleasant aspects of our experience. As described in the Joni Mitchell song "Both

Sides Now" (from the album *Clouds*, 1969), if we pay attention to both sides of our experience, we may find that we begin to loosen the hard certainties of our lives, the stories that keep us stuck. We may start to open up into the wonderful mystery and richness of a life fully attended to.

The power of mantra

For centuries, many spiritual traditions in Africa and Asia have used mantras to heal the soul. One of the oldest mantras is the sacred syllable *om*. It is often used to close a yoga session, and precedes many other mantras. It is said that when we chant this syllable, its vibration assists our psychic integration. Many schools of Buddhism use the practice of chanting mantras. There are all sorts of mantras in Buddhism, which can evoke compassion, kindness, joy, and equanimity.

Sometimes words, concepts, and exercises can just be too much in the moment when we are suffering. The Buddhist teachings offer the practice of chanting mantras, which are sacred syllables that resonate in the body and bring about positive emotions. These mantras often belong to archetypal *bodhisattva*s or Enlightened beings. We can think of *bodhisattva*s as mythical beings who have committed to help alleviate all the world's suffering, or as representations of the Awakened mind. We can relate to *bodhisattva*s as forces outside of us that we can tap into, or as symbols for what we can become at our best, our potential residing deep in our minds and hearts. Two of the best-known *bodhisattva*s are Tara and Avalokitesvara. When we chant their mantras or bring them to mind, we can imagine them radiating compassion.

One of the most famous mantras belongs to Avalokitesvara: *om mani padme hum*. If we chant this mantra, it is believed, we will develop compassion in our hearts. Another figure associated with compassion is the female *bodhisattva* Green Tara. Tara is said to protect people from ordinary worldly dangers, and from the three factors that cause human suffering: greed, hatred, and delusion. Green Tara's mantra is a playful chant of her name: *om tare tuttare ture svaha*.

If you are a more devotional type of person, the chanting of mantras may work for you. They can most definitely help quiet the mind, if you feel that the meditation and reflection exercises are too hard because of all the chatter going on inside your head.

For some people, the thought of sitting down to reflect or meditate can be their worst nightmare. If our minds are very busy, or we are experiencing strong, painful emotions, we might feel that right now we can't face sitting with these experiences with just the breath.

One quite simple thing that we can do when we feel consumed by something negative is chant a mantra. This can enable us to take time out from our toxic, obsessive thinking. At times of difficulty, a mantra may be able to hold our attention more easily than the breath. By not feeding our unhelpful thinking, we can start to break some of the hold it has over us.

The power of mantra can help us to change our lives. Reciting mantras could be seen as similar to repeating an affirmation like "I love myself," or "I matter." Nobody knows exactly how mantras work, but people who recite them know they have the capacity to purify the heart. Mantras are believed to protect the mind from anger, hatred, and fear, and bring about psychic integration. Reciting mantras helps bring the whole body alive.

You can listen to mantras on our website (http://thebuddhistcentre.com/eightsteps) and hear how they are chanted. Try your best to pronounce the mantras correctly, but don't get too caught up in the enunciation: intention is the most important thing.

Chanting mantras

Put this book down and sit somewhere you feel comfortable. You may wish to light a candle or some incense. Begin to ground yourself, connecting with your breath, and with the soles of your feet and your sitting bones. And just breathe. Put your hands together in a prayer position and raise them to your heart. Or sit with your hands in your lap, palms facing up and with your hands on top of each other with thumbs touching.

When you feel settled, try chanting one of the mantras below for about five minutes. Pause before going on to the next. Or do some research into mantras and find one that resonates with your heart. Then repeat it over and over, not worrying too much about pronunciation, but with the desire to transform your anger, hatred, and fear, or with the desire for true happiness. If you get tongue-tied, just pause and start again, finding your own rhythm and sound.

Chant for at least five minutes and see how it feels. If this feels more comfortable than meditating, then begin with chanting mantras as your practice. These are some of the mantras that we use in our Buddhist tradition:

- *om mani padme hum*
- *om tare tuttare ture svaha*

While chanting a mantra, you could imagine your whole self being transformed. Feel a sense of compassion filling your whole body. Trust that the moment will pass. Trust that all moments of craving are impermanent.

Once your mind is settled and feels more quiet, you could begin to reflect on the following questions:

- What has changed in your life during the past ten years?
- What has changed in your life during the past five years?
- What has changed in your life during the past year?
- What has changed in your life today?
- What has changed in your life in the past hour?
- If there was an end to suffering, what would it look like in your life today?

Recap

In Step Three, we embrace the fact that there is an end to suffering, that everything in our lives is impermanent, including our addictions, compulsive and obsessive behaviors. We accept that change is possible. We begin to pay attention to small changes in our lives. We do this by practicing one of the meditative exercises to help us slow down.

This is a gentle reminder for us to pause at the end of Step Three, and take a three-minute breathing space.

 Three-minute breathing space, AGE

Awareness of thoughts, feelings, and body.
Gather the breath, notice the breath, become aware of the breath.
Expand the breath throughout the whole body – connect to the whole body.

Step Four

....

Being willing to step onto the path of recovery and discover freedom

Vision and transformation

In the last three steps we have painted a vision of existence. In particular, we have drawn attention to the nature of suffering and the universality of impermanence. Everything changes. We can relate to change in a fearful way that keeps us on the path of suffering, or we can open up to change. We can begin to see that we can change and our lives can change. We can get a glimpse of a different sort of life: a life without addiction and one that has the taste of freedom.

If we want this life of freedom, we will have to make some changes. We can describe the way to freedom as a path of vision and a path of transformation. First of all, we see that change is the nature of existence, and that we could be different; we could be free from suffering. This is the path of vision. Then we need to choose to step onto the path of transformation, if the vision is to be more than just a good idea, like an old book gathering dust on our bookshelf.

To recover, we need a vision that is bigger than our addiction. We need to want the vision to be realized, more than we want the glass of wine, line of coke, that gamble, chocolate bar, or our compulsive behaviors. We need to listen to our heart's whisper that actually does want recovery, more than to the loud clashing thoughts of our addictions.

Seeing things clearly

Seeing things as they really are is critical to recovery. All too often, we tend to think that the only people with addictions are those dependent on drugs or alcohol. It can be tempting to underplay our own problems. If we can admit that we have compulsive behaviors, or are addicted to things like food, pharmaceutical drugs, smoking, shopping, working out, or indeed alcohol or illegal drugs, we have begun to see clearly. However, it does not stop there. Staying awake to this can be tremendously challenging.

There are things we can do to help us see more clearly, and to act on what we see. We may think that we want recovery, but if we are still manifesting compulsive behaviors, still dependent on our addictions, maybe we don't see how we can change, or maybe we want our addiction more than we want recovery.

If we can admit that we want the food, the drug, the cigarette, the avoidance strategy more than we want recovery, we can begin to see clearly what is getting in our way. It's hard to admit, but if we are still engaging in our addiction, it is a fact that we don't want recovery enough to change. We have to stop playing the game of recovery, and admit the truth to ourselves.

Take a moment to reflect on this question: what do you want more, your recovery or your addiction? If your answer is "your recovery," and you are still addicted, then you are not seeing clearly. If you really wanted recovery more, you would have it.

The moment we decide to pick up our drug of choice, we are blocking out what is at stake. That choice may mean losing our families, our jobs, our relationships. But once we have made that decision, we tell ourselves: "It's too late now, why stop?" If we were choosing the things that we believe matter to us, we would not turn to our addiction.

This can be uncomfortable to accept. But every time we reach for our addiction we are making a choice. To recover, we must find or be inspired by something that we want more than our addiction. We need vision.

When we step onto the path of recovery, we have to want recovery more than our drug of choice. Using the breath, the three-minute breathing space, AGE, and kindness toward ourselves can give us the space to choose something different.

Kindness to help us step onto the path of recovery

It is as if we have been sitting for a long time in a darkened room with the curtains closed. The last time we looked out, it was a cold, gray winter's day, scarcely any lighter than in our room – no point in going out there. But we are completely fed up with our life in here, feeling like a prisoner in our own home. So we get up and draw back the curtains a little way, to peek out again.

It still looks cold out there, but some of the clouds have parted and there is some weak sunshine glistening on the rooftops. There is a sense that spring is on its way. Maybe it is time to put on a coat and brave the world outside. It's not going to be comfortable and maybe we hesitate at the door. The familiarity of the darkened room draws us back. But the world out there is brighter, bigger, and richer. We step over the threshold and meet the world.

Step Four is about getting ourselves ready to move out into the world. It's about making the decision to risk stepping into the unknown. We are invited to step onto the path of recovery. That's not an easy step to take. It probably won't be a one-time decision, but one that we will have to make again and again. We will keep coming back to this theme throughout the book to remind us to hold the ideal of recovery in our minds.

The decision to choose recovery, to move toward freedom, is a matter of the heart. If our emotions are not involved in the decision to change, or if we approach change in a bullying or forced way, without kindness, we are unlikely to be able to sustain any changes we attempt. We have to want recovery because we want it, not because somebody else wants it for us.

Kindness can help us to face up to the difficult thoughts and emotions that we experience. It can help to strengthen our desire to move toward recovery.

Throughout this step, we suggest several reflective exercises. Don't feel you have to do all of them. We suggest you do what resonates for you. We are all different and each reflection will speak to different people.

The most important thing is that you give yourself kindness. We all need kindness if we are to step onto the path of transformation and recovery. Take a moment to reflect on the four basic needs of the heart that we spoke about in Step Two: attention, affection, appreciation, and acceptance. Take three minutes to check in with yourself and give yourself some attention by noticing yourself, your thoughts and feelings, and give yourself some affection, appreciation, and acceptance. You can stop what you are doing at any moment and cultivate these qualities.

Tania's story

Tania had worked a lot on her various addictions over the years. She had had an eating disorder, misused stimulants, and been dependent on alcohol. For periods of time she had managed to get abstinent, stop bingeing and vomiting, and come off all drugs. She would eat healthily, do yoga, and make contact with her non-using friends.

For a few weeks or even months she would think that she had conquered her addictions. She would feel great for a while, then, almost imperceptibly, things would start to unravel.

A few times she got into relationships. She enjoyed the intimacy, but after a while she would feel taken advantage of. She noticed a pattern: she felt that she had to take care of her boyfriend, and felt criticized by him if she ventured to share some of her difficulties. This would get worse until she found herself bingeing and vomiting again or back on drugs.

At other times she avoided getting into a relationship, but she would start to feel lonely. In her loneliness she might turn to drink as a solace. Or she might throw herself into activity: intensive yoga, lots of twelve-step meetings, and volunteer work in three different places.

Sooner or later she would feel overwhelmed by all of this, crash, and start bingeing or using drugs and alcohol again.

Each time Tania would pick herself up. Usually she would seek some professional help to get back on track. This time, when she stopped drinking and stimulant use, she felt particularly wretched. She felt hopeless about ever getting to a place of sustained recovery.

Talking about Tania's attitude to herself and her approach to recovery, her therapist mentioned one word: kindness. Tania burst into tears. In that moment she recognized that kindness had been lacking in how she went about things.

Tania's approach to herself had been to push, cajole, and criticize. When she did yoga she was pushing her body, and usually criticizing it for not being flexible and fit enough. When doing volunteer work, she chastised herself if she was not working harder and longer than the paid employees. Even the men she chose to get involved with were a project in which she ended up not being good enough. It was time for a different approach. She needed to soften her heart.

Even though Tania knew that kindness was what she needed to move on in her recovery, she wasn't sure how to go about it. It took some time to find ways to bring more kindness into her life.

 Kindness reflection

Take a pause from reading just now. Give yourself five minutes. Settle your body into a comfortable posture. If you are sitting, allow your body to come into an upright posture without forcing or straining. If you are lying down, become aware of your spine. Take one or two deep breaths, exhaling slowly. Say to yourself gently and slowly the word "kindness." Notice any effects in your body, any images that come to mind, or any thoughts or feelings that appear. As best you can, try to be interested in any responses, whether pleasant or unpleasant. If there is no response, that is completely fine too.

How we practice this step

Approaching kindness

Kindness is integral to successful recovery and finding freedom from our suffering. However, it is something that many of us struggle with, especially being kind and loving toward ourselves.

To begin, it is worth recognizing what we associate kindness with. Some of these associations may have appeared when you did the short exercise above. Perhaps the connotations of kindness are for you wholly positive. If so, that is a good foundation on which to bring more kindness onto your path of recovery.

For many of us, the idea of being kind to ourselves or others can bring mixed or uncomfortable feelings. It's worth catching the negative connotations. Do we feel kindness is weak, soppy, and sentimental? Do we feel that being kind means to be a doormat that others will walk over? Do we feel that we should be kind to others, but it is wrong to be kind to ourselves or that we don't deserve it? Whatever our responses or associations, we can try to bring a friendly curiosity to them.

By kindness, we mean a quality of friendliness and interest in whatever is happening. It includes warmth, consideration, and thoughtfulness. True kindness sees to the heart of the matter and meets whatever is there with a desire to help and support. Importantly, real kindness is both for ourselves and others. Just as the sun shines impartially on the whole earth, touching with warmth wherever it lands, so kindness – in the way we mean it here – reaches out and touches all beings, including ourselves, without discrimination.

We can think of kindness as having three aspects: feeling, thought, and intention. The feeling side of kindness includes warmth, care, and sympathy. Our thoughts are involved, in that true kindness sees what is really happening. It has an element of understanding or wisdom. The intention side of kindness is the urge to be helpful, and will lead to constructive action wherever that is possible.

How kindness looks in practice will depend on the context, and may not always be obvious. For example, if we have been working hard, taking a break with a cup of tea and a slice of cake might be an act of kindness toward ourselves. However, if eating cake, biscuits, or chocolate becomes our default response to stress, so that we regularly eat for comfort, reaching for the cake may no longer be a kindness.

How we are kind to others is also not straightforward, as the following examples illustrate.

Angela and Bill's story

Angela had been married to Bill for over twenty years. Bill had started to develop numbness and weakness in his legs due to his drinking. When he was drinking particularly heavily, this got worse, and he could no longer leave the house to buy alcohol. He would then beg Angela to buy it for him. Seeing her husband helpless, Angela felt it was only kind to do what he asked. Only later in therapy did Angela see that she was buying the alcohol for Bill to avoid conflict and to feel needed. True kindness for Angela meant not colluding with Bill's drinking. It meant finding the courage to stand up for herself and find her own worth independent of being needed by Bill.

Doris and Eve's story

Doris had begun to get withdrawal seizures when she stopped drinking. Her partner Eve had never previously obtained alcohol for her. Doris had been advised not to stop drinking suddenly and to continue drinking until arrangements for medical detoxification could be made. As Doris was finding it harder to get out, she asked Eve to buy her alcohol. Eve was reluctant to do this, but she saw that it was the best way to keep Doris safe until the detoxification could happen. She agreed to do it on this occasion.

Both Eve and Angela were faced with requests to provide alcohol to partners with a drinking problem. For Angela to buy alcohol was not really kind, since it did not help Bill to change his damaging drinking, whereas for Eve it was a means to assist Doris to become free of her drinking.

Cultivating kindness

There are many ways of bringing more kindness into our lives. Meditation, or taking time out to be quiet, can be a kind act, as it can be a way to take care of ourselves and gain perspective on our lives. Tania had a special place in her local park where she liked to sit on the grass among a group of birch trees. She enjoyed looking at the silver-white bark, the graceful branches, and the leaves dancing in the breeze. For her it was a good way to be quiet and content, without the compulsive need to do something.

Back at her apartment, she would bring this place to mind. Sitting on a chair with her eyes closed, she could find a sense of ease with herself. At these times she was more able to discover what she needed to do to look after herself. Sitting in meditation like this, she would also bring to mind friends and other people, inviting them to join her in her special place and wishing them well.

Creating a safe and kind space

Take some time now to pause. Give yourself five minutes. Settle into your body and take one or two deep breaths. Bring to mind a place where you feel at ease. It could be a real place that you have visited, perhaps on holiday, or it could be somewhere completely imagined. Alternatively, it could be a mixture of the two – your favorite beach high up in the sky, but without the garbage and just the weather and temperature that you like. Bring the place as vividly to mind as possible. What can you hear? What can you see? What smells and tastes are there? What can you feel with your body? Don't force or struggle. Just ask yourself the question for each sense and see what happens. If nothing particular comes to mind, that is fine. Allow yourself to enjoy being in this special place. Let yourself be at ease and wish yourself well and to be at peace.

Sometimes we find it hard to feel kindness toward ourselves. If we have developed a habit of being harsh and critical toward ourselves, it can take time and patience to cultivate a more loving, kinder attitude. Perhaps we could remember ourselves as children. Or bring to mind a child that we know and care about. If that child were suffering, how would we like to meet and be with him or her? If we could give the child something, what would it be? That child is within us too. We could allow ourselves to feel with that child, to find out what he or she needs. Perhaps we could imagine taking the child in our arms and responding to him or her with love and kindness.

If we are unkind to ourselves, we will inevitably be unkind to everything around us. We will love everything the way we love ourselves. When we begin to cultivate self-kindness, everything in our life will begin to change. Just try for yourself.

Weighing the benefits and costs of addiction

Addictive behaviors don't just come out of the blue. There may be an element of chance – we may have been invited to a party with people we didn't know and offered a drink or some cocaine, and that high we experienced set us off on a road to addiction. Once we have tried the substance or engaged in the behavior, we return to it for certain reasons. We want to enjoy the high again or we want to be part of the in-crowd. Maybe we drink because it makes it easier to socialize. Perhaps control of our food intake helps us to feel more self-confident, or heroin helps us to forget all our worries. We may have grown up in homes where the abuse of alcohol, illegal or pharmaceutical drugs, food, or money was the norm, and so it may seem normal for us as adults too. As the addiction takes hold, these reasons may change. In the end, it may be just that our behavior relieves withdrawal symptoms, and we don't feel we could live any other way. Nevertheless, whatever our addiction, there is something that we get from it.

The other side is that there are costs to our addiction. At first, these costs may be insignificant. Smoking perhaps leaves the young body with a dry mouth or a morning cough. Serious trouble such as cancer or chest disease may only arrive years later. For others, there may be big costs early on, such as contracting hepatitis C from a first injection, or getting pregnant from unprotected sex while intoxicated.

In this respect, addiction is like almost any other behavior: there are benefits and costs. Shopping online saves us time, and we may find what we want at a cheaper price, but we may end up buying more than we had intended (because it is so easy to click the "add to shopping cart" button). If we go to the movies with our friends, we might have an enjoyable night out, but then struggle to get up early the following day and feel tired at work.

Since most actions have two sides to them, we often have mixed feelings about what choice to make. It may be relatively easy to just go to the movie and not worry about being tired the following day, or to say to our friends: "Not today, I need to get to bed early. How about we go out on Saturday?" Where the stakes are higher, such as changing one's career in mid-life or moving to another country, there may be much more soul-searching and ambivalence.

Once addiction is entrenched, stepping away from it onto the path of recovery is a big decision, and there are likely to be mixed feelings. Thus, we need to make this choice with open eyes. We can do this by reflecting on the costs of our addiction. What troubles and difficulties has it caused in our lives? What will we lose by giving it up? What advantages or benefits do we gain from our addiction? What will it mean for our lives to let go of these benefits?

Tom's story

Tom was trying to change his gambling. Here is the list of benefits and costs he came up with:

Benefits of gambling	Costs of gambling
• I find it exciting. • I may be able to make a lot of money quickly. • I forget about my worries. • I feel confident.	• I lose a lot of money and am in debt. • It makes me unreliable. • My girlfriends leave me. • I neglect other important areas in my life like my family. • Gambling rules my life.

For this exercise to have any meaning, it requires us to be completely honest with ourselves. It may take some time to see all the consequences, positive and negative, of our addictive behavior.

And it is not just about numbers. Tom listed four advantages/benefits and five disadvantages/costs to gambling, but that did not immediately mean that the costs outweighed the benefits. The various items will weigh differently at different times. When Tom was feeling bored or anxious, the draw of the excitement of gambling seemed to outweigh everything else. He chose gambling over his family. After his flutter he would feel even more guilty, and the cycle of his gambling was perpetuated.

The cost that Tom found most painful, which led him to want to change, was neglecting his family, especially his young daughter. He was haunted by the image of his beautiful daughter in tears because he had failed to show up for her birthday. This image caused a turnaround for Tom. Whenever the craving for gambling arose, he pictured his daughter in tears. He had finally connected to something he wanted more than his gambling. He began to choose his daughter instead of the gambling every time the urge to gamble arose.

Weighing up the benefits and costs of our addiction

You can fill in your own list below:

Benefits of my addiction	Costs of my addiction
•	•
•	•
•	•
•	•
•	•

The time for courage and compassion

When we start to examine what our addictions have cost us – the damage we have done to ourselves and the hurt we have caused to those dear to us – it can feel overwhelming. This in itself can lead us back to our addictions as we seek to block out the painful experiences.

Molly's story

When Molly first began to think about giving up drinking, although she was concerned about the health effects, like Tom, the desire to be a good parent was her strongest reason for wanting to change. However, recollecting how she had failed her children again and again filled her with pain and self-recrimination.

She thought of herself as the worst mother in the world. She taunted herself with just how bad a mother she was, that she could put drinking before the care of her darling daughter and son. Many times she had promised to give it up altogether, only to start drinking again in secret. It would then escalate, and her own mother would have to take over the care of the children. Now her mother had complete custody of her children and Molly could only see them if she was supervised. Molly found this humiliating. The whole situation felt hopeless. She felt that she could never make it up to her children. The more she thought about it, the more pointless it seemed to make an effort. The very pain of it all drove her back to drinking.

It is at these times that we need some courage and self-compassion to face the situation. Compassion literally means to feel or suffer with. To break out of the cycle of pain–addiction–recrimination–pain–addiction requires kindness. When loving-kindness meets suffering, it is transformed into compassion. It is the compassion that is able to sit right alongside pain and sensitively feel with it, and then respond in a caring way. Like a willow tree, with leaves fluttering, compassion bends in the storm but is not broken. In the storm of our painful emotions and negative self-criticism, it is compassion that can see us through.

Compassion toward the costs of our addiction

Take a pause right now. Give yourself five minutes. Settle your body and allow it to come to rest. Bring to mind one of the costs of your addiction. Allow yourself to notice the effect of bringing this to mind, especially in the body. If you find your mind is spinning off into critical thoughts, try to keep coming back to the sensations in the body, particularly in the chest or heart area. Use your breath to breathe with whatever is happening. Allow the breath to be like a friend, touching whatever is painful with compassion. Breathe with whatever pain or hurt there is, whether caused to yourself or to others.

When we bring kindness and compassion to our pain, it is not to let ourselves off the hook for what we have done, or to gloss over or to make it OK that we have hurt others. We may well feel regret, but beating ourselves up with recrimination is not going to help. Bringing compassion to what we have done allows us to accept what has happened, rather than flee from it (usually back into addictive behavior). As in Step Two, we allow ourselves to feel the pain – any regrets or remorse – without making the pain worse by adding more suffering to it, so that we can move on. What has happened has happened and, if we want things to be different, we can only change our behavior from now onward.

Letting go of our addiction stands between us and recovery. The pain of the costs of our addiction also stands between us and our recovery, and makes it harder to let go. It is like saying goodbye to a friend. It can feel like a bereavement. The pain of letting go is the grief that we can be scared to experience. What will comfort us now? What will keep the messy feelings at bay? The fear of letting go of our addiction and facing the pain in our lives, including the pain of the costs of our addiction, is like a fast-running river that blocks our path. We are scared to enter the river for fear of being carried away or drowning – and sometimes that is how our pain can appear to us.

Unfortunately there is no way around it. Though we look up and down the riverbank, there is no way to the other side without crossing it, and there is no easy bridge. We may have spent a lot of time trying to circumvent the pain: trying to ignore it or argue with ourselves that it doesn't matter. Or we may wallow in it, tell ourselves how bad we are, and then return to our addiction. That's like stepping into the river and sitting down in it near the bank, feeling miserable, and then stepping back onto the same side of the river. Compassion is like a life raft or a floating log that can help us cross the river. It will help make a gentler ride over the sometimes turbulent water.

Ask yourself: what does my addiction give me? Do I need what it gives me? If I do: how can I give (some of) those things to myself without turning to my addiction?

Compassion can help us cross the river of our pain, because it changes our relationship to pain. When we bring kindness to our suffering and that of others, this is compassion in action. When we can stop fighting or avoiding our pain, we no longer need our addiction, which was perhaps the best way that we had found to cope with our pain. Kindness and compassion offer a different response to our pain, instead of reacting with addictive behavior.

Molly needed to find compassion to come to terms with the damage she had caused herself and the pain she had brought to her children. She had to find the courage to admit what her drinking had led to, but without falling into harsh self-blame. It took her some time to steer a way between self-pity and self-blame. Each time she felt herself drawn toward one or the other, and had the urge to block out the pain with a drink, she stopped what she was doing, took a deep breath, and then felt the sensations in her body. She imagined the breath like a warm, kind light, so that, with each in-breath, she imagined her body was filling with kindness. Paying attention to the bodily sensations and the breath in this way enabled her to let go of her painful thoughts, and contain the difficult emotions in an atmosphere of kindness, which made them more bearable.

Admittedly, it can be hard to give ourselves compassion when we are in the throes of an addiction, or suffering physically or mentally. However, if we can be kind to ourselves in our darkest moments, or when someone has abused us or hurt us, we begin to conquer self-criticism, self-judgment, self-doubt, and self-hatred. We can learn to cultivate kindness toward ourselves and all other beings through loving-kindness meditation. We encourage you to try this practice. Practicing loving-kindness meditation has transformed many people's lives, including our own.

In the box below, we explain the first stage of the loving-kindness meditation, which focuses on cultivating kindness toward ourselves. The rest of the practice, in which we cultivate kindness toward others, is described in the tools section at the end of the book.

 ## Loving-kindness meditation

Read the following instructions and then put the book down. Give yourself ten minutes to reflect on loving-kindness.

There are different ways to approach this meditation, so it's worth experimenting to see what works best for you. You can also combine some of the different approaches together. Here are some suggestions:

Imagine your heart as a flower opening up, or use another image that evokes loving-kindness for you.

Put your hand on your heart and breathe into your heart, feeling your chest rising and falling.

Imagine moving kindness around your whole body, or filling your whole body with kindness.

Say a phrase to yourself, wishing yourself kindness. Imagine that each phrase is like a tiny pebble and your body is like a pool or lake. As you say each phrase, imagine the pebble dropping into your body and kindness rippling throughout your body.

Begin by making yourself comfortable. Prepare yourself by cultivating the basic attitudes of the heart. Pay attention to yourself. Notice yourself. Be affectionate to yourself by giving yourself a metaphorical hug. Appreciate yourself for opening up this book and being willing to read what we have to say. And then just accept yourself in this moment right here and now.

Start to imagine loving-kindness radiating in your body. Try to visualize yourself in your mind's eye. If this is tough, then think of a photo you like of yourself and imagine that, or imagine yourself as a baby. If this still feels uncomfortable, then just whisper your name silently until you feel connected with yourself. If this feels overwhelming, you could imagine a helpless puppy or kitten, and radiating loving-kindness toward it. Once you feel that loving-kindness, radiate it toward yourself. It is important for us to work at cultivating this. For many of us, it can feel challenging to begin with, but, the more we do it, the more our heart opens up toward ourselves. Sitting with our direct experience of discomfort or fear, without pushing it away or getting caught up in the stories about it, can be an expression of loving-kindness. When we can sit with these feelings, compassion for ourselves will eventually appear, and loving-kindness will begin to flow.

The most important thing is to have the strong wish for yourself not to suffer. So if you cannot take on any of the above suggestions, just sit with the strong wish for yourself not to suffer and see what this feels like.

Then begin saying silently to yourself the following phrases, which can also help with cultivating loving-kindness:

May I be happy.
May I be well.
May I be kind toward my suffering.
May I be free of all suffering.

Then pause, perhaps use one of the suggestions above to help radiate loving-kindness. After a few minutes, say the phrases again, seeing if you can feel them drop into your body on a visceral level. Don't worry if you can't feel loving-kindness. Having the intention of loving-kindness is enough right now. You may even feel sadness and have some tears. This is an opportunity to be kind to yourself and not criticize yourself for feeling tearful or crying.

Now put the book down and practice. Of course, pick it up again if you can't remember everything.

Developing compassion

One method of cultivating compassion is called "giving and taking." We take the suffering and, in return, give compassion. As a preparation, we give ourselves some loving-kindness for at least a few minutes. Then, as we breathe in we imagine the breath as dark smoke. We imagine that we are breathing in the pain. As we breathe out we visualize or sense the breath as pure white light like moonbeams, soothing the suffering. We can do this with our own pain or with the suffering of others.

At first it can seem a little strange to deliberately breathe in pain. In fact, what we are doing is opening up to whatever is already there. It is a turning toward and accepting what is. We just do it moment by moment, breath by breath. If it becomes overwhelming and unbearable, it usually means we have got caught up in a story about the pain. Our thoughts have spun off, as they easily do. So we try to stay with the bodily sensations, coming back to them again and again, one breath at a time.

The out-breath is like a wish. We wish from the bottom of our hearts to alleviate all pain, and we imagine that wish contained in the moonbeams of our out-breath. Sometimes our wish is a bit shaky or not very strong. That's OK. We just do what we can for now, and remember that it's a practice. We are gradually building up the capacity of our hearts to be able to meet more and more pain with compassion, to be able to hold more and more of what life throws at us.

Reflecting on the benefits of recovery

Counting the costs of our addiction, especially with an attitude of kindness and compassion, can help motivate us to step onto the path of recovery. The other side to this, which can also help our motivation, is reflecting on the desirability of recovery. We can give our imaginations free rein to feel what recovery would be like for us. Perhaps there was a time earlier in our lives when we weren't so caught up in our addictive behavior. Recalling that time may bring us something of the flavor of how recovery could be. Perhaps we know somebody who is already further along in recovery than we are. Contact with people who have already made steps in their recovery is extremely helpful. It is inspiring to meet people who have made significant changes in their lives and it can give us a sense of what recovery can look like. It also lets us know that recovery really is possible. No matter how much our addiction is costing us and how attractive recovery might seem, if we don't think that it is possible, any motivation to change is likely to fall away.

Giles's story

Giles had started his drug-using career with LSD. He saw himself as an explorer, pursuing altered states of consciousness. He tried other hallucinogens, Ecstasy, and stimulants. Although he barely noticed it, his experience changed from exploring to managing his mood. Eventually, he became dependent on stimulants and benzodiazepines. He needed the lift to enable him to go out, and diazepam to manage the comedown and his increasing anxiety. He became thoroughly fed up with himself and his life. He desperately wanted to be free of his addiction, but despaired of ever finding a way out. He hated himself for wasting his life.

One day he bumped into an old friend he hadn't seen for some time. They had used drugs together, but his friend had stopped. He meditated now and suggested to Giles that he give meditation a try. Giles's first response was cynical: he couldn't imagine it working for him, and he felt critical of his friend.

Back home, Giles turned over in his mind the meeting with his friend. He realized that he had felt envious of him. He had a certain ease and confidence that Giles had not known in his friend before, and Giles wanted something of that. He saw that his envy was just another trap that would keep him stuck. He thought that, after all, his friend had really been trying to help him. In the safety of his own home, Giles reflected that perhaps he could put his pride and arrogance aside, and appreciate his friend for who he appeared to have become and for wanting to help him.

As he reflected, he recollected his early trips on LSD. What he remembered was the drive that was in him then to find meaning and significance in his life, which he had sought through chemically induced altered states of mind. He had been seeking a sense of real freedom. Meditation was partly attractive because it might be another way to altered states of consciousness. It might also bring him something that he had glimpsed in his friend, a sense of ease and freedom. Maybe he could get out of this trap of addiction after all and find what he had been looking for all along.

Just as counting the cost of addiction needs to be done with compassion, so too, when we reflect on the benefits of recovery, we need to be held with kindness and appreciation. Without any kindness, when Giles contemplated recovery, he spiraled back down into self-criticism for having wasted his life and into hopelessness. The turning point for him was being appreciative of his friend. This allowed him to have a kinder attitude toward himself, making it possible for him to turn toward recovery.

Benefits and costs of recovery

To help strengthen your desire for recovery, it can be helpful to reflect on the benefits and costs of recovery. You can reflect on your own recovery and think about its benefits and costs, filling in the list below.

Benefits of recovery	Costs of recovery
•	•
•	•
•	•
•	•
•	•

Cultivating appreciation and gratitude

Appreciation and gratitude are helpful allies on the road to recovery. So often our minds habitually turn to what is wrong and what we are lacking. This only feeds ill will and despondency. Starting to appreciate what we do have can turn our lives around. We can notice the simple things in our lives such as the sunshine, the fresh air, the trees in the park, and the food we eat. In a cynical frame of mind, this can all sound trite. However, if we can let go of that mind-set, we can open up to the beauty of our lives.

Appreciating other people can sometimes be more difficult. Like Giles, we can get caught up in pride and envy. We may feel that, if we admit that we are grateful to someone, it puts us in their power and demeans us. However, true gratitude is not like that. Gratitude and appreciation are more like gifts that we can give to others, and in doing so we bestow an open heart on ourselves.

Making changes

Take five minutes to reflect on making changes. Settle your body and follow a breath or two. Ask yourself: what do you not want to change in your life? If it were possible to erase parts of your life, including your memories, what would you not want to rub out? What do you appreciate in your life? You could include people and relationships, animals, education, possessions, the planet and nature, music and art – whatever your mind turns to.

Notice the effect of doing this, especially in your body and your emotions. If you were in recovery, which of these could you have more of or appreciate and enjoy more fully? What could be the benefits for you of stepping onto the path of recovery?

Finally, if we are to be able to transform ourselves, it will help us to begin to cultivate more gratitude in our lives. Every night before you go to sleep you could ask yourself: "What do I have gratitude for in my life?" It could be having clean water to drink, or having a job, or being able to read this book.

Recap

In Step Four, we need to be willing to step onto the path of recovery and connect to a vision that is greater than our addiction or compulsive behaviors. We need to begin to identify things we want more than our addiction. We can begin to discover this new freedom by cultivating loving-kindness in our lives. It is like blowing onto coals: after a while, a flame arises. We must keep on diligently practicing loving-kindness toward ourselves, so that one day we will choose the path that leads to recovery instead of the path that leads to our addiction.

This is a gentle reminder for us to pause at the end of Step Four, and take a three-minute breathing space.

 ## Three-minute breathing space, AGE

Awareness of thoughts, feelings, and body.
Gather the breath, notice the breath, become aware of the breath.
Expand the breath throughout the whole body – connect to the whole body.

Step Five

··

Transforming our speech, actions, and livelihood

Watch your thoughts; they become words.
Watch your words; they become actions.
Watch your actions; they become habits.
Watch your habits; they become character.
Watch your character; it becomes your destiny.[1]

Transforming our speech, actions, and livelihood is part of the ethical and moral spring-cleaning we need to do to help maintain recovery and cultivate sobriety of mind. We explore these three aspects as gateways to recovery. We need to become aware of our ethical life and its consequences if we are to maintain our abstinence and sobriety of mind.

Our thoughts and emotions drive our actions

In Step Two, we explored the impact of our thoughts and emotions, and how they can trigger us into a vicious cycle of relapse. It is important for us to be reminded of this, because our thinking can help us maintain recovery or set off a relapse. Everything we think and all our emotional responses have an impact on us and everything around us, even if we don't act on them.

Our thoughts and emotions can be so fleeting and subtle that we might believe they don't matter. However, they shape our speech and bodily actions. If our hearts were full of love all the time, our thoughts would be full of love too. Having a tinge of resentment, greed, hatred, or delusion in our hearts guarantees that toxic thoughts will still arise, leaving us prey to our stinking thinking. When we are in the throes of addiction, we constantly grasp onto our thoughts and act them out, often taking no responsibility for the impact our actions have on others.

Remember, if we let our thoughts arise and cease, they will have less impact on us. Yet when thoughts come into being, we often grasp at them, and they develop into stories that we tell ourselves about our experiences. The problem is, we begin to believe these stories and behave as if they were true.

Our actions have consequences

We explored briefly that our actions have consequences in relationship to the Buddhist teaching of the four reminders. In this step, we expand on this. It is essential to recognize this if we are to transform our speech, actions, and mind. All of our thoughts and emotions – the words that we say or write and everything we do with our bodies – have an effect on ourselves and on the world. Put simply, actions (of body, speech, and mind) have consequences. Even our thoughts can be considered to be a kind of action, insofar as they affect us and determine how we act. In this step, we learn to notice the consequences of our actions and to find ways of acting that are beneficial and life-enriching. Where those actions have been unhelpful – often associated with our addiction – the consequences can haunt us and cause us trouble. However, there is also a tremendous freedom to be found, because at any moment we can shape our actions in ways that lead to greater happiness.

Our past unhelpful actions can ripple forward, creating self-loathing and guilt. We need to find a way to move forward rather than staying stuck in unhelpful recrimination.

As we discussed in the last step, kindness toward ourselves can help us to face painful recollections of our past actions. However, we can do more to come to terms with our past and move forward. In particular, there is a process we can use to acknowledge the past so that we can let it go, and we can take fresh actions that help to create happiness and boost self-esteem.

Both acknowledging past regrets and acting in new, beneficial ways help to transform us and support recovery. We will come to dealing with the past later in this step, since it can be easier to start with developing new, beneficial actions.

James's story

James would find himself seeking sex, usually from a prostitute or, failing that, Internet pornography. For a long time he could not understand what led him to engage in his addictive behavior, especially since afterward, he would feel humiliated and ashamed. Eventually he began to see that quite small changes in his mood would trigger this behavior. Feeling bored or angry could lead to him to want sex. In particular, he discovered that, if he felt put down in a situation, he would have negative critical thoughts about himself, castigating himself, as well as angry attacking thoughts toward the person he felt had put him down. These were quiet thoughts that he had scarcely noticed before. As he became more aware of them, he also became aware of wanting to escape the uncomfortable feelings that went with them, through engaging in sexual activity.

As James found, there are many thoughts we don't even hear, because we are so unaware of what is going on in our minds. Even though we are not conscious of them, these thoughts can have a great impact on our bodies, speech, and minds. The subtle thoughts that lurk about in our psyches can affect our mood, just as our emotions can bring into being elusive thoughts that we may not be aware of. This can affect what we do and how we communicate with others. It is sometimes these subtle thoughts that can lead us back into our addictions. We may wonder how on earth we ended up in a relapse once again. It is important to connect to the heart's whisper, because sometimes this whisper is putting us down. The loud thoughts we can hear, but the whispers go unnoticed unless we have created the pause for them to emerge.

The mindfulness practices described in earlier steps are a great way to bring more awareness to these whispers, subtle thoughts, and feelings. As our mindfulness gains strength, through repeated practice, we can learn to spot unhelpful thoughts and emotions as they arise, before they have taken hold of our minds. It is then easier to let them go.

In addition, mindfulness can help us to watch uncomfortable thoughts and feelings, without getting involved in them. By just watching them, we don't feed them through struggling against them or getting into a narrative about them. Once we develop more awareness of our thoughts and emotions through mindfulness, practicing kindness (especially the loving-kindness meditation) can help us to not react in unhelpful ways to the painful experiences that we become aware of. Loving-kindness meditation can help us to create happier, more beneficial states of mind. Mindfulness and kindness are valuable tools to transform our minds. We have also spoken about cultivating the four basic needs of the heart that help to shape a more positive outlook on life. When we bring more attention, affection, appreciation, acceptance, and loving-kindness into our lives, our mental states will become more positive. At the end of Step Four, we spoke about cultivating gratitude, which is another helpful way to develop more positive thinking in our lives. If we want to transform our speech, actions, and livelihood, it will help us to commit to taking on some of these practices.

Transforming speech

As someone once said, once the habit of untruthfulness begins there is no knowing where it may end. Does this message sound familiar? Untruthfulness can be the stumbling block of our recovery. Tell one small lie, and we may have to keep on telling more small lies to cover our tracks. Add all those lies up and they will amount to a whopping lie. Whether small lies or whopping lies, lies create anxiety, the fear that we may be found out. Lying can help perpetuate the cycle of addiction.

James's sexual activity was a secret. To keep his wife ignorant of his liaisons, James had to make more and more excuses and tell more lies. He would say he had to work late or was going out with the boys for a drink. Sometimes he would go out to see a prostitute during work hours and would have to cover his back to his colleagues. This created more and more anxiety as he had to remember what he had said to whom. Always there was the fear of being found out.

However, truthfulness is more than not lying; it is about factual accuracy, letting go of exaggeration, and being as sincere as possible. Sometimes in recovery we can conveniently miss out important details, or exaggerate about how well we are doing, and then wonder why we have ended up in the familiar place of using.

Mumtaz's story

Mumtaz would tell her counselor and her family that she was doing fine when asked about her credit-card shopping addiction. She would say that she was back on track and this time she was sure she was not going to relapse again. However, she was ignoring the tension she was feeling and the cajoling, critical inner voice. Even though she had some awareness that she wasn't feeling that great, she would put on the face that she believed her counselor and family wanted to see. As the gap increased between how she said she was feeling and how she actually felt, she became more and more vulnerable to relapsing. She would then end up walking out of a counseling session and going on a credit-card shopping spree. In order to change this pattern, Mumtaz needed to be more aware of what she was actually feeling. Only then was it possible for her to be more truthful.

Practicing the three-minute breathing space, AGE, can be a good way to catch what we are feeling, before we speak to someone – especially if we anticipate that the communication is likely to be tricky. As we practice mindfulness, we are likely to notice more the emotions behind our speech and the effect our speech has on others. For example, we might notice that, when we are tired or irritable, we speak more harshly to our partners. If we have been hurt by what someone else has said to us, we may retort angrily or take it out on another person. Wherever they start, exchanges like these can quickly build into big arguments, which can then be a trigger to relapse. Through mindfulness, we can notice the intention behind our speech. For example, is our aim to hurt someone, to hide our own discomfort, to hide a lie, or to help the person we are speaking to?

Our words can be like weapons that harm us and others. Transforming our speech is part of the ethical spring-cleaning we need to do in our lives if we want to maintain our recovery. This involves more than being truthful. It is also the practice of taking small steps in our lives to have the intention to be kind and helpful in our communication. When we appreciate something someone has done for us, we can let them know.

In intimate relationships especially, it can be easy to take each other for granted and assume that our partner knows we appreciate them. However, letting someone know that we care about them and what we value, even when we think they already know it, can improve the quality of our relationships. It can be a gift to the other person, which can also have a positive effect on us.

Before speaking, ask yourself:

How kind is my speech?
What is the intention of my speech?

Practice saying only kind things today and see what happens.

Transforming actions

Actions have consequences. This is what we mean when we talk about karma. For example, if we continue having that pint of beer, injecting that needle, having that extra flutter, turning to whatever our addictive behavior is, we will perpetuate the cycle of craving and suffering. Every time we act out of craving we will multiply the seeds of craving and suffering. Therefore, karma is not about fate: it is recognizing that our actions have a cause and effect. If we change our actions, we will change our karma.

Transforming bodily action entails that we stop doing things that hurt ourselves or others, and take actions that help ourselves or others. Despite having performed unwholesome actions, we can always retrain ourselves to do things differently. By not harming ourselves or others, abstaining from fraud, robbery, and stealing, we can begin to cultivate a sober mind that will support our recovery. We can make efforts to be kinder and more generous. Small actions such as helping someone who is lost with directions or giving a small gift to a friend, especially when it is unexpected, can bring happiness to us, as well as to the recipient of our actions.

Creating positive states of mind through our kind actions helps us to feel better about ourselves, and can help to counteract regrets from past hurtful actions. In this way, transforming our speech, actions, and livelihood forms the backbone to abstinence and to letting go of our addictions.

Our thoughts may be elusive, and we may hardly notice the quality of our habitual speech, but the actions we take with our bodies can be easier to notice, and often easier to change. If our actions hurt ourselves or another – such as hitting someone or self-harming – they will have an adverse effect on us, creating negative states of mind like anger and resentment. Conversely, if we act with kindness and generosity toward ourselves and others, this will have a beneficial effect. If we are to stop hurting ourselves, this will mean letting go of our addictions. Though we often take our drug of choice to feel better, in the end we feel worse.

The process of transformation can be slow and gradual. It takes time and practice to recognize what is helpful and what isn't, and to act as best we can in ways that are helpful and to let go of unhelpful actions. Often our old habits are deeply entrenched, having been repeated over many years. When we are in the grip of our addictions, we may feel powerless over our speech, actions, livelihoods, and minds. Under the sway of addiction, usually without fully recognizing it at the time, we act in ways that cause us and others harm. We build up habitual ways of thinking, speaking, and acting that are unhelpful and have their own momentum that is hard to resist.

We can lose control over our everyday actions. Whether we are under the influence of an intoxicant like alcohol, or caught up in the drive to gamble, we can lose awareness of our speech, bodily actions, livelihoods, and minds. Lack of awareness renders us powerless. To attain sobriety of mind and abstinence from our addictions, we must have awareness of what we are saying when we speak, what we are doing with our bodies, what we do for a living, and what thoughts are in our minds.

Silas's story

Time was running out for Silas. He was troubled by the memories of what he had done when he was a drug dealer. He alluded to violence, but could not bring himself to speak openly about what had happened. By injecting heroin, he had contracted hepatitis C and HIV. He really wanted to be clean and had stopped all drug use. He wanted to build bridges to some of his family and make up for his neglect of them. However, now he drank to drown out the thoughts and feelings that tortured him from the past. When he was drunk he was not able to take medication regularly, so his HIV was worsening and he could not start treatment for hepatitis C. His liver was failing with the combination of hepatitis and alcohol.

Silas had reached an impasse, with the troubles of the past holding him in addiction and stopping him from acting in ways that would support his recovery in the present. He was unable to transform his actions, putting his life at risk. He did not want to die. But in the moment of craving for a drink and faced with the choice between his life and the alcohol, he was choosing the alcohol.

If you have been trying to recover for many years, and have not been successful, you may want to take a look at what you are doing in your life. Ask yourself: "What could I do to help clean up my life?" Reflect on this question; be honest with yourself. Take some time to review your life.

> What actions do I need to take to transform my life?
> What ways could I act that would bring my life more in
>   line with how I would like to be?

Practice doing only kind acts today.

Transforming livelihood

> But if you can create an honorable livelihood, where you
> take your skills and use them and you earn a living from
> it, it gives you a sense of freedom and allows you to
> balance your life the way you want.[2]

When we are in recovery, it is important to set up the right conditions to maintain sobriety and abstinence. If we were honest while in the throes of an addiction, and reflected on our lives, we would be able to see that the conditions we set up for ourselves support us living an addicted life. This may mean that we will have to let go of a social network that we have socialized in for years. It may mean changing jobs, because the way we earn our money is inconsistent with our recovery. Transforming our speech, actions, and livelihood means we must look at every aspect of our lives.

Jennifer's story

Jennifer was a veterinarian, and part of her job was putting down sick animals. On the days she euthanized animals, she often went out on a binge. It was clear that her job was one of the main triggers for her to binge drink. Although she could see this clearly, she refused to let go of her job. She convinced herself that, since she knew the reason she was drinking, she could manage it. Two years later Jennifer voluntarily put herself in an alcohol-detox unit, and she resentfully let go of her job. A year later, after her recovery, Jennifer realized that leaving her job was one of the best decisions she had made in her life.

Some of us may have to acknowledge that our way of living is facilitating our addiction. For example, some of us living with addiction have fallen into the rut of unemployment. We have nothing to get up for in the morning and are left with the whole day to pass with minimal amount of responsibility. Having too much time on our hands can be a major stumbling block for recovery. Of course, if you choose not to work and have put yourself in a recovery program or are engaging in other activities that are supporting your recovery, then your time is being used wisely.

Reflecting on our livelihoods, we could ask ourselves: "What are we doing to pay the bills? Are we earning money legally and peacefully?" Livelihoods that harm other living beings, such as working in the armaments industry, raising animals for slaughter, prostitution, or selling intoxicants like alcohol and drugs, are likely to have an adverse effect on us and not be supportive of recovery. Some in particular, such as dealing drugs, could lead us to become addicted. There are many reasons that we may earn our living in an unsupportive way, such as things that happened to us in childhood, or being involved with an inappropriate social circle. There are also the conditions we create that support our addictive behavior. Often, like Jennifer until she entered the detox unit, we may be unaware that our way of living or of earning money keeps us caught up in our addictions.

We need to review this, look at what we are doing, and perhaps make some hard decisions. We must ask ourselves: "Are we willing to commit our lives to recovery?" Committing to recovery wholeheartedly can have a huge financial impact on ourselves and our families. In some cases it may mean having more money, but in other cases it may mean a drop in income, even to the extent of having to leave your job for the sake of your recovery.

We need to find livelihoods that support our recovery. More generally, we need activity in our lives that supports recovery rather than habitual addictive behavior. Lack of meaningful activity and boredom are a sure road to relapse.

If you are in an unhealthy work situation, you might consider taking a sabbatical. It might mean acknowledging that you are unwell and need some time to heal or work on yourself. If you are unemployed, you could take up a new hobby, get back into something recreational you used to do, or do some volunteer work. If you are not able to stop or change your work, you could reflect on how you could improve your work situation or change your attitude toward it. For example, you could practice being kinder to people at work. In Step Four, we saw how kindness can be a great tool for recovery.

How we practice this step

Training principles to guide our actions toward sobriety and abstinence

The Buddha offers guidance to cultivate good karma through the practice of the five precepts (training principles), which help train the mind and provide the moral framework for us to surrender to recovery, transform and live our lives more skillfully.

These training principles can help us transform our bodily actions, speech, and livelihoods, which will guide us toward abstinence and sobriety. They are also reminders of how we want to live our lives, and can support our endeavors to transform our actions. Listed below are five principles, which are from the Buddhist tradition. Each one has a negative and a positive form – what to avoid doing and what to put into practice. The positive form is described as "purifying" the body, speech, and mind. Purification is another way of talking about transformation. For some people, purification will have negative associations – if that is the case for you, just ignore the word or replace it with "transform." Some people find the image of purification helpful. When we act in ways that bring benefits to ourselves and others, and we don't have to berate ourselves for actions we regret, our lives can feel simpler. Some people experience this lack of complexity as feeling purer – undiluted, like pure orange juice. So use the metaphor if it speaks to you.

	Negative form	Positive form
1	I undertake to abstain from harming life.	With deeds of loving-kindness I purify my body.
2	I undertake to abstain from taking the not-given.	With open-handed generosity I purify my body.
3	I undertake to abstain from sexual misconduct.	With stillness, simplicity, and contentment I purify my body.
4	I undertake to abstain from false speech.	With truthful communication I purify my speech.
5	I undertake to abstain from taking intoxicants.	With mindfulness clear and radiant I purify my mind.

1. *Abstain from harming life; practice loving-kindness*: this principle includes avoiding violence toward all living beings, such as domestic violence. The positive form covers acts of kindness, such as helping others in practical ways or taking care of ourselves.
2. *Abstain from taking the not-given; practice generosity*: in the negative form, this principle concerns more than

stealing. It is taking anything that does not belong to us, including emotions that don't belong to us. Forcing someone to do something they don't want to do is also taking the not-given. We can act generously through giving gifts, time, attention, or encouragement – opening our hands and offering kindness and generosity.

3. *Abstain from sexual misconduct; practice contentment*: this principle is about avoiding harm in sexual relationships – giving up sexual harassment, sexual assault, sexual abuse, infidelity, and secret non-monogamy. In the positive, it is about living a life with more contentment and stillness. This principle is a great aspiration to hold in our hearts. The craving of addiction is the opposite of contentment, so working on this principle can help to counter some of the driving force of addiction.

4. *Abstain from false speech; practice truthfulness*: communication is essential to all relationships. It is the pulse of life. As well as lying, this principle covers all areas of harmful speech including harsh, frivolous, useless, and slanderous speech. And in addition to truthful speech, the positive form includes helpful and harmonious speech.

5. *Abstain from intoxicants; practice mindfulness*: if we can train our minds to adhere to this principle, all the other principles will be easier to live by. Once we indulge in any amount of an intoxicant, we are at risk of breaking all the other principles, through lack of awareness.

If we choose to follow these principles, it's worth remembering that they are guidelines. They are reminders to help us act in ways that will benefit us and others. They are individual choices to follow if we wish. We start from where we are. We do not beat ourselves up about our past actions, or criticize ourselves. The five precepts are not rules or commandments, and you will not be punished if you don't follow them. The only person who will give you a hard time is yourself. In fact, we don't need anyone to punish us, not even ourselves. If we pay attention, we will notice that going against the principles causes us trouble and suffering, and following them leads to greater happiness and contentment. However, you don't need to take our word for this. You can test it out for yourself in your own experience.

Devising your own training principles

In addition or as an alternative to the five precepts, you could write one which is relevant to your addiction or compulsive behavior and include an action plan with it. For example:

- Training principle: I undertake to abstain from bingeing on food. With serenity and courage I purify my mind.
- Action plan: I will seek help. I will record what I eat so that I notice exactly what I am doing with my food.

Reciting the training principles

We can recite the principles daily to help our minds to sober up, which in turn will support us in abstaining from our addictions. We could look at these principles as a coaching script to retrain our minds.

Valerie

I found this especially helpful in my recovery. Over twenty years ago I was still addicted; however, I began reciting the positive and negative precepts daily. My addictions began to fall away. The experience of using a substance to move away from a strong emotion just did not have the same impact. Without my being aware of it, these principles trained my mind so much that I was able to let go of the gross intoxicants of drugs and alcohol.

When we recite the training principles daily, we are creating new thoughts and changing existing habits of belief. Reciting the precepts helps us to become more aware of our actions – especially whether they are harmful or beneficial – since it helps

Reflecting on the five training principles

Take a couple of minutes to reflect on each principle. You can say them out aloud or silently to yourself.

> I undertake to abstain from harming life.
> With deeds of loving-kindness I purify my body.

Now reflect on this question: what deeds of loving-kindness can you do to help transform body, speech, and mind?

> I undertake to abstain from taking the not-given.
> With open-handed generosity I purify my body.

Now reflect on this question: what acts of generosity can you do to transform your body, speech, and mind?

> I undertake to abstain from sexual misconduct.
> With stillness, simplicity, and contentment I purify my body.

Now reflect on this question: how can you bring about more stillness, simplicity, and contentment in your life?

> I undertake to abstain from false speech.
> With truthful communication I purify my speech.

Now reflect on this question: how can you make your communication more truthful and kind?

> I undertake to abstain from taking intoxicants.
> With mindfulness clear and radiant I purify my mind.

Now reflect on this question: how can you transform your mind so it becomes more clear and radiant?

to keep the guidelines in mind. When we become aware of what we are doing, it becomes more of a choice, and so we can choose to do something differently.

Reciting these precepts is a strong and rewarding practice. We could perhaps begin with the fifth principle, reciting it daily.

Old habits, addictions, and compulsive behaviors will fight for survival. We may need to visualize ourselves living much healthier lives. This could be done while reciting the precepts. Many athletes visualize winning to help them achieve their dreams. It's said that it takes twenty-one days to change a habit and begin to create new beliefs. If we recite the principles daily, we will gather momentum and begin to achieve what we most deeply value.

After a week of daily recitation of one precept, we could up the ante and take on a few of the others. Make a commitment to do this regularly for at least twenty-one days and see what happens. There's nothing to lose. Start putting your recovery into action now. Why wait for tomorrow?

Coming to terms with past and ongoing unhelpful actions

We have all done things in the past that, when we look back, make us wince and wish we could change. We have to accept that we can't change what has happened. If we beat ourselves up for what we have done, we are adding more difficulties that can get in the way of recovery. When we chastise ourselves, we keep our past actions alive, leaving us feeling helpless and hopeless and, often, continuing the same behaviors.

Many of our clients have stayed in the vicious cycle of addiction exactly for this reason. They have felt so awful and guilty about some of the things that they have done, the awareness has been so overwhelming, that they have beaten themselves up and continued to use. "What the hell, I've gone this far, who cares now? Who's going to forgive me?" can be the lament.

Fear of looking at the past, and of becoming aware of our past actions, is also a major stumbling block to recovery. We can feel shame and guilt about our behavior. We don't want to face the wreckage of our past, so we spiral back down into our addiction. For both Silas and James, the fear of facing up to their past behavior kept them in the grips of addiction.

It is clear that, if we are to stay on the path of recovery, we need to sweep out the cobwebs of the past that haunt us. Memories and secrets can also be stumbling blocks to our recovery.

There are three stages that can help in coming to terms with our unhelpful actions. These are acknowledgment and regret, making amends, and a promise to act differently.

Acknowledgment and regret
The first part of coming to terms with past and current unhelpful actions is to acknowledge them. We acknowledge the fact that our actions have caused suffering to us or to others. We do this with an attitude of kindness. This is not to minimize the consequences of our actions or let ourselves off the hook. Rather, it is to avoid adding yet more suffering through beating ourselves up.

Reflecting on our actions that have caused harm, we are likely to feel regret. However, it is important to distinguish regret from guilt. Guilt is fearing the loss of approval or love. It is likely to lead us to berate ourselves. Sometimes it is as if we are criticizing ourselves to avoid criticism from others. Regret has a "cleaner" quality to it, in which we are willing to fully accept the consequence of our past actions. We often have a mixed response, with feelings of both regret and guilt. Whatever our emotions, we acknowledge them with kindness. We try to see as clearly as we can the pain or suffering we have caused, allow ourselves to feel that pain, and let go of any self-chastisement. Feeling the pain is enough, without making ourselves suffer more.

The reality is that some of us have committed past actions that have had devastating effects. In this case, we need to find a way to forgive ourselves, and work with our minds so the memories of these actions do not keep tripping us into relapse.

Nothing is unforgivable. We have to start from where we are, and spring-clean our minds.

Sometimes we can see that our behavior is causing us to suffer, but we are not yet ready to give it up. We are not yet in a position to say that we won't repeat the behavior that is troubling us. Particularly if we have been secretive about our habit, we may have kept it even from our own awareness, so it can be helpful first just to acknowledge what we have done.

To begin with, we can acknowledge our actions by reflecting on them and on their consequences. If we wish, we could write them down. A stronger practice is to tell another human being. If we choose to do this, we need to pick the person with care. We want to share this with someone who will both understand our concern and not judge us negatively. It's important that we trust this person to hear us in an open-hearted way. Telling someone else can be beneficial because, when we keep our unhelpful deeds to ourselves, our memories of them can fester in our minds as we so easily go over them with recrimination, but without making any changes. To open up to another person can help to give us a little more mental space around our actions. We may then find it easier to make changes, so that in time we can let go of our unhelpful behavior more fully. As telling someone else can be such a strong practice, we need to go at our own pace. James started to tell a friend with whom he was meditating about his sexual activity. At first he could only mention the pornography. It was only later, as their friendship developed and James felt more trust in the relationship, that he could talk about visiting prostitutes.

Making amends

As we reflect on our past actions, if we feel regret for some of them, we may wish to apologize. Apologizing can be a helpful step toward making amends, although we need to accept that some people may not want our apology. If this is the case, we can try to be gracious and compassionate toward the person. They may be in a different place from us in coming to terms with what has happened, and may not be ready to receive an apology.

As well as apologizing, we can take action to make amends. For example, if we have stolen, we may want to make an anonymous donation to the person or the institution. Sometimes we need to make amends to people who are no longer alive. We can still be creative, and offer amends to the family. Sometimes it would be too inflammatory to approach someone to make amends. When this happens, we can ritually write an apology that we don't send, and wish that person well.

A promise and a plan
The final stage in coming to terms with our unhelpful actions is to promise not to repeat them, and to make a plan that can support us to act differently in the future. Many of us have made promises that we failed to keep, throughout our history of addiction. All too often we promise never to repeat an action again, without acknowledging our past actions, and everything else that needs to precede a promise. How many of us have promised ourselves or another person that we will not repeat a certain behavior, or apologized, or said it is the last time we will do something – only to break our promise hours, days, weeks, or months later?

A promise is a vision. On its own it is not enough, which is why so many people mess up after making a promise. There needs to be a clear plan of action to back up our promise, if we are to keep it. If we are sorry, it will help to express exactly what we are sorry for, so we can come into relationship with the past, feel some kind of remorse, and feel inspired or motivated to set the plan of action to support us in keeping our word.

Making a promise

For example, before you promise your partner never to drink again, it may well be best to make the promise to yourself first. Doing something for somebody else is not enough. We have to change our lives because we want change, not because it will please somebody else. This is the barometer of a promise: are you ready to make a pact with yourself? If so, reflect on these questions for the next five minutes:

- Are you aware of the impact of your past actions?
- What have those past actions been?
- What plan of action are you going to take so that you don't repeat the same behavior?
- When is this going to happen?
- What are the new things that you can bring into your life to help you?

Now take a moment to reflect on this fifth step of transforming speech, actions, and livelihood, and what it means to you. Take the next ten minutes to recite these phrases and reflect on the questions below:

- Body like a mountain – just as a mountain is strong, firm, and present, let my body be strong, firm, and present.
- Heart like an ocean – just as the waves in an ocean arise and cease, let my thoughts and feelings arise and cease.
- Mind like the sky – just as the sky is big, wide, and open, let my mind be big, wide, and open.
- Speech like honey – just as honey is sweet and soft, let my speech be full of sweetness and softness.
- Livelihood like a bird – just as a bird flies happily in the sky, let my livelihood create happiness in my life.
- Breath like an anchor – just as an anchor steadies a boat, let my breath steady my thoughts and feelings.

Ask yourself:

- How do my bodily actions impact my life?
- How does my speech impact my life?
- How does my mind/thinking impact my life?
- How does my livelihood impact my life?
- What do I need to do to transform my body, speech, and mind?

Now ask yourself: "Am I ready to make that promise?" If you're not, go back to your plan of action, and break it down even more.

Ritual approaches to coming to terms with our past

Some of us find that ritual can be a powerful way to come to terms with our past unhelpful actions. Ritual, for example a wedding or a funeral, is a way to emphasize the significance of what we are doing. If we want to make a big change in our lives, a ritual, especially when we do it deliberately and consciously, can be a way to strengthen our resolve. Ritual can help to get more of us behind what we are trying to do. Two rituals that can support our efforts to come to terms with the past are using a prayer and chanting a mantra.

Prayer
Positive affirmations are a daily practice for some people. Some of us meditate daily, some of us get down on our knees and pray, and some visualize or chant for what we want to see emerge in our lives. These are all helpful ways to help bring about positivity in our lives.

A prayer can also be helpful if we have a sense of something or someone higher or beyond us. Even if we have no concept of a higher power, praying for something that we would like to happen can be very helpful. We can recite the prayer in a special place. This could be a place of beauty that we like to visit. Alternatively, we could make a place in the corner of our bedroom or living room. We might wish to clean the room and then sit in front of a photo or photos that are significant for us. We could have some flowers and light a candle. We could sit quietly for a period and then recite our prayer. Below, we have rewritten a traditional Buddhist prayer and put it into more accessible language (see p.137).

Having recited the prayer, we resolve not to commit the actions again. We clearly state our plan of action, including the time frame in which we will begin to act. Then we can sit quietly again, allowing the ritual to have its effect.

Admitting our faults with compassion

So be it!

Dear Buddha, *bodhisattva* (or God or Higher Power of my understanding), please listen to me as I admit my faults.

I (state your name _____), who have been in the vicious cycle of addiction, have created suffering in my life. I have been overpowered by my addictions, attachments, aversions, and ignorance. I admit I have lost awareness of my body, speech, and mind, and because of my lack of awareness I have been perpetuating negative actions. I ask that you guide and support me as I begin to transform my bodily actions, speech, livelihood, and mind.

I have been unkind to my family, friends, and people I don't even know. (Include what is appropriate to you.) I confess I have been unkind to all beings, including animals.

I have committed actions harmful to myself and to others. (Include what is appropriate to you.) I have taken the not-given, I have committed sexual misconduct, I have spoken harshly and told lies, I have taken intoxicants. I have had a livelihood that has been harmful to me and others. These and many other destructive actions I have done. I admit I have created my suffering and the obstacles that have hindered my recovery. I have been stuck in a rut of misery.

Now in the presence of a trusted human being (or in the presence of the Buddha, a *bodhisattva*, God or the Higher Power of my understanding), I confess all my negative actions. I will not pretend they have never happened. I will confront my past actions and acknowledge my unskillful misdeeds. I promise to refrain from doing these actions again in the future. By confessing my unskillful actions I allow myself forgiveness and will now rest in stillness, simplicity, and contentment. I will move toward more happiness in my life.

Sadhu, Sadhu, Sadhu (well done, well done, well done).

Mantra

Another approach to help us come to terms with past unhelpful actions is mantra. We spoke about mantra in Step Three. We could chant any mantra that resonates with us. Before reciting the mantra, we reflect on our past actions that have caused harm and suffering. We continue reflecting until we feel some kind of remorse, and realize that we need to change and not continue with our way of life. Remember, this is not about giving ourselves a hard time, it is simply bringing awareness to how we have harmed ourselves and others. As we chant we could lightly hold a wish to be able to let go and move beyond our past troubles.

One of the blocks to overcoming past unhelpful actions is feeling that something deep within us has been permanently damaged by them. We can feel irretrievably soiled by our past actions. This seems to be especially the case if we have experienced trauma. Vajrasattva is an archetypal figure from the Buddhist tradition that is associated with overcoming past unhelpful actions. In particular, he represents the realization that our deepest nature was never impure or soiled; that our addiction had covered up our well-being and goodness.

The short version of the Vajrasattva mantra is o*m vajra-sattva hum*. You could repeat this mantra for ten minutes daily. There is a long version of the Vajrasattva mantra for those who want to take up the practice more seriously (see p.139). You can listen to the full-length mantra chanted online at our website: http://thebuddhistcentre.com/eightsteps.

Vajrasattva Mantra

Oṃ vajrasattva samayam
anupālaya
vajrasattvatvenopatiṣṭa
dṛḍho me bhava
sutoṣyo me bhava
supoṣyo me bhava
anurakto me bhava
sarvasiddhiṃ me prayaccha
sarvakarmasu ca me
cittaṃ śreyaḥ kuru hūṃ
ha ha ha ha hoḥ
bhagavan sarvatathāgatavajra
mā me muñca
vajrī bhava
mahāsamayasattva
āḥ hūṃ phaṭ

Translation:
Oṃ Vajrasattva! Preserve the bond!
As Vajrasattva stand before me.
Be firm for me.
Be greatly pleased for me.
Deeply nourish me.
Love me passionately.
Grant me success and attainment in all things,
And in all actions make my mind most excellent. *hūṃ*!
ha ha ha ha ho! [Be joyful as you recite this laughter of liberation.]
Blessed One! Vajra of all the Tathāgatas! Do not abandon me.
Be the Vajra-bearer, Being of the Great Bond!
āḥ hūṃ phaṭ

Another mantra believed to help transform body, speech, and mind is one we also mentioned in Step Three, *om mani padme hum*. This is one of the best-known Buddhist mantras, and is the mantra of the male *bodhisattva* of compassion, Avalokitesvara. Reflecting on our past actions can bring up difficult emotions, so it can be helpful to cultivate compassion. Chanting Avalokitesvara's mantra is one way to put us in contact with compassion. The mantra is a popular one. You can find it on our website (http://thebuddhistcentre.com/eightsteps) and hear how it is chanted.

The fourteenth Dalai Lama says:

> It is very good to recite the mantra OM MANI
> PADME HUM, but while you are doing it, you
> should be thinking on its meaning, for the meaning
> of the six syllables is great and vast. The first, OM [...]
> [symbolizes] the practitioner's impure body, speech, and
> mind; [it also symbolizes] the pure exalted body, speech
> and mind of a Buddha.[3]

As we chant the mantra, if we find it helpful, we can imagine the different syllables of the mantra transforming different aspects of our bodies, speech, and minds:

- When we chant *om* we can feel we are transforming pride and selfishness, and cultivating generosity.
- When we chant *ma* we can feel we are transforming our jealousies and cultivating an ethical life.
- When we chant *ni* we can feel we are transforming our craving and cultivating patience.
- When we chant *pad* we can feel we are transforming our ignorance and prejudices and cultivating diligence.
- When we chant *me* we can feel we are transforming our possessiveness and cultivating letting go of attachment.
- When we chant *hum* we can feel we are transforming our hatred and aggression and cultivating wisdom.

Now chant *om mani padme hum* for ten minutes. Then sit for a few minutes, absorbing the impact of the mantra.

Making the most of opportunities to change our lives – GIFTS

Transforming our bodily actions, speech, livelihood, and mind is not easy. In fact, it is a lifetime commitment. However, there are GIFTS (Great Indicators For Throwing Stuff out). There are always moments of clarity, even in the midst of addiction, and these are GIFTS staring us in the face. We have to learn to value them and act on them.

For example, there may be an important life event, like a new relationship. This can be a great indicator for throwing stuff out, like our addictions or other unhelpful behavior. For some of us, taking these opportunities can bring about temporary recovery, and for a few it may lead to prolonged abstinence.

Sometimes the GIFT may be painful, as happened with James. James's wife finally found out that he had been seeing prostitutes. He saw the hurt in her eyes and he could see that their marriage was over. He felt wretched and, at the same time, could feel the same old urge that he had begun to recognize as the buildup to escaping into anonymous sex. The whole process – the discomfort, the urge to flee into sex, the sex, and then the humiliation – passed through his mind. He had done enough damage to himself and his wife: now it was time to act differently. This was a GIFT in his life. He finally took it as an opportunity to throw stuff out, to let go of his unskillful actions and act differently, despite the fact that his marriage was over.

Often our GIFTS can be subtle, like the tiny positive whisper telling us: "I want to stop." We must try to hear the heart's whisper and act on these GIFTS, seizing the opportunity to throw stuff out of our lives.

This came to Silas in the middle of the night after he had been admitted to hospital with a failing liver. For a while the ward was quiet, but Silas could not sleep. His body was itching and his mind was restless. He knew that he might not have long to live, especially if he continued to drink. For a moment he let go of the struggle: let the ghosts of the past do what they would. He was determined to move forward in his life, however long or short that would be.

Recap

In Step Five, we learn to transform our speech, actions, and livelihood. With an attitude of kindness, we review our past actions. We acknowledge them and their impact on us and others. We make amends, and plan to do something different. We take our GIFTS to move forward in our recovery and commit to living our lives more in line with the five training principles. We acknowledge the consequences of our addictions and have healthy compassionate regret. If we make a promise, we make a plan of action before promising to let go. And, if we are able, we admit to another human being the exact nature of our actions and give ourselves forgiveness.

This is a gentle reminder for us to pause at the end of Step Five, and take a three-minute breathing space.

Three-minute breathing space, AGE

Awareness of thoughts, feelings, and body.
Gather the breath, notice the breath, become aware of the breath.
Expand the breath throughout the whole body – connect to the whole body.

Step Six

....

Placing positive values at the center of our lives

Changing ourselves and our lives to overcome our addictions can be hard work. Finding recovery on our own is also hard. Without other people to support and encourage us, it is difficult to make the challenging changes that recovery demands. We can fall back into old habits all too easily.

We have emphasized the inevitability of suffering in life and the need to face up to this – mindfully and with kindness. At times this can become grueling, as we battle with old habits and meet painful experiences again. So it's worth reflecting on why we have chosen to do this. We started this reflection in Step Four, when we looked at the costs and benefits of our addiction and of recovery. However, we can take this further by reflecting on what is truly valuable to us, what we really want our lives to be about, and what sort of person we deeply want to be. If we are clear about what is important to us and what we really value, it is easier to steer our lives in a meaningful direction, and it helps us to keep on track when the going gets tough.

In this step, we will explore values in general and how to approach them. We will then look at the Three Jewels, which are seen in Buddhism as the most important values. The Three Jewels are the Buddha (Awakened mind), the Dharma (the nature of reality and the teachings of the Buddha), and the sangha (the spiritual community). In looking at the Three Jewels, we will have the chance to see how values can support a rich life free of addiction. We hope that the perspective of one spiritual tradition – Buddhism – will be helpful whether you are Buddhist, from another spiritual tradition, or from none.

....

Exploring values

Our values are very precious to us, which is why in Buddhism they are called jewels, treasures, or gems. Sometimes, because they are precious, we keep them hidden, even from ourselves. We might then feel that we have no values. Particularly if our lives have been difficult and we have struggled with a lot of suffering, we may have lost sight of our values, or it may have felt too dangerous to have any. We may have had the experience of expressing something important to us, only to have someone else belittle it. Or we might have tried to act on our values, only to be thwarted by difficulties in our lives.

We have two ways to start to get in touch with our values, two ways of finding out what is important to us.

Connecting to our values

First, take a breathing space, AGE, to help center yourself.

Now, reflect: if you could change everything about yourself, what would you not want to change? What characteristics about yourself would you want to keep? In terms of how you approach the world, how you behave toward other people, what would you like to keep the same? What does this tell you about what is important to you? What is important in your life? What qualities or values matter to you?

Imagining a party at the end of your life

In this exercise you imagine that from this day onward, you live your life in the way that you would most like to live it, according to your most precious values. Now imagine a party toward the end of your life, perhaps a birthday celebration. You could imagine it as a small and intimate affair or as a big ball in a grand palace. Allow yourself to imagine freely the sort of celebration it is.

At the party there are various friends and perhaps family. (As it is in the imagination, you could have people there who might no longer be alive.) As part of the celebration, some of the guests speak about the good qualities that you have displayed during your life. Bring to mind someone who cares about you, and imagine this person stepping forward and rejoicing in some of your qualities. What does this person say? What do they particularly rejoice in about you? As you do this exercise, remember to keep breathing and, as best you can, allow whatever feelings show up.

Now bring to mind another person. They too step forward and speak of your fine qualities. What do they say? Pause for a moment and notice your breathing.

Finally bring to mind a third person. Allow this person to step forward and describe your qualities and how you have lived them out. What does this person say? Pause again, following your breath, before leaving the party in your mind.

Take some time now to write down the responses of the three people.

Values as a direction and as a refuge

There are two ways in which we can look at values: in terms of a direction in our lives and as a refuge.

Values as a direction

Values act like a compass that shows us which way to go. For example, if honesty is an important value, then this will guide how we endeavor to act in our relationships. Values are pointers of the way rather than a destination. We don't ever arrive at perfect honesty. Instead, honesty is something we try to bring into our relationships moment by moment as best we can. Inevitably, we won't be living by our values all the time and will sometimes go against them. The good thing about values is that we can always get back to them in the next moment, as soon as we remember.

As well as showing us how to act, values can direct us toward important goals. For example, if we value helping other people, we might decide that we want to move away from our administrative job to one that has an element of direct caring for others, or we may wish to free up some time to do volunteer work that involves helping others. If creating beauty is important to us, we might decide to join a choir or enroll in an art class. When we act on our values and move toward goals that express them, we are likely to feel more satisfied and nourished in our lives.

Values as a refuge

In everyday language, a refuge is a place to go when we are in danger. It is a place of safety, like a hut on a mountain that can keep us warm and dry in a raging storm. In the face of suffering, recollecting our values and trying to act on them can give us strength. For example, if a loving relationship with our children is important, keeping this in mind may help us when our child is misbehaving – or when we are separated from our children – and we are tempted to return to our addiction to drown the pain.

We can reflect on what we do when things are difficult, what we go to for refuge. We are likely to have used our addiction as a refuge to cope with difficulties, and we may have engaged in other damaging behavior, such as self-harm or getting involved in destructive relationships, to manage painful emotions. We call these refuges that don't help us in the long run false refuges. False refuges look like they are going to be reliable, are going to relieve our pain, but they let us down. They don't work, except perhaps in the short term. They are like a derelict house, empty, without life or breath, with weak walls and a leaky roof. We flee from the storm only to find that the rain starts to come through the roof. Then, as the wind picks up, the whole structure blows over, and we are left exposed to the elements with pieces of the building falling on us. We are no nearer to safety. Instead we are soaked and have cuts all over from the fallen timber.

So as well as reflecting on where we go for refuge, we can reflect on how helpful our refuges are. Perhaps we will want to let go of some, and we may be able to find others that reflect deeper values, that are more helpful and constructive. We can look at our refuges as the things we place at the center of our lives, or what we choose to turn our lives over to. Our addictions or compulsive behaviors will be among the things at the center of our lives. This means that we spend the majority of our time thinking about things related to our addiction, and that most of our decisions will be based around the addiction. It means that we have gone for refuge to the addiction, in the hope that it will support us, help us, keep us safe.

Placing what you value at the center of your life

Pause now and reflect on some of the following questions:

- What do you take refuge in?
- What do you turn to when life gets difficult?
- What is at the center of your life?
- What occupies your thoughts?

Having identified what you turn to for refuge, reflect on how helpful it really is when times are hard.

Are there refuges that you would like to let go of?

If you could put the three most valuable things to support your recovery at the center of your life, what would they be?

Janet and Bob's story

Sometimes we are not aware of what we use as a refuge until circumstances change in our lives, as Janet discovered after her husband stopped drinking. Janet had grown up in a drinking environment. Her father had been a heavy drinker and died of complications from alcohol misuse. Janet had never touched alcohol, but found herself married to a man who drank excessively.

She was devoted to her husband, Bob, and supported him as he tried to give up drinking, relapsed, and went back on the bottle. Bob was never sober for very long. Although he wasn't violent when drinking, he would become argumentative, and gradually his health declined so that he needed more and more care from Janet. Janet would complain to her friends about her husband's drinking. She rarely criticized Bob directly, although in some of their bigger fights she would threaten to leave him if he did not stop. Finally Bob made a more determined effort to give it up. His health improved and he was less irritable.

At first Janet was delighted. Then she found herself becoming more on edge, depressed, and touchy. She could not understand herself. After a big argument, largely provoked by Janet, Bob hit the bottle again. Janet told her friends she was disappointed that Bob had started drinking, but at the same time she began to recognize – with some discomfort – that she was also relieved. Without her role as Bob's caregiver, she did not know who she was and felt lost. Caring for Bob had become a false refuge for Janet. This was the thing at the center of her life.

Janet had built her self-worth on her identity as a caregiver. She had taken refuge in Bob – the drinking Bob – and, when he changed, she felt let down.

It is a real test of a relationship when someone dear to us changes. Of course people are changing all the time, but we may not notice it unless the changes are more marked, such as when someone becomes seriously ill, embarks on a spiritual path, or gives up an addiction. To the extent that we have gone to them for refuge as a particular, fixed person, it is a false refuge and we will be let down. Individuals are not the best thing to put at the center of our lives, because they are human and will let us down. We have no control over another person. However, putting a relationship at the center of our lives is different because we have more control, and, if it becomes unhealthy, we are able to choose something different to support our recovery.

How we practice this step

Exemplars of values, teachings, and community

We are likely to have associated with our values one or more of the following: people who exemplify our values, teachings on how we express our values, and other people – a community – with whom we share the values. We may find these three aspects not just with positive values that support recovery, but also when our values are caught up in addiction.

For example, a parent who was dependent on alcohol may have influenced us – more or less consciously – to take up drinking heavily. The drinking may have served the value of appearing strong or confident. Alternatively, with a value of wanting to explore altered states of consciousness, our drug use may have been inspired by figures from popular or alternative culture.

As we became more involved with our addiction, we may have learned and talked a lot about the effects of different types of drugs, and how best to obtain the maximum effect from them. We have probably associated with other people who shared our addiction.

Where our values are tied up in addiction, we will need to find either new, more positive, values or a different way of expressing our values – new exemplars, new teachings, and a new community. For example, in recovery, if a value that is dear to us and that we want to pursue is truthfulness, we may find it helpful to find out about people who have exemplified speaking truthfully. It will support us to learn how we go about being more truthful in our lives, and we will benefit from being in contact with other people who share our value and also are trying to be truthful in their lives.

To understand how we can make the most of our positive values, we will look at how values, with their exemplars, teachings, and community, are enacted in Buddhism. The core value in Buddhism is the realization of reality, of how things really are, which is called Awakening or Enlightenment. By "reality" we mean the nature of human existence, such as the inevitability of suffering, which we explored in Step One, and impermanence, which we looked at in Step Three. Realization of reality, from this perspective, means understanding deeply and coming to terms with the transient, ever-changing nature of life. It means seeing how we cause ourselves suffering by trying to hold on to things that are changing. The chief exemplar in Buddhism is the historical Buddha, who realized reality through his own efforts and gained Awakening. The Buddha's teachings that help us to realize reality are called the Dharma, a term also used to refer to the nature of reality itself. The spiritual community (or followers of the Buddha) is the sangha. The Buddha, Dharma, and sangha are refuges in the sense that they can give an orientation to our lives, which provides meaning, support, and direction. We speak about going for refuge to the Buddha, the Dharma, and the sangha in the following pages, but we are aware that Buddhism may be completely new to you, or you may have a different religion or no religion at all. So use this as an example, and think about what could be the equivalent for you to place at the center of your life. It could be God, Allah, nature, something that offers you a vision of potential.

Going for refuge to the Buddha

When we go for refuge to the Buddha, we are taking the Buddha as an example of what is possible for human beings. We are taking refuge in the ideal of an Awakened mind, a mind that has wisdom, knowledge, compassion, and insight. Just as the Buddha became Enlightened, so too, we can become Enlightened. Buddhism holds that this is possible for all men and women. We all have Buddha nature, that is, the potential for Awakening. This can be very encouraging. Even though our minds are often full of craving and ill will, and clouded by spiritual ignorance, they also have the seeds of liberation within them. It can be inspiring to reflect on what is possible for human beings. Especially when we are struggling, it can be helpful to recollect that we have the potential for tremendous positive change.

By reading about the Buddha's life, we can get a feeling for what one who is fully Awake is like. We can see how the Buddha behaved in different situations; how he responded to the people he met. This can be a touchstone for our own lives. We could ask ourselves: how might the Buddha act in this situation that we are facing?

Around the time of the Buddha, or perhaps shortly afterwards, his disciples developed a practice called "recollection of the Buddha" (*Buddhanusati*). His disciples were widely scattered across northern India. Without the benefit of rapid transport or telecommunications, they had to rely on what they knew of the Buddha from his teachings, from the stories they had heard about him, and, if they were lucky, from having met him. They would turn this over in their minds, holding the Buddha in their hearts, and perhaps seeing him in their minds' eyes. Through doing this they would develop an inner sense of the Buddha upon which they could draw.

We too can practice recollection of the Buddha. We can't meet him in the flesh, but we can find out about his life and reflect on him, so that we too can develop an inner sense of the Buddha. We can call on this inner sense of the Buddha when we are distressed, struggling, or not sure what to do.

As we get to know the Buddha in this way, we may feel gratitude toward him, both for his example and for his teachings that have come down to us, to help us find freedom from our suffering. Many of the rituals in Buddhism are both a reflection of this sense of gratitude and a means to develop it and our inner sense of the Buddha. These rituals include chanting mantras and reciting devotional verses. We might also visualize the Buddha. To help us, we create a beautiful shrine, which usually has an image of the Buddha, often with flowers, incense, and candles. Flowers represent the Dharma, and especially – with their fleeting beauty – the teaching of impermanence. Candles represent wisdom and the light of the Buddhist teachings. Incense represents the sangha, as the perfuming effect of the spiritual community on the world.

In this context we speak of "worshipping" the Buddha. By worshipping the Buddha, we are not making him a creator God or expecting him to intercede in the affairs of our daily lives. Rather, worship in Buddhism is a practice of cultivating respect, devotion, and gratitude for someone who can show us, through their example and teachings, a way to free ourselves from suffering. We are developing an inner feeling for the Buddha, which can encourage and guide us. In worshipping the Buddha we are cultivating a sense of appreciation for the direction and meaning in our lives that the Buddha points to.

Where is your special place at home where you can sit quietly on your own and reflect on the potential of human beings? If you don't have a special place at home, perhaps you could create one and build a small shrine/altar out of things that inspire you.

Going for refuge to the Dharma

The word "Dharma" has the dual meaning of reality (the way things are), and the teachings that show us the way to realize reality. When we go for refuge to the Dharma, we are putting the teachings of the Buddha into practice in our lives and moving toward reality. We are aligning our lives with how things are.

When we go against how things are, it is like bumping into furniture in a room, and we suffer. For example, if we are on a train that is running late or sitting in a car in a traffic jam, we may find ourselves getting tense and irritated because we are delayed. The reality is the train is running late or there is a traffic jam that we are stuck in. No amount of cursing or getting annoyed about it will change the facts. Wanting it to be different is of course understandable, and we may choose to take actions to ameliorate the situation, like calling a friend to say we will be late. However, the response of becoming irate is us moving against reality, and so we suffer. When we go for refuge to the Dharma (as reality), we are accepting how things are.

When we are in a difficult or uncomfortable situation, we can ask ourselves: "What is the reality of this situation?" Is our response to it – our thoughts and emotions – helping or making it worse?

Inevitably, we carry expectations about how the world is or should be. Sometimes we don't realize that we are holding expectations until they are not met. For example, we expect our normally reliable friend to meet us when they said they would.

Paramabandhu

I was waiting for a friend at the Tate Gallery. At that time (some years ago) I did not have a mobile phone. As the time passed with no sign of my friend, I felt mounting frustration, with thoughts alternating between concern that something untoward had happened to my friend and thoughts of how inconsiderate he was in not turning up. In fact he had turned up on time – but at the other Tate Gallery (there are two in London). We had failed beforehand to clarify which one we were meeting at. Or rather, each of us had assumed it was clear which Tate we were referring to. My unconscious assumption was that my friend should have understood which Tate I meant.

Experiences like this can show us how we expect things to be a certain way and how that expectation can cause us to suffer. The more rigidly we hold to our expectations, the more we are likely to suffer. Generally, the way we expect things to be is our way. We unconsciously hold ourselves at the center of the universe. The train should not be running late and there should not be a traffic jam that is delaying me.

In the bigger picture, traffic jams and train delays are just what happens. When we go for refuge, we see this bigger picture. This creates space around what is happening and our immediate emotional response. We are not so caught up in the grip of our emotions. The space and clarity allow us to see what might be the most helpful thing we can do in this situation.

Humor helps. If we can smile at what is happening – seeing the absurdity of feeling that we are or should be at the center of the universe – we may be able to loosen the hold of unhelpful emotional responses.

So we can go for refuge to the Dharma by asking ourselves: "What is the reality of this situation? What is really happening now?" This is the Dharma as reality. The Dharma is both reality and the teachings that move us toward alignment with reality. Hence we can also go for refuge to the Dharma by asking ourselves: "What teaching or practice would be helpful right now? What quality is needed in this situation? What quality is being asked of me right now?"

For example, the traffic jam could be an opportunity to

practice patience. We could use the moment to reflect that probably other people in the traffic jam are feeling frustrated. We could sympathize with them and wish them well. Alternatively, we could use the moments to practice mindfulness of the body. We could feel the body's contact with the car seat. We might notice tensions in the body and try to let them go, perhaps with an out-breath. If we are feeling irritable, we could use the traffic jam as an opportunity to reflect on anger and ill will. We might observe how being irritable affects the body and mind, causing contraction and suffering. We could see how futile and unhelpful this response is.

Then again, it might be a chance to cultivate compassion. Perhaps we are feeling ill will in the traffic jam and finding it hard to let go of, even though at some level we know it is unhelpful. So we could try to bring some kindness and compassion toward ourselves, as suffering beings caught yet again by our painful emotional responses.

We can always go for refuge to the Dharma. At each moment we have the chance to try to see things more clearly and to put into practice the teachings of the Buddha. Of course, a lot of the time we are likely to be running on automatic pilot, being ruled by our habits. Yet, as soon as we come to, we have the opportunity to get back into the driver's seat of our lives. We can recollect ourselves and go for refuge to the Dharma.

Sometimes we may feel disappointed in ourselves for not having lived up to our ideals. We may reprimand ourselves for having acted unhelpfully, being on autopilot, or taking shelter in false refuges. Yet this too is an opportunity to go for refuge to the Dharma. Rather than create more suffering by wishing that what was done had not been done, we can reflect on how to respond creatively to where we are now.

Life happens moment by moment. Only in the moment that we are in right now can we make changes, respond differently. We can reflect on the past in order to learn from it, but we can only act in the present. So each moment is a fresh opportunity to go for refuge to the Dharma and to try to live our lives fully, in accordance with what is most important to us.

What teachings do we go to for refuge? Take this opportunity to reflect on some of the teachings we have shared with you in the book so far. Which one resonates for you? Which teaching or teachings would you like to put more at the center of your life? There may be other teachings that have helped you on your journey to recovery. Include those too.

Going for refuge to the sangha

It is important to find a like-minded community, a community of people who want recovery. Placing the recovery community at the center of your life can be a real jewel. We see this very much in the twelve-step community. Part of its success lies in providing meetings and fellowship for its members. If you are not part of a twelve-step community, it is important to find a group of people who have similar ideals to yours, so that your recovery will be supported. This can mean going forth from unhelpful relationships that have kept us stuck. Letting go of friends we used to drink, smoke, or take drugs with. As you can see, it's not easy. We need a lot of courage to move on and make new friendships.

Graham's story

Graham had tried a number of times to give up drinking. He had ended up several times in hospital in excruciating pain with pancreatitis due to his drinking. Each time he came out of the hospital, he swore that he would not touch another drop. The trouble was, everyone he knew drank. All of his friends drank, his father had died of complications from alcohol misuse, and his remaining family, his brother and mother, also had drinking problems. Once out of the hospital he would avoid his friends. He didn't answer his phone or respond to texts. When someone came to the door, he pretended he was out. He would only go out after dark so that he wouldn't bump into drinkers he knew.

Sooner or later, something would happen. The first time, his brother came to stay. His brother had pleaded with him to put him up for a while. They reached an agreement that his brother would not drink in Graham's home. His brother kept to this for a while, then he brought in a bottle and Graham was soon sharing it. Another time, when he ran out to buy some milk, he was accosted unexpectedly by an old drinking friend. His friend persuaded him to come to the pub, "just for one drink," and soon Graham was back to heavy drinking. This time, more determined than ever, Graham was still more vigilant at keeping to himself. However, he found himself pacing his small apartment, restless, irritated, and bored. He felt hopeless about ever sustaining abstinence.

In this mood of resignation he went out, thinking maybe he would buy a can of beer. He ran into an old drinking friend, Trevor, whom he hadn't seen for some time. He expected Trevor to talk him into going to the pub for a drink, to which Graham would put up no resistance. However, it turned out that his friend had been sober for almost a year. Trevor had sought help from the local alcohol-treatment services, had been attending Alcoholics Anonymous (AA) meetings, and had started going to meditation classes. Trevor had had a long-standing interest in eastern religions and had dabbled in Buddhism in the past. Now that he was sober, he had renewed his pursuit of Buddhism and was enthusiastic about meditation. Rather than go to the pub, Trevor persuaded Graham to come along to AA meetings and a meditation class.

Both marked a turning point for Graham. He found that he responded to meditation and to the teachings of the Buddha. Prior to this, he had in a sense been "white-knuckling" sobriety. It was only at the point of meeting Trevor that his recovery really began. What was key for Graham was seeing someone who had made the sort of changes that he wanted to make. Trevor showed him that it was possible to break out of the cycle of addiction and find a more fulfilling way of life.

We can see the benefit of mutual aid in setups like twelve-step groups or "Self Management And Recovery Training" (SMART Recovery). Aside from any benefits of these particular methods, they provide compelling evidence for the possibility of breaking free from addiction. This is an important function of the sangha. When we go for refuge to the sangha, we take inspiration from other people who have put into practice the teachings of the Buddha. We may not need a spiritually advanced person, let alone a fully Enlightened being; someone who has a little more experience than we do can show us that it is possible to make meaningful changes in our lives.

Once we have started to make changes, it is helpful to have other people around us who support us in our recovery. Graham found it helpful to get to know some people at the meditation class. He also derived considerable support from his ongoing friendship with Trevor and from AA meetings. When he was struggling, he would call Trevor, or Trevor would call him, and encourage him to keep going. Sometimes Graham did not understand what a teacher was getting at, and Trevor would have the knack of explaining things in simple terms or lending Graham an inspiring book to read.

Which of your friends support your recovery by way of example? Take a look in your life. You may have friends who go to meditation classes, twelve-step meetings, yoga, and all sorts of other self-development courses. Ask them about what they are up to. If you don't have any friends who could support your recovery, search online and you will find plenty of information about places to meet other people in recovery.

Taking refuge in the sangha is not all plain sailing

The sangha can be the most practically helpful of the three refuges. When it works well, we can gain support and inspiration from other people in the sangha. Making friends with others who share our values, who are making strides in their recovery and cultivating a more enriching and satisfying life, can be both rewarding and enjoyable. However, the sangha is made up of aspiring individuals, with their faults and shortcomings. Even if someone is ordained into a spiritual or religious tradition, a teacher or a nun or monk, it does not mean they are a Buddha or an impeccable individual.

The real sangha refuge consists of those people with true spiritual insight. The greater someone's insight, the more likely they are to be reliable. Their behavior is more likely to be skillful and, should they knowingly make a mistake, they would want to make amends. Yet even outstanding followers of the Buddha can have blind spots, or be more developed in some areas than in others. Moreover, it is very difficult to ascertain how spiritually advanced someone is, and only then after sustained contact over a long period. Add to this our own shortcomings and conditioning, and we have the potential for interpersonal challenges and difficulties.

Sandra's story

Sandra had been inspired by watching a TV program on Buddhism. She was fed up with her life, which revolved around skunk, crack, and other drugs. After seeing the program, she decided to pay a visit to a local Buddhist center that she had walked past many times, but never been in. Still coming down after a crack binge, she attended an introductory class. She felt extremely awkward. Everyone there seemed to be middle-class, white, and professional. Sandra was from a black, working-class background and had never held a job. Although she could not connect to the other people attending the class, she enjoyed the humor and teachings of the class leader. She sensed that there was something important for her here and, being determined, decided to give it a go.

It took Sandra a long time to make friendships in the sangha. She attended sporadically, falling back into drug use, but slowly and with difficulty built up connections, eventually finding some people in the sangha she could feel at ease with.

To go beyond our background and our conditioning is a big challenge. It requires patience and perseverance to see through our individual particularities and connect to others through our common humanity. Going for refuge to the sangha is seeing the way in which others – despite differences in temperament and background – are putting the teachings of the Buddha into practice in their lives. When we can do that, we can feel a connection and resonance within the sangha that is deeply satisfying.

Elaine's story

Elaine had recently stopped using stimulants and Ecstasy. In contrast to Sandra, Elaine felt comfortable in the sangha right away. Like most of the people in the room, she was white, and recognized others from a counterculture background that she identified with. She warmed both to the other participants she met at classes and to the teachers. She felt at home practicing the Dharma and was glad to have found a drug-free environment where she felt safe and welcomed. She attended a weekend retreat, which went well, and then decided to do a ten-day retreat. During the longer retreat, she was disappointed that the food was not vegan and mentioned this to one of the leaders. To her surprise, the teacher did not seem interested in the issue of veganism, either from the perspective of animal life or from that of climate and ecology. She raised it with another teacher, whom she experienced as being dismissive. Elaine felt put out and her confidence in the teachers wavered. They had seemed such good people, but now they appeared to her to be seriously flawed.

Elaine had a bumpy time coming to terms with this. Over the ensuing period she came to value the qualities that she saw in other members of the sangha, while at the same time seeing they were not perfect human beings. She found a few people who were as passionate as she was about veganism. However, she was able to appreciate that other people – though sincerely following the teachings of the Buddha – did not feel so strongly about this area of ethics. She recognized that, just as she could fall into righteous indignation and ill will, others, even with more experience than her, were still prey to unskillful states of mind that could sometimes be expressed in speech or behavior.

Inevitably, as human beings with our varied backgrounds and personalities, we will have different issues to work with and will place greater importance on some areas of practice than others. For example, if we are trying to practice avoiding taking life, we might decide to be vegan (since the dairy industry generally relies on keeping cows lactating but kills many of the young calves that are born as a result of repeated insemination) and feel strongly about this, as Elaine did. However, someone else might be more concerned about working on avoiding harsh speech and creating kind, harmonious speech.

As we get to know each other, we will bump up against each other's differences. We may experience those differences as fascinating and stimulating, or they may feel wrong and annoying. Either way, there is the potential to learn about ourselves, and to find creative ways of responding skillfully to one another. If we can remember to be patient and inquisitive, and to recollect that each person is doing their best within their own limitations, then we may find the sangha a rich practice.

The sangha can be a place where like-minded people gather together. If we are in recovery this may well be a twelve-step group, a social-networking group like Meet Up that you have organized, or a therapy group. If you are in recovery and are looking for a spiritual community that is open to discussing issues of addiction, your sangha may be at a place where people gather together and meditate or pray. It is important to surround ourselves with people who share similar ideals to ours, because they will help us to grow and develop. Once upon a time we may have surrounded ourselves with people who had addictions or compulsive behaviors, and therefore it would have been a lot more challenging to get well. Not impossible, but this company would most definitely be a pull away from our recovery.

Going for refuge moment by moment

The three refuges are always available to us. We can at any moment bring to mind the example of the Buddha as a source of inspiration. We can reflect on what is really going on, what aspect of reality is manifesting now. We can consider which teaching of the Dharma would be helpful at this point in time.

We have in this and earlier steps explored the teachings of the four noble truths, the four reminders, the practice of admitting our faults, the five training principles, the practice of cultivating loving-kindness and mindfulness, and going for refuge to the Three Jewels. Choose one of the teachings and explore it more.

We can recollect the sangha either by considering what someone we respect would do in this situation, or recalling that we are part of the sangha. To the extent that we go for refuge to the Three Jewels, we can feel ourselves part of a web or movement, which extends across space and through time, of people endeavoring to create wiser, kinder, and more fulfilling lives on this planet.

We won't manage to go for refuge all the time. We will fall back or forget the refuges. However, we can always come back to them, as soon as we remember. As we take refuge more and more deeply and more and more frequently, the urge toward addictive behavior moves to the edge of our minds, and healthier things begin to emerge at the center of our lives.

What this means is that our addictions never totally go away. They can go into remission, and therefore have less of a gravitational pull on us. We may one day be able to look at a bottle of alcohol, or a doughnut, and not feel we have to grasp it and consume it. But these gravitational pulls can always surface. This is why it is so important to set up the conditions for recovery. It is easy to become distracted, and before we know it our obsessive thoughts will emerge at the center of our lives. Then the acting out of those thoughts follows.

When we go for refuge to the Three Jewels, we are recognizing the importance of the conditions we need to keep us safe. The Three Jewels are refuges because they lead us away from addiction and allow our recovery to blossom.

Many people who have had recovery for fifteen or more years, sadly, have relapsed. Many did not have a spiritual path, or had gone for refuge to their work or relationships. Although a spiritual path is not foolproof, placing values at the center of our lives will inspire us and help us to grow. That can be a refuge, and, especially when we are struggling, will most definitely help to maintain our abstinence and sobriety.

Becoming aware of what inspires us

Pause now, take a few breaths, and then give yourself five minutes to reflect on the following questions:

- What values are most important to you?
- Who have you seen, read about, or heard about that most embodies your values?
- What teachings are you inspired to reflect on?
- Who do you know that shares your values? Or how could you get to know more people who share your values?

Recap

In Step Six, we place positive values at the center of our lives, values that will support us in our recovery. We recognize that our addiction is a false refuge and cannot bring about true happiness and contentment. We go for refuge to a community that offers the ideal of recovery, sobriety, and abstinence.

This is a gentle reminder for us to pause at the end of Step Six, and take a three-minute breathing space.

Three-minute breathing space, AGE

Awareness of thoughts, feelings, and body.
Gather the breath, notice the breath, become aware of the breath.
Expand the breath throughout the whole body – connect to the whole body.

Step Seven

....

Making every effort to stay on the path of recovery

Every effort needs to be made to stay on the path of recovery. The nature of addiction makes it easy to relapse and for our old habits to reassert themselves. To make matters worse, when we do fall off the path, strong feelings of failure, of not being good enough, and all sorts of negative put-downs can arise. Staying on the path takes a lot of courage, a lot of kindness to ourselves and letting go of who we have been in the world. When we are overwhelmed by an addiction, there is only room for us to be center stage. There may be moments of concern for the people we are harming, but under the weight of addiction it can become all about us, to the extent that some of us may say if we relapse: "Who cares? Nobody cares about me. I'm just harming myself."

Staying on the path of recovery

We remind you of recovery throughout, because our addictions can confuse us and delude us. We need to keep recovery at the center of our lives if we want it. We have to be prepared to put effort and energy into our recovery and not give up at the first, second, third, or fourth temptation. To stay on the path of recovery we have to make that our priority. It has to be the thing we want most in our lives.

If we are to stay on the path of recovery, we have to stop clinging to a rigid sense of self. We hold a largely unconscious belief in a fixed experience of ourselves at the core of our being. We then feel we have to protect or defend ourselves. So when someone criticizes us, or says something that we believe is a criticism, we feel hurt and want to hide or strike back. We have not been struck with a stick or other weapon, but we experience words that we perceive as attacking our sense of self as painful. Or, because we fear others will judge us, we step in first and harshly criticize ourselves. This can lead us to beating ourselves up when we have a slip or relapse.

Staying on the path of recovery is about being in the present moment without any narratives, judgments, or interpretations. The work of embracing impermanence (Step Three) can help us to see what is happening without the filter of a fixed self. Instead, we have a mind full of our present moment and in touch with our own truth.

Early in our recovery we may feel confident about changing our lives and leaving behind our addiction. Sometimes our recovery is precipitated by a dramatic event or a flash of insight, and we feel we can never go back after that.

Liam's story

After seeing his friend die, Liam felt he could never use again. Liam was a recreational drug user. He took Ecstasy every weekend and smoked marijuana during the week. All his friends did this. One weekend, he and a group of four of his best friends bought a batch of Ecstasy. They all swallowed their pills, and five minutes later one of his friends began gagging. There was nothing they could do. They called an ambulance but before it arrived their friend died in front of them. This shook up Liam and his friends. His friends continued to take recreational drugs. As far as they were concerned this was a tragedy, but there had been a one-in-a-million chance that it would happen in their circle of friends. Liam was different – he recalls seeing his friend die. "I was absolutely helpless. As I dared to look at my friend I could see my face in his. I felt sick. I knew in that moment it could have been me. If I didn't begin to change my ways, I could be dead too." This tragedy upset Liam, and he began his journey of recovery.

A year after his friend died, however, Liam was desperate. He knew he was at risk of hanging out with his other friends and taking recreational drugs again. He took part in one of our Mindfulness-Based Relapse Prevention courses. In this course he learned to meditate and to slow down, which helped him to maintain his sobriety. He learned to work with his thoughts and emotions to keep himself in a positive frame of mind, and understood how to take care of himself when he was at risk of relapsing.

Although we may begin our recovery in full confidence that we will never use again, our resolve can wane over time. A day, a week, a month, or even a year later, we are back doing what we said we would not do. On its own, a flash of insight or experiencing painful consequences from our addiction is not enough. It takes sustained effort to keep our recovery alive. We will need to keep working on our minds and taking actions to support our recovery.

Great effort is needed to stay on the path of recovery. Applying effort is more than just reading a book on recovery; it is about bringing some of the tools that have been suggested into action. If it were easy, there would be no such experience as a relapse. If we relapse, we can take this as a salient reminder not to give up, even when the going gets tough. We need to pick ourselves up out of the relapse, give ourselves a gentle, firm, kind talking to, and move on. Beating ourselves up and dwelling on the past keeps us stuck and overfocused on ourselves.

The harder we are on ourselves, the more likely we are to relapse. Yes, we need to acknowledge our mistakes, but we also need to forgive ourselves. Relapse may be part of our process of recovery. Shame, anger, frustration, and aversion will not get us better; compassion will. We could use the three-minute breathing space, AGE, as described below.

Breathing space, AGE, after a slip

After you have had a slip, and woken up the next morning, become **aware** of any anger, resentments, or ill will that you have toward yourself. Notice your feelings and thoughts.

Then, as you **gather** and notice your breath, just acknowledge that this slip was part of your process, and this is a new moment, or perhaps a new day to do something different.

And as you **expand** the breath throughout your body, give yourself words of encouragement, as if you were sponsoring or coaching a friend through a relapse. Tell yourself that you have done well: you are still on the path of recovery and this slip is an opportunity to put all that you have learned about recovery into practice.

Relapse is painful, and we need to experience the ordeal of recovery if we want freedom from addiction. We will have to ride the agonizing wave of desire that arises, and watch it calmly peter out, if we want to be liberated. We will have to apply effort every day. The good thing is, the more effort we apply at the beginning of our recovery, the less effort we will need further down the road. But don't be fooled. Effort is always needed. There is no time of recovery; recovery is a full-time job, a lifelong journey. A wave of desire seductively luring us toward an old habit can arise at any time without notice. But if we work hard, give recovery all our energy, it will not feel so agonizing two years down the road. Our addictions will not have the same hold on us, will not lure us in the same way, will not speak to us in the same way, and we may even feel repelled at the thought of something we once loved to do.

When we are caught up in our addiction, we can sometimes be proud. We may think we can deal with everything on our own. And many of us have, but at what cost? Asking for help is another tool for recovery that we need to begin to make use of. When we ask for help, we have succeeded in taking some more responsibility for our recovery. We have most definitely not failed. When we ask for help, we are no longer isolating, keeping our secret mess to ourselves. We have found the courage to accept help on our journey of recovery.

Being kind to ourselves by asking for help

If you find yourself white-knuckling it, take a breath and pause, and ask for help. If you are unable to ask another human being for help, you can call on the *bodhisattva* of compassion, Avalokitesvara, and chant the mantra introduced earlier in the book: *om mani padme hum*. What we need is compassion when we are struggling. We can recite loving-kindness aspirations to ourselves, like: "May I be well; may I be happy; may I be free from all my addictions; may I be free from all suffering."

How we practice this step

The four efforts are Buddhist teachings that are part of the path to help us become more awake to reality. They help us become more aware of our inner and outer experiences. These efforts can support our recovery.

The four efforts are: preventing, eradicating, cultivating, and maintaining. In the context of recovery, preventing is exploring ways to prevent us from turning toward our habits, preventing unhelpful thoughts that can lead us to addiction. Eradicating is overcoming existing mental states that create obstacles to our recovery. The effort of cultivating helps us to develop kindness and awareness in our lives. Cultivating new habits and helpful thinking will aid our addictions to stay in remission. Maintaining is the effort of keeping sober and abstinent by encouraging kindness and awareness that has arisen through developing new and positive habits.

Preventing unhelpful states of mind arising

Part of the art of recovery is anticipating when we will be at risk of relapsing into addictive behavior. Once we know what situations put us at risk, we can either avoid them or rehearse how to cope with them. For example, if boredom is a trigger to our addiction, ensuring we have sufficient activities to keep us occupied may be an important part of our recovery. If irritation arises when we see a particular friend or relative, and anger leads us to addictive behavior, then we might choose to minimize our contact with this person, or work on staying patient.

Sometimes we can find ourselves unexpectedly in situations that trigger our addiction.

Liam's story continued

Liam was on his way home from the Mindfulness-Based Relapse Prevention course. He had been asked before he left where he would go after the course finished that evening. He told the group that he was going straight home. But, on his way home, he bumped into some old friends who invited him for a drink. He felt confident in saying yes, as alcohol had never been much of an issue. He drank Diet Pepsi in the bar with his friends, and then made his excuses and said he had to leave. His friends said: "Hey, we haven't seen you for ages, come back and watch some movies." Liam told us he panicked, and lost awareness of his body, thoughts, and feelings. He said: "Yeah sure," without thinking. He went back with his friends. And they all sat in front of a flat-screen TV and watched a movie.

Ten minutes after the movie began, a pipe full of marijuana was passed around. The sight of it made Liam panic again. He lost his breath, and his head became full of thoughts of puffing on the pipe. Then the doorbell rang. "I saw this as a GIFT. I leapt up and said 'I'll get it.'" Liam walked out, and practiced his three-minute breathing space, AGE, for just ten seconds. He opened the door, let the person in, and walked back into the room, saying that he needed to get home, as he had to get up for work in the morning. "I was already standing up, and as I spoke I was edging out of the room. Some of my friends grumbled, but soon forgot I was standing there, and I could slip out without much fuss, and return to my plan of going home."

Liam had applied effort through mindfulness. The door knock was a GIFT, a great indicator for throwing out the influence of his friends. When he was able to slow down, he became aware he was at risk and had to get out of the house, so he didn't relapse.

Taking a breathing space can be a good first action when we find ourselves unexpectedly at risk of relapsing. It can provide the space to allow the beginnings of unhelpful thoughts or emotions to pass, before they become too strong to resist.

Mental chatter
One area that we need to be vigilant in is our habitual mental chatter. This can go on in the background without us really noticing that it is happening. For example, we might have the thought: "If I have a drink now it won't be so bad, I'll be able to limit it to just one drink," or "I'm having such a hard time, I deserve a little treat," or "I've created so much trouble in my life, there's no point in being sober." These thoughts or rationalizations can creep up on us and lead to craving. Our job is to see them just as thoughts; mental events that come and go. We could even smile at them and recognize our minds being

up to their tricks again. Or we could think of them as being like the radio playing in the background, which we don't need to pay much attention to. We just acknowledge it's there, and then continue with what we need to do to look after ourselves.

Eradicating unhelpful states of mind

In the Buddhist tradition, there are five hindrances that can arise to obscure the mind. They are thoughts and emotions that tangle and overgrow in the mind like weeds, hindering all possibility of seeing things clearly and putting us at risk of relapse. It is important to know what our main hindrances are, so we can begin to pull out those weeds that have taken root in the mind. These hindrances are obstacles of the mind and will get in the way of recovery. If we don't recognize them, they will contribute to our relapsing. It is extremely helpful to get to know all five hindrances so we are not tripped up on the path of our recovery. They will distract us, sabotage our recovery, and cloud our awareness. So we must be vigilant, as we all experience them to some degree. They can come in pairs, the fifth hindrance underpinning all of them:

> sensual desire – ill will
> sloth and torpor – restlessness and anxiety
> doubt and indecision

Sensual desire
Sensual desire is part of the dis-ease of addiction. It is the desire for happiness through sight, smell, sound, taste, and touch. We walk past a shop and something catches our eye in the window display. It makes us feel good, we may even salivate, and, before we know it, we are wanting it. We are out in a restaurant happily enjoying the meal, and a waiter walks by with a meal for somebody else. It catches our eye and the next thing we know, we are wanting it. We catch a whiff of smoke, and soon we are craving a cigarette or a joint. We hear a cork of a wine bottle pop or the sound of a can opening, and we begin wanting a drink. We make accidental physical contact with someone, and this can trigger a sexual

desire for this person. We taste something, and we want more before we have finished what is on our plate.

There is the sensual desire for the experience of satisfaction that we try to obtain through our addictions. There is also the sensual desire for material things, such as money, property, technological gadgets, and much more. While it is a natural part of being human to experience desire, when it takes over and rules our life, it becomes a hindrance. Most of us want more than we need. Just take a look in your basement, in your garage, in your cupboards, and see how much you have that you don't even use. Sensual desire is a dominant hindrance for many people with addictions. We need to learn to quell the licking flames of craving.

Moderation in all our desires is said to be an antidote to sensual desire. If we can bring more moderation in our lives, and begin to appreciate the imperfections of life, the weeds of sensual desire will begin to wither. When we seek perfection, we multiply our cravings. Nothing in the end is ever perfect. We can seek perfection, but we will never be satisfied in the end.

Ill will

Ill will includes negative mental states like resentment, envy, jealousy, anger and aggression, hatred and complaining. If we have been overcome by craving, ill will comes into being. Ill will punishes and hurts us as well as hurting others. We give ourselves ill will when we have relapsed, because we are unable to let go of our addiction. People who go on a bender (a binge on their drug of choice) can feel much shame and fear when they pull through, which often manifests as ill will. They experienced the hindrance of craving while they were on a bender, and the hindrance of ill will takes over when they come down from their bout of hedonism.

Cultivating loving-kindness will transform ill will (this meditation practice is described in Step Four). In addition, we can begin to respond to the four basic needs of the heart, that is, giving ourselves more attention, affection, appreciation, and acceptance to help uproot the weeds of hatred and ill will (see

Step Two). The hindrance of ill will can only be pacified with the practice of self-forgiveness and compassion.

Restlessness and anxiety
Restlessness and anxiety can manifest as worry and agitation of the mind. We worry about our families and friends who have been affected by our unhealthy habits, but we do nothing about it, except worry. This in turns agitates the mind so much that we can find ourselves turning to our drug of choice to calm our minds down. If we find ourselves not in touch with the breath, our heart racing, our palms sweating, we have probably moved into restlessness. Dissatisfaction can often propel restlessness. And most people with addictions will experience a lot of dissatisfaction. It's one we need to watch out for, because it is cunning. Living life at a fast pace is a distraction from what is actually going on in our lives.

To counter restlessness and anxiety, we can occupy the breath by engaging in our breathing, and becoming aware of the palpitations in our body. We can stop and pause throughout the day to calm our agitated minds by using the three-minute breathing space, AGE, and through longer mindfulness meditation (as described in Step One). The practice of mindfulness will also help to uproot restlessness. Keeping company with people further along the path of recovery will also help to calm the mind. Learning to become aware of our minds darting all over the place will help us to slow down.

Sloth and torpor
Sloth can be seen as inertia in the body, and torpor as the stagnation of thoughts and feelings. Slothfulness is a heavy laziness. It can be brought on by overindulgence and by not facing our unskillful actions. Torpor is a dullness of mind and disinterest in things happening around us. Sloth and torpor and natural tiredness shade into one another and can accentuate each other. This hindrance has been likened to the person we call a "couch potato." Lethargy of the body often kicks in after a spurt of restlessness, which can manifest as surfing the Internet,

manically looking for jobs or for information about campaigns we believe in, or other useless or compulsive behaviors.

We have to take ourselves to task to work with the hindrance of sloth. Literally get ourselves off the sofa, out of bed, and into the fresh air. Pull our ears, even jump up and down to get the vitality back into our bodies. When torpor arises, we have to try to engage our interest, find something that inspires us and gets us motivated. A regular lifestyle and routine will help to maintain our energy, and so make us less prone to sloth and torpor. Inertia and sloth/torpor often mask unskillful actions. We put the duvet over our head and don't have to think about anything. Overindulgence will also bring about this hindrance. In the end, we need to commit to living a more ethical life. Reciting the five training principles daily will help too.

Doubt and indecision
Doubt and indecision underpin all of the hindrances. Doubt undermines our recovery. It hijacks our recovery. Doubt is the hindrance that says: "It's not worth it. Recovery is not for me. I'll never make it. I won't be able to face up to all the harm I have done." If you keep ending up in the same place, like a relapse, or in negative mental states of anger, resentment, and ill will, doubt has overgrown in your mind. If doubt and indecision are the dominant hindrance for us, it is likely that we find it difficult to commit fully to our recovery, and we will suffer from inability and unwillingness to make up our minds. There is always some element of doubt if we experience the four other hindrances.

Taking time to clearly reflect on our values, on what is important to us in our lives (as in Step Six), can help to uproot doubt. We need faith and confidence in the journey of recovery if we are to succeed. When doubt overgrows in the mind, fear arises, which can be a major obstacle in our self-development. Try not to listen to the thoughts that can tell you: "It's a waste of time. What's the point: my partner is going to leave me anyway." Don't let doubt make you treat these thoughts as facts. Paying attention to the things that undermine our faith and commitment to recovery is necessary if we are to weed out the hindrances in our minds.

Swinging between different hindrances
For many of us who have addictions or are dependent on a behavior to move away from uncomfortable experiences, our dominant hindrances will most probably be craving and ill will. When we are not feeling good we may move into resentment, and feelings of ill will can arise. To anesthetize those feelings we will move toward something that will make us feel better. "What is wrong with that?" you may think. It's not a matter of right or wrong. It is just that we will end up playing a game of sensations, our mind swinging like a pendulum from craving to hatred, hatred to craving. And inevitably that will cause us suffering, because nothing will bring about lasting happiness.

Veronica's story

Veronica told us she was addicted to feeling high. When we asked her what she meant by that, she said: "Whenever I am sad, I make myself happy. Whenever something awful happens I make myself feel better. I hate feeling unhappy. It feels so horrid in my body. I can't bear it. I'll do anything to feel better. As soon as a tinge of pain arises I'm out of my body reaching for something to calm me." When we asked her if reaching for something calmed her, she smiled and said: "For a few minutes, then I'm feeling hatred at myself and I need to do something else to feel better. I am never satisfied; I'm always chasing that high. I'll never let myself go down. I am proud of that." And then she cried. "Let's do something to make us all feel happy. This is so depressing." Nobody in the group responded and Veronica was left to sit with her tears. A few weeks after that session, she told us that this had been a turning point for her. In that moment when nobody changed the subject, she could see clearly how she had created a life of misery for herself. Making herself high was like a piece of duct tape that had lost its stickiness over the years.

Beware of sloth and torpor and restlessness when you step onto the path of recovery. In recovery we begin to face up to things that we have kept a secret or at bay for years. There will be many of us who will swing from sloth and torpor to an agitated and restless state of mind. These hindrances are more likely to be dominant if we are out of touch with the impact of our habits and addictions on others, or if we have done things in our past that we do not want to face. Slothfulness will manifest as sleepiness, drowsiness, and laziness, and torpor will manifest as boredom. So it is important to be vigilant, because, when we are abstinent and sober, we may find life boring. We need to find new sources of interest in our lives. When we are abstinent and sober we can also feel more alert. There can be great agitation in our minds, because we are trying so hard to keep the lid on our unskillful past actions. Once again we are playing a game of sensations. The mind becomes so agitated and restless that it wears us out, and makes us sleepy and drowsy, and when we feel alert again we are wrestling with the agitated mind.

The hindrances

Stop and pause. Reflect on the next few questions. We often have more than one chief hindrance. If that is the case for you, then go through the list with each hindrance in mind, one at a time.

- What is my main hindrance?
- How does this hindrance manifest in my life?
- Which hindrance do I need to watch out for in my life, to support my recovery?
- What are some of the things I can do to address my hindrance?

Cultivating helpful states of mind

When we follow the training principles outlined in Step Five, we will create states of mind that support our recovery. When we act with generosity or kindness, for example, our actions will tend to promote our happiness and a feeling of blamelessness.

Living by our values leaves us with a clear conscience. The experience of a clear conscience can feel like a great weight is lifted from our shoulders. Without anything to blame ourselves for or to beat ourselves up with, we are much less likely to need to resort to our addiction. Practicing responding to the four basic needs of the heart in ourselves, by giving ourselves attention, affection, appreciation, and acceptance, along with loving-kindness, cultivates helpful states of mind. Practicing loving-kindness is one of four meditations that are called the four immeasurables, or the sublime abodes. The other three meditations are based on cultivating compassion, sympathetic joy, and equanimity. When we can nourish a helpful relationship with ourselves, it will affect every other aspect of our lives.

The four sublime abodes directed toward ourselves

Loving-kindness: let yourself have the strong wish to experience more kindness and happiness in your life.

Compassion: allow yourself to respond to your suffering with kindness and have the strong wish for the suffering to be alleviated.

Sympathetic joy: let yourself have the strong wish to recognize all your good qualities.

Equanimity: let yourself have the strong wish for peace, simplicity, contentment, and stillness in your life.

Maintaining helpful states of mind

We have spoken a lot about the importance of responding to the four basic needs of the heart, and cultivating loving-kindness and compassion. These are some of the things that constitute helpful states of mind, free from mental states like ill will. Developing positive mental states will have a huge effect on our recovery.

One aspect of maintaining helpful states of mind is keeping up our motivation for recovery. Motivation tends to wax and wane, and this may be influenced by the external circumstance of our lives.

Tracey's story

Tracey was a cigarette smoker; she smoked forty cigarettes a day. When she became pregnant, the doctor told her that she was at risk of damaging the fetus if she continued. Tracey went home that night, distressed. She lay awake in bed and told herself it was impossible to stop smoking.

"I can't have this baby. I'm going to have an abortion. It will be easier. I can still smoke." She shuddered at her thinking. She knew deep down it wasn't easier, and that she really wanted this baby. She heard a little whisper in her head saying: "You can have the baby if you really want it," and she screamed inside herself: "Oh yeah, what planet are you on; Mars?" The whisper got louder and said: "You don't have to smoke." She woke up in the morning inspired. She wanted her baby. For the first time she could see that she had a choice. She could stop smoking and have the baby. She stopped smoking throughout the whole pregnancy. However, she relapsed once her baby was born. She decided she could smoke in the other room. She lost motivation. There was nothing inspiring her to stop, even though the doctors had told her that her own life was at risk if she continued to smoke forty cigarettes a day. The moment she picked up a cigarette, she was choosing smoking over her own life. She no longer wanted recovery more than smoking.

Two years after the birth of her baby, she came to our Relapse Prevention course. She soon became aware that she was smoking again because, although she wanted to stop, she didn't want to deal with the difficult feelings, from which she distracted herself by smoking. Now that the baby was born, she had to face the agony of recovery. She was so blissed out by her pregnancy, she hardly had to struggle with the urges to smoke. Once her daughter was born, the urges became too much, and she chose smoking rather than staying in recovery.

Are you willing to do what it takes to stay in recovery? How much effort are you putting into keeping up your recovery?

Recap

In Step Seven, we make every effort to stay on the path of recovery. We are likely to have to feel the unbearable pain of not turning to our addiction. We ride the harrowing waves of recovery with calm, and know that, every time we surf the pain of recovery, the waves will become calmer. We surf the waves with calm by preventing unhelpful states of mind from arising, eradicating them when they do arise, and cultivating and maintaining helpful states of mind. We get to know our minds by identifying our dominant hindrances. And we breathe.

This is a gentle reminder for us to pause at the end of Step Seven, and take a three-minute breathing space.

 Three-minute breathing space, AGE

Awareness of thoughts, feelings, and body.
Gather the breath, notice the breath, become aware of the breath.
Expand the breath throughout the whole body – connect to the whole body.

Step Eight

....

Helping others by sharing the benefits we have gained

So far, the focus of this book has been mainly inward-looking. We have described a Buddhist understanding of how our minds work and the nature of reality, and then used this to offer practical steps we can take to free ourselves from addiction. Some of the steps do have an other-regarding aspect to them, especially Step Five, where we looked at the importance of skillful actions in our lives. However, the emphasis was still on self-transformation: coming to terms with and overcoming our past unhelpful habits and actions, as well as setting up new skillful habits. In Step Six, in going for refuge to the sangha we aim to develop friendships, yet here too the stress is on the crucial support and inspiration that friends can provide for us.

The focus on self is entirely necessary. Early in our recovery we need to find ways to pick ourselves up. We need to take addiction seriously and create the time and space to be able to make the potentially big changes that our life requires. Once we are in the grip of an addiction, it is a large undertaking to break free. It demands determination and our full attention.

The fourth sight

Yet, if we remain entirely focused on ourselves, our recovery is not complete, and that focus can even be an obstacle to recovery. In the final step we look at the place of helping others. We referred in Step Four to the importance of believing that recovery is possible. The Buddha, before he was Enlightened, needed to see the example of a truth-seeking wanderer (the fourth sight) to prompt him to leave home in quest of liberation. It wasn't enough for the Buddha to recognize that life was full of suffering (the first three sights of old age, illness, and death). Without the possibility of a solution, he might have tried to reconcile himself with ordinary life as it is – as many did before and have done since. In his case, he might have attempted this by enjoying as best he could the pleasures and power of a worldly ruler. In the same way, when we are immersed in addiction and beginning to think about making a change, it can be really helpful to come into contact with someone who has made significant recovery from their difficulties. It demonstrates in a tangible way that recovery is possible.

Step Eight invites us, once we have made some progress with our recovery, to be that person for others. We can stop looking out there for our fourth sight to inspire us to change. And we can become the fourth sight for someone else. This can be a quite natural response. As our lives become more satisfying as a result of letting go of our addiction, we may feel some gratitude for having our lives back and some appreciation for the people and conditions that have supported our recovery. In return, we might want to give something back. In reaching out to others we have the opportunity to give back, and at the same time we are given a means to consolidate our recovery. We do not have to be perfect. We can still have many things that we are working on in our lives. What inspires people is seeing that our recovery is still alive, that we are working hard at transforming our lives. A renunciant begging for alms was the fourth sight for the Buddha, which inspired him to transform his life.

Recovery is always changing, and once we are on the path of recovery we can be an inspiration for someone who is not yet on that path.

We can be the fourth sight that inspires the group to recover and change. If we want recovery, it will take more than reading books about recovery. It will take faith in the process, self-surrender, belief in something bigger than ourselves, and putting recovery into action. We can stop going to meetings or groups and feel disillusioned and critical because most of the people still seem sick with their habitual behavior. Or we can go to that same meeting or group, and be the recovery we want to see in others.

If we want recovery, we must be the recovery. When we have recovery, it can be enough to have an impact on others. When we heal ourselves, we help others just by our natural way of being. Perhaps this can motivate us enough to see that we want recovery more than our dis-ease of mind.

In helping others, we also help ourselves, just as by helping ourselves (through the first seven steps) we put ourselves in a better position to help others. Helping others can be a reminder of where we have come from, it can give us a sense of purpose in our lives, and it can bring us closer to how things really are.

Helping ourselves and others

Reminding ourselves of where we have come from

Once we have made some changes and stopped, at least temporarily, our addictive behavior, we may forget just how much suffering our addiction caused us. In Step Six, we met Graham, who relapsed a number of times despite his drinking having caused him pancreatitis. There were various reasons why he relapsed – it is rarely just one thing – some of which we outlined in his story. One of the ideas that allowed him to start drinking was a thought that maybe drinking wasn't so bad after all. That thought in particular nearly led him to start drinking again on the day he met Trevor.

We have a tendency to minimize past problems, whereas current difficulties loom larger. When Graham first had pancreatitis, it was so painful that he swore another drop of alcohol would never pass his lips. After a period of abstinence, the memory of just how painful pancreatitis was faded. Intellectually he still knew that drinking would cause him pain, but gradually this held less weight. By contrast, his present difficulties – feeling bored and fed up – held more and more sway over him. In his mind, drinking changed back from something that would cause him a lot of pain to a solution for his discomfort. Besides, he argued with himself, he could just have one or two drinks; his period of abstinence surely indicated that he had some control over his drinking now. In his heart, he knew this wasn't the case. He knew that, if he had one drink, he would just keep on drinking. However, as the attractiveness of alcohol became stronger, he put this thought out of his mind.

Fortunately, on the very day that he had finally decided to drink, he ran into Trevor, who saved him from returning to drinking. At the same time that Trevor was helping Graham, unbeknownst to Graham, he was helping Trevor. Seeing Graham in an ambivalent state, unhappy and close to going back to drinking, reminded Trevor of his early recovery. He recalled times when he had thought of giving up and going back on the booze. Now he felt much more confident about sobriety and was pleased to be abstinent, but it was salutary to see Graham wavering. As Trevor heard Graham's description of pancreatitis, he remembered the time he had had DTs (delirium tremens), and how frightening that had been. After their meeting, Trevor came away even gladder that he was sober and more grateful for his life.

Helping other people who are still in the clutches of addiction or in the precarious, early stages of recovery can refresh our memories of the pain of addiction. Seeing the adverse effects more vividly can help to deter us from returning to addiction when it lures us as an easy solution to our difficulties or appears attractive and free from negative consequences. In addition and perhaps more valuably, it can give us a positive appreciation of our lives, as we see how far we have come.

Creating good karma

In Step Five, we discussed how to live skillfully. We live skillfully by being mindful of the principles of karma. The Buddha put it like this:

> Experiences are preceded by mind, led by mind, and produced by mind. If one speaks or acts with an impure mind, suffering follows even as the cartwheel follows the hoof of the ox (drawing the cart) [...] If one speaks or acts with a pure mind, happiness follows like a shadow that never departs.[1]

The basic idea of karma is that willed actions have consequences. When we act (with actions of body, speech, or mind) out of mental states rooted in craving, ill will, or confusion, we will suffer. Conversely, actions based in contentment, kindness, and clarity will have a beneficial effect; that is, they will create positive karma. When we help someone, particularly when we do this in a relatively unselfconscious way, we are likely to be acting out of kindness, and this will have a positive effect on us.

In this step of our recovery, we are not helping others primarily because of the positive effect on us: rather, it is a happy coincidence, a win–win, that, when we help others, both they and we benefit. To deliberately try to help others because we want the positive effect is likely to backfire. It's like the young scout who tries to help the elderly person across the road – even though they don't want to cross the road. If we are doing it primarily for our own gain, that will come across, even if only subliminally, to the other person, and they are likely to feel coerced. Feeling manipulated, they are likely to resist, leading to tension and difficulties between the person being "helped" and the one trying to help.

The attitude we are trying to foster in this step is an interest in other people for their own sake. Real helpfulness comes from a place of abundance. We are grateful for and appreciative of our own lives, and out of this comes the heartfelt desire for others to enjoy recovery in their lives. From this perspective we can be more objective toward others. We are likely to see what really would be helpful and offer help in a more unobtrusive way.

A sense of purpose

Having a sense of purpose in our lives can be a great support to recovery. It gives us a broader perspective, which can help us through the struggles that we will inevitably face. To find recovery – as we have mentioned a few times – we need, at least at first, to take care of ourselves; we need to put ourselves first. However, in the end, self-concern becomes limiting. Focusing on ourselves eventually narrows us down, unless there is something bigger than us in our lives. Helping other people can draw us away from self-preoccupation and can be one way of providing a sense of meaning to our lives.

Justin's story

Justin had been a professional musician before his career was wrecked by drug use. During a lengthy period of treatment for his addiction, he came to the conclusion that he could not go back to the music industry, as it would be too risky for his recovery. Once he was able to think about working again he changed careers and retrained as an electrician. He heard about a self-help project for people in recovery and decided to see if he could help out. In the project he assisted in setting up a music group. This was a way for him to use his musical skills, since music had been such a passion in his life, and to help others who were at an earlier stage of their recovery. Justin really enjoyed the group and it gave a new sense of satisfaction to his life.

The wisdom perspective

When we help others, we are aligning ourselves with reality. Most of us, most of the time, behave as though we were separate, independent units. It is as though we see ourselves as an island state in an ocean with many other islands. We feel that we have to defend and protect our own special island. Buddhism refers to this as having a belief in a fixed self. We create a sense of self-hood through our beliefs and the narratives we tell ourselves. These stories are often about what sort of person we are, our likes and dislikes. In this way we mark ourselves off from other people, holding a boundary in our minds between us and the rest of the world.

In the early steps we explored the inevitability of suffering and the reality of impermanence – the fact that everything changes. These two concepts belong to an essential Buddhist teaching called the three characteristics. These are characteristics of all phenomena, including human beings. The third in this group is the characteristic of no-self. This is somewhat hard to grasp, but we need to have an understanding of this concept. No-self means that there is no fixed, unchanging core of our being. The mind is not self because it is subject to change. However, many people identify with their mind, fixing it and calling it "self." We identify with the thoughts in our mind and then all we can see is the person with the addiction. However, if we could see that there is no fixed self, that we are always changing, this could free us to recover.

Many people in addiction believe they cannot change, that addiction is their destiny. They have fixed themselves into a particular state, giving themselves no way out of addiction. However, we could ask ourselves the question: what is the I, or me, or mine in the person who was once a one-day-old baby, who was once a child, and is now an adult, with gray hair? Where is the I, me, or mine in the person who was once upon a time clean and sober, and who is now in the throes of addiction (or vice versa, if you are no longer engaged in addictive behavior)? What we are trying to highlight is that there is no fixed self: the self is always changing. If we believe in a fixed self, that implies we cannot transform ourselves.

Valerie's story

Twenty-three years ago I walked into a Buddhist center with "I hate myself" ranting around my head like some sacred mantra. The practice of loving-kindness restored me to sanity, helping me to cultivate a calm and sober mind. The undermining voice began to cease, and I would hear: "I love myself." However, I resigned myself to the fact that sometimes the voice of "I hate myself" would arise, and I would just match it with "I love myself." But somewhere I still believed this thought. Then one day the voice arose: "I hate myself." And I spoke to it loud and clear, telling it: "There is no self to hate. There is no self to identify with." Finally I was beginning to let go of this thought. The undermining voice becomes quieter and quieter as every day I continue to practice loving-kindness and remember there is no self to identify with.

I began to see how my thoughts are an illusion, a game of misinterpretations, assumptions, and judgments. My thinking had been the dis-ease of resentments, jealousies, dissatisfaction. They had kept me trapped in suffering. I had spent so much time restricting food that I had missed the point. I needed to just let thoughts arise and cease, let go of all the assumptions and illusions that had created a self I had fixed as unlovable, which could never be lovable.

How could I let someone love me if I could not love myself? Realizing there is no self has allowed me to change radically. I look back at my past fifty years and hardly recognize myself. If I live another fifty years I hope it will be the same. Can't change, won't change – we are always changing, whether we like it or not.

From an everyday practical perspective it can be helpful to think of having a self. We look in the mirror in the morning and see roughly the same person we saw the night before. We go about our familiar daily routines. Friends and family call us by our name, which we recognize and respond to. And we do need to look after and protect this thing we think of as "self." However, from another perspective, our selfhood is a fiction. When we look at our experience more closely, we cannot find a fixed self at our core. It is as though we perhaps imagine a "me" at the center of our experience, who directs all our actions and thoughts, like an operator sitting in a little cabin in a crane. Instead we are an ever-changing process amid a world of flux. We depend upon and cannot be fully separated from that bigger world. If you stand on a bridge spanning a big river, you can see all sorts of eddies within the river. The eddies have a certain constancy, and yet you could not separate one eddy from the rest of the river, which is continually moving toward the sea. Our "self" is like an eddy in the bigger river of life.

When we try to separate ourselves from the rest of life, by holding onto a fixed sense of self, we suffer – as we have indicated in the earlier steps. We might notice this when someone holds a belief contrary to ours. We might then feel threatened and want to argue with them. Often we can hold on to views of who we are, even when they are not helpful. When we are underweight with anorexia, we may continue to believe that we are fat, or we may adhere to a view that we are essentially unlovable. Our views about ourselves are peculiarly sticky: they are hard to shift and we have a force, like gravity, that pulls us back to our concerns about ourselves. Thus our basic tendency is one of self-preoccupation, even when that is a negative self-preoccupation about how bad we are.

Addictive behavior, because of its sense of urgency and compulsion, accentuates this preoccupation with self. It can render us vulnerable to being obsessed with me, mine, and myself, which inevitably leads us to suffering. When addictive behavior is at the center of our lives, all we can think of is ourselves. We feel ourselves to be at the center of the universe. Since everyone else believes that they are at the center of the universe, conflict and suffering are bound to follow. In order to recover, we have to move beyond the delusion of self and break free from the clinging to self. Our self-view is like a distorting lens, which creates stories in our minds about our experience, interpreting what happens in terms of me and mine.

When we seek to help other people, we move beyond this self-preoccupation. We become concerned with someone outside of ourselves. When this is not done out of self-denial (see below on the dangers of being a helper), we can forget ourselves in a positive sense. We move into the flow of life. We can then experience more connectedness with others. Since reality is an interconnected, interfused whole, by helping others we are moving closer to how things really are. In effect, we are no longer resisting reality, by holding on to a separate sense of self. We let go of the guards patrolling the borders of our selfhood.

While helping others, a strange thing may happen: we may find we can access a new source of energy. When we are defending our sense of self, we use up energy in resisting reality. All the time, reality is throwing evidence at us that we are not a fixed, stable center of the universe. We use energy to manage the signs that we are aging, reiterate to ourselves our familiar and reassuring likes and dislikes, or get angry at others who seem to think that they are the center of the universe. Taking an interest in other people can help us to let go of unhelpful self-preoccupation and free up energy.

The two main characteristics of Awakening are wisdom and compassion. Wisdom is seeing the nature of reality. It is understanding on a deep level that everything changes and is interconnected. The natural emotional counterpart of this is compassion. Compassion is not something added on, rather it is the spontaneous outpouring that comes from understanding how things really are. In fact, it is said that the Buddha does not think in terms of "being compassionate"; it's just the natural way for him to behave, which we, who are not Enlightened, experience as compassion.

We may not be Enlightened just yet, but we can make efforts to move beyond the grip of our sticky self-preoccupation. Stepping past our self-concerns can open our eyes to a bigger universe. It can help us to see and feel our interconnectedness with all life – or at least with something bigger than our small and narrow sense of self. The more we have this larger perspective, the easier it is to reach out to others. We create a positive reinforcing spiral, freeing up energy, causing ourselves less distress, and moving closer to being in harmony with life.

How we practice this step

Ways to help others

There are many ways in which we can help other people. Justin was lucky enough to find a way that used his skills and helped other people with addiction problems. This need not be the case. We don't need to have special talents. But first, as we mentioned in Step Seven, we need to be able to ask for help for the sake of our own recovery. When we can accept help, we can help others from a gentle and compassionate place. The most important thing is to cultivate an attitude of wanting to be of help to others and then acting on that intention when we see the chance.

There are many small opportunities as we go about our daily lives. Being friendly and courteous to people we happen to come across, including strangers, can make a difference to someone's day. An extra smile or a few friendly words to the shopkeeper, or helping a mother with her stroller down the stairs, doesn't cost us much, but can be part of building larger patterns of helpfulness. We can be on the lookout for occasions to give small gifts. A bunch of flowers or some chocolates can provide delight to a suitably chosen recipient, especially when the gift was not expected. We might see a book that we feel someone would appreciate, or pass one on that we have found enjoyable or helpful.

If we have skills or talents like Justin, we may be able to make them available to other people. We might offer to help someone with some DIY or gardening, or provide some complementary therapy if that is our skill. Volunteering in a charity can be a good way of using our skills to benefit others.

In particular, we may want to find a way to help others who are not as far along in their recovery. This might be by befriending others. Extending the hand of friendship to someone more entrenched in their addiction can make a real difference. Just being around, we can act as the fourth sight for others. If we do this, we need to be confident in our own recovery, so that we don't end up being talked back into our addictive behavior. A safer way might be to help out in an addiction service, perhaps with the administration where we won't be directly exposed to others in full addiction, or in a situation where there are others around who are more confident in their recovery than we are.

If we have found that a spiritual approach, like the one described in this book, has helped us, we may wish to support that. This might mean making tea at a meditation class or encouraging a friend to try meditation or a retreat. Some people have set up their own groups where there has been nothing available locally, either teaching meditation themselves or inviting more experienced people to come and teach. Adopting the practice of anonymous random acts of kindness is another way some people have contributed to helping others.

Helping others

Take a moment now to pause and ask yourself:

- How could I help other people?
- What could I do or give – perhaps just something small – to a friend or a loved one?
- How could I be a little more friendly to people I meet?
- Is there an organization that I would like to support in some way that would help others?
- What is one thing I can commit to doing to help another person?

Perhaps the best way we can help anyone living with addictions is to be an example. We can live our own lives without addictions.

The challenge of helping others

Valerie

When I worked with female alcoholics, who had been ordered by the courts to go to rehab and take part in an anger-management course or go to prison, I had to face my own relationship with alcohol. I didn't identify as an alcoholic, but there I was, talking to women about never drinking again. Did I really believe it was possible to live a life without alcohol? This was a flash of insight. I decided to let go of alcohol and see if it was possible in my own life. I have not looked back, staying awake to the reality of my own relationship to addictions.

If you are reading this book because you have a relative, a friend, or even a client who is living with addiction, seeing things as they really are can begin with looking at your own life: looking at what you are dependent on, recognizing what you turn to when things get tough.

Winsome's story

Winsome's husband was an alcoholic; he had lost many jobs because of his dependence on alcohol. Winsome wanted him to stop. When she came to a support group for family members of people with addictions, she realized that she had her own addictions too. She was a compulsive overeater. When her husband drank, she would eat. None of her grown children ever said anything about her eating, because the focus was on their father. She realized that the best way to help her husband was to begin dealing with her own addictions. She wanted him to be well, but she was unhealthy herself, weighing almost 300 pounds.

Attending the Mindfulness-Based Relapse Prevention group was a turning point for Winsome; she could see clearly that her recovery would have an impact on the whole family. Our own recovery can be the best thing for someone living with addiction. We can be an example of what is possible.

If you are caring for a person with an addiction, then this could be a good moment to practice the three-minute breathing space, AGE.

Then ask yourself:

- What am I dependent on?
- What might be my addictions?

The dangers of being a helper

Helping others is the final step because, as we stressed earlier, our first need is to take care of ourselves and to free ourselves from addiction. Nevertheless, we don't need to be too cautious and overprotective of ourselves. We don't need to be a Buddha before we can start to help others. Once we have made some progress in our recovery, we can turn our attention to how we can also be of benefit to others.

However, it is worth taking some care over timing and how much we do. If we are too enthusiastic and take on too much too soon, we may experience a kickback. Ideally, helping comes from a place of abundance: we feel that our lives are rich and, out of that bounty, we desire to benefit others. If we take on a lot and neglect ourselves and what we need for our own recovery, we may end up struggling. What may have started as a genuine impulse to help can become a drain or a weight on our shoulders if we are not sufficiently resourced. In the worst case it may lead us back to our addiction. Sadly, there are too many people working in the drug and alcohol field who are abusing substances in their personal life.

Be honest with yourself. When you are in the position of helping another being with their addictions, ask yourself: who needs help? We're not saying that you can't do good work if you are abusing substances, because, ironically, as the "wounded healer" we can help others. However, we have to admit if the only people who are recovering are our clients or the people we are working with, while we are still sick with our own compulsive behaviors and/or addictions. Is this what we really want? We don't teach recovery, we exemplify recovery.

Paige's story

When I was twenty-one, I began my working career on the front lines in the downtown of a large Canadian city. I did this for thirteen years. I can't believe how I managed to do this. The only environment I understood from growing up was one of crisis and chaos and addiction. I grew up experiencing everyone around me drinking, everyone. I started blackout drinking when I was fifteen. As soon as I started drinking, I could not stop. This is how I drank. On the military bases where I grew up, this was normal. When I started social-service work, I was already an alcoholic but had no idea. I couldn't even do a cleanse because it would require me to stop drinking for ten days. As a way to debrief the grief, loss, and injustice we faced in our work, my colleagues and I (including my mentors and supervisors) would regularly get together at the end of the day and drink and drink and drink and drink. It was built into the structure of the work culture; staff parties and meetings took place in bars. Now I can see the parallels with how all the dads in the military also used to get drunk at the "mess" hall after their work. This was normal, expected, and designed in these workplaces.

I was actively teaching courses and working one-on-one with people in their addiction, while completely unaware that I was deeply immersed in my own realm of alcoholism. It still shocks me to look back on that time, knowing I had no understanding, awareness, or control of my own alcoholism, even though I logically was well versed in and on a daily basis practicing harm reduction with others.

We may wish to ask ourselves, especially before taking on something fairly substantial like a regular commitment or working in the field of addiction:

- Is this the right time for me?
- Do I feel secure in my recovery?
- What will I be doing as well to continue to look after myself and my recovery?

Marianne's story

Not long after completing some treatment for her bulimia, which included MBRP, Marianne started helping out at an art group for people in recovery. She had a talent for teaching art and was popular in the group. Marianne felt pleased to be able to help out and enjoyed the appreciation she received. As time went on, people in the group began to open up more and more to her, telling her of the difficulties in their lives. Then the person who had been leading the group left and Marianne was asked if she would take over as leader and consider starting up a second group.

Outwardly appearing to be thriving, Marianne agreed to both proposals. She felt honored to be asked and convinced herself that she was doing well and that the teaching was helping her. However, she felt increasingly weighed down by the sense of responsibility for running the groups, and found it hard to bear the suffering of the participants. She felt that she was not helping people enough, with all their pain.

She started a relationship with a man who was attending one of the groups. Initially this helped her, as she felt she had an ally in the group and felt cared for. As the relationship developed, she experienced her boyfriend as increasingly critical of her. In addition, he pressured her to give him money to support his crack habit. Marianne felt more and more stressed and found herself bingeing and purging again.

Eventually it all came to a head, and Marianne gave up both groups and left her boyfriend. She felt wretched and that she was a complete failure. Marianne went back into therapy. She was then able to see how she had been driven by a desire to feel needed. Growing up with arguing parents who had often ignored her, she had developed a strategy of trying to be helpful and minimizing her own needs. Marianne felt guilty about looking after herself and the art group had been a way of walking back into that role of being a helper.

As well as having therapy, Marianne went back to meditation, especially loving-kindness meditation. She also started doing her own artwork again.

It is neither unusual nor surprising that our motivations to help others are mixed. Sometimes, like Marianne, we may not be aware of some of the driving forces behind our desire to help other people. While not waiting to have perfectly pure motivation, it may be prudent to watch out for our investment in helping others. We may have a habit of wanting to please or wanting, like Marianne, to feel that we are needed. Helping others may be a way of distracting ourselves from our addiction and not addressing our own problems.

We may get clues that all is not right if we feel that people are not appreciative enough of our help, or if they seem to resist our help. Also, we should be concerned if we start to notice that we are neglecting ourselves and feel ourselves being drawn back into addictive behavior.

If we notice any of these warning signs, we can take it as a cue to pause and take a three-minute breathing space, AGE. We could be curious about what is happening. If we are feeling stressed, we could ask ourselves what expectation is not being met. If we see that we have stopped doing the things that supported our recovery, we should make reintroducing them a priority. It can be helpful to remind ourselves that we can only give to others if we have something to give. By ensuring that we take our own needs into account, we will be in a better place to give to others, and what we can give is more likely to be of a higher quality.

It is likely that sometimes we will err on the side of trying to give too much, just as at other times we may veer toward being overcautious and self-focused. If we keep up a practice of daily mindfulness, even just doing a regular breathing space to check in with ourselves, we can observe as we head toward either extreme. We may be surprised at times by how much we are able to give, just as at other times we may be caught out by discovering unhelpful hidden motivations. By continuing to explore the edges of self-care and of benefiting others, we will gradually purify our motivations and learn to find the right balance in our lives.

In time Marianne was able to go back to helping others, especially through teaching art. She found a way to do it from a different place, which wasn't so fueled by being needed. She made sure that she kept up her own artwork and meditation practice. This gave her the inner resources from which she was able to give more freely. With this balance, Marianne did not return to her addiction.

The journey of recovery

It is sometimes said that people who have recovered from an addiction have happier lives than those who never had that problem. Whether or not this is true, to recover is a remarkable thing to do with your life.

As we progress in our recovery, we may find patterns of addiction at more and more subtle levels. Sometimes people give up class-A drugs only to get dependent on alcohol or remain addicted to smoking. Perhaps we give up alcohol, but then find we have a dependent obsessive quality in our intimate relationships. Some of us will find we are addicted to fantasizing and to our stinking thinking. More subtly we are hooked on a fixed sense of self.

Although we are born with a tendency for addiction, we also have the capacity to find true freedom and happiness. Recovery is like a journey on which we gradually free ourselves from more and more limitations.

In terms of the eight steps presented in this book, we could think of our journey as like a path ascending a mountain. However, the path would not be straight up one side of the mountain, but more like a spiraling path that gradually ascends while going round and round the mountain. This is a journey of faith, energy, mindfulness, concentration, and wisdom. We need all five of these spiritual faculties for this arduous and rewarding journey.

Faith

The journey may take you around and around the mountain with the feeling that you have made little progress and that you have got nowhere in your recovery. Have faith and trust in the process. We are moving, and never end up in exactly the same place. And if it feels like the same place, just trust and believe that you are not mentally in the same place and that you are a different person from when you began your journey of recovery. When you have faith, you go beyond what you have been told and try new things for yourself. When we step onto the path of recovery we have faith. We need to remember this before we tell ourselves we are not a faith type.

Energy

This journey may be one where we fall down to the bottom of the mountain and, when we look back up, it feels all too overwhelming to pick ourselves up and begin the journey again. We need energy if we want to achieve recovery. Picking ourselves up, being kind to ourselves, and continuing with the journey is all part of the process. We need persistence if we are to keep going on the ascent of the mountain to recovery. Recovery is strenuous and it takes great effort and perseverance. We may tumble down the mountain many times, but, each time we pick ourselves up and make the ascent, we are making new habits in our lives.

Mindfulness

We need to recollect and remember that we have committed to a life of abstinence and sobriety. We may meet people on our journey as we spiral up the mountain and they may be our downfall. Before we know it, we are sitting on the mountain enjoying the view, and thinking about how a drink, or a joint or some food, will make this the perfect day. And five minutes later we are indulging with the friend we have met on our journey. We need mindfulness in every aspect of our journey of recovery so we are not taken by surprise. And if we are caught out, we need the energy to be kind to ourselves, and know that the present moment is always an opportunity to do something different.

Concentration

We can become complacent on our journey. We have been spiraling up the mountain for many months or even years, and we stumble and the honeymoon is over. We can also become bored because our recovery seems to be taking too long. Our boredom and lack of concentration can be a trigger for desire and craving to erupt with full force. Desire and craving become stronger, we lose all concentration and focus, and before we know it we are relapsing. So we need every bit of concentration not to pick up our addiction again. Recovery must come first. We have to narrow our focus for those first few years in recovery. We need to continually sharpen our concentration through practicing the three-minute breathing space, AGE, meditating, and chanting mantras. It may take shouting out aloud to our demons of desire and craving: "Stop! I want my recovery!"

Wisdom

We may make it to the top of the mountain, sit down and think: "Yay. I've made it, I'm cured." And before we know it, we are tumbling down the mountain. Recovery does not stop when we reach the top of the mountain. When we make it to the top, we can catch our breath and pause, but if we look out we will see there are more mountains, hills, and humps to journey over. A new life is about to unfold, if we can accept that recovery is a lifelong journey. It is the beginning of something new. We need to practice faith, energy, mindfulness, and concentration at the top of the mountain if we are to stay up there and discover wisdom, if we are to discover the true meaning of our lives.

The cultivation of wisdom is realizing that our craving will be transformed, but this does not mean it will be entirely removed. There is craving and desire before recovery. And craving and desire during recovery. And craving and desire after recovery. When we are sitting at the top of the mountain, we may well feel waves of craving and desire, but they will not have the same gravitational pull on us. We will not feel compelled to act on the energy or be overwhelmed by it. There will be more mountains to climb and they will become smaller, but know that a wave of craving can arise in us after one year or twenty years of recovery. With time, we will have the tools to sit and be calm, to give ourselves that three-minute breathing space, AGE, or meet the four basic needs of the heart. If we practice these tools regularly, we will be prepared for that unexpected wave of craving and desire.

These five spiritual faculties are what the Buddha said we need to help shape everything that we do. They are like five new senses that we need to begin developing and using. We cannot do recovery for you, we can only give you pointers. But know that, if you are able to embrace some of the Buddhist teachings in your journey, it will be one with less suffering. The path of recovery does not have to be continually grueling, or one where you have to white-knuckle it all the way up the mountain. It can be a bittersweet journey with much joy on the way. However, in the spirit of the Buddha's words, perhaps if we really want recovery this is how we should go about it:

> Just as one whose clothes or head had caught fire would put forth extraordinary desire, effort, zeal, enthusiasm, indefatigability, mindfulness, and clear comprehension to extinguish [the fire on] his clothes or head, so that bhikkhu [monk] should put forth extraordinary desire, effort, zeal, enthusiasm, indefatigability, mindfulness, and clear comprehension to abandon those bad unwholesome qualities.[2]

So we have a glimpse of how our addiction is causing us to suffer and the possibility of a different life (Steps One to Three) and this may affect our willingness to make changes in our life (Step Four). As we work on cultivating more kindness and compassion, this will change how we speak and act (Step Five). Then, as we transform our speech, actions, and livelihood, we may feel the need to explore our values and consider what refuges can support our recovery (Step Six). This will make it easier to keep applying the effort that we need to make to stay in recovery (Step Seven) and to be attentive to our experience and reality. As we practice all this, our lives will have more of a focus and we will increasingly embody a state of recovery and may feel the urge to help others (Step Eight). The more we embody this state and the more fully we have contact with others who are caught up in their addictions, the more we will see the unnecessary suffering we cause in our lives and will know more directly that our lives can be different (Steps One to Three again). And so we go on with ever deeper or fuller understanding and transformation of our lives.

The important thing is not so much where we are on the journey; rather, that we accept the challenge and take to the road. We hope that this book helps you to take some steps on the road of recovery and we hope that you enjoy the journey!

Recap

In Step Eight, we learn to help others from a place of kindness and share our recovery with others. We continue to cultivate our five new senses of faith, energy, mindfulness, concentration, and wisdom. We don't teach recovery: we radiate recovery. We live our lives as people who have stepped onto the path of recovery and freedom from their addictions.

We are almost at the end of the book, and endings can be bumpy affairs. A whole host of sad feelings and thoughts can emerge. "I'm still using, it hasn't worked." In this moment you are reading this book, in this moment you have turned your life over to recovery. Allow yourself to face the pain of where you are right now in your recovery. It is a journey, not a test of willpower. Trust that, if recovery is what you really want, it will emerge in your life. Maybe not as fast as you would like. Have compassionate patience, keep on picking yourself up and give yourself a hug of loving-kindness. If the three-minute breathing space, AGE, responding to the basic needs of the heart – attention, affection, appreciation, and acceptance – and the practice of loving-kindness have not benefited you, then keep on seeking. If living a more ethical life, transforming your speech, actions, and livelihood does not inspire, you, then seek something else that will motivate you and inspire you.

In the spirit of the Buddha's words:

> Do not go by oral tradition, by lineage of teaching, by
> hearsay, by a collection of texts, by logic, by inferential
> thinking, by reasoned cogitation, by the acceptance of
> a view after pondering it, by the seeming competence
> of a speaker, or because you think, "The ascetic is our
> teacher." But when you know for yourselves, "These

things are wholesome; these things are blameless;
these things are praised by the wise; these things,
if undertaken and practiced, lead to welfare and
happiness," then you should engage in them.[3]

This is a gentle reminder for us to pause at the end of Step Eight,
and take a three-minute breathing space.

 Three-minute breathing space, AGE

Awareness of thoughts, feelings, and body.
Gather the breath, notice the breath, become aware of the
breath.
Expand the breath throughout the whole body – connect to
the whole body.

Tools for recovery

Here is a recap of some of the teachings that can be used as tools to help you with your recovery. We are all different and not all the things we offer to help with recovery may work for you. So we invite you to try them out and discover which ones resonate most with you.

The most essential tool for anybody's recovery is the breath. When we notice the breath, connect to the breath, it will slow us down and help us to pause. In these pauses we get to know what we are thinking and feeling, and can begin to make choices with clarity.

Recap of Dharma tools in the book

As outlined in the "Accessing the guided meditations" section (p.xi), some of these tools are included as free downloads. There are additional meditations (21-day meditation recovery) at http://thebuddhistcentre.com/eightsteps.

- Three-minute breathing space, AGE (see p.23).
- Understanding the four noble truths: there is suffering; a path that leads to more suffering; an end of suffering; and a path that takes you away from suffering (see p.15).
- Counting the costs of your addiction (see pp.103–5).
- Understanding the four reminders: life is precious; death is inevitable; actions have consequences; suffering and dissatisfaction are part of everyday life (see p.34).
- Recognizing your triggers and high-risk situations (see pp.54 & 56).

- Understanding that thoughts are not facts (see pp.62–5).
- Understanding impermanence: everything changes (see p.79).
- Mirror-like wisdom (see p.87).
- Chanting mantras: *om mani padme hum; om tare tuttare ture svaha; om vajrasattva hum* (see pp.92, 139 and website).
- Kindness reflection (see p.99).
- Creating a safe and kind space (see p.102).
- The four basic needs of the heart: learning to give yourself some attention, affection, appreciation, and acceptance (see p.76 and website).
- Learning to give yourself some loving-kindness, compassion, sympathetic joy, and equanimity (see p.175).
- Practicing the five training principles to help train your mind (see pp.126–31 and website):
    - I undertake to abstain from harming life; with deeds of loving-kindness I purify my body.
    - I undertake to abstain from taking the not-given; with open-handed generosity I purify my body.
    - I undertake to abstain from sexual misconduct; with stillness, simplicity, and contentment I purify my body.
    - I undertake to abstain from false speech; with truthful communication I purify my speech.
    - I undertake to abstain from taking intoxicants; with mindfulness clear and radiant I purify my mind.
- Experiencing regret for past actions (see p.132).
- Making amends (see p.133).
- Making a plan before a promise (see p.135).
- Admitting your faults with compassion (see p.137).
- Placing positive values at the center of your life (see p.143).
- Connecting to your values (see p.144).
- Practicing the four efforts: preventing and eradicating unhelpful mental states, and cultivating and maintaining helpful mental states (see p.167).

- Recognizing the hindrances (see p.169).
- Being kind to yourself when you have had a slip (see p.165).
- Helping others (see p.189).
- Developing the five spiritual faculties: faith, energy, mindfulness, concentration, and wisdom (see p.195).

Meditation

We have also spoken a lot about meditation and how this can aid recovery, how it can help cultivate a sober mind, a mind that is calm, still, and peaceful. We introduced short versions of the Mindfulness of Breathing and loving-kindness meditation. For those of you who have enjoyed practicing them, we outline below fuller versions of both of these meditations. They too can be most helpful for recovery.

The Mindfulness of Breathing

> For as long as the meditation subject is connected with counting it is with the help of that very counting that the mind becomes unified, just as a boat in a swift current is steadied with the help of a rudder.[1]

This meditation is all about coming back to the breath. Every time you find your mind caught up in thoughts, planning the next things to do, or distracted by a conversation you had earlier, you just come back to the breath. With kind awareness you notice you are distracted and gently come back to the breath. The more you notice how distracted your mind is the more you are engaging with the practice of meditation. So let's begin.

Prepare yourself for this meditation by using the three-minute breathing space, AGE. Use this as preparation for settling yourself in a chair or on meditation cushions. Once you have settled down, become aware of your breath, allow yourself to appreciate your breath, rejoicing in every in- and out-breath, because without the breath there would be no life, no beauty, no opportunity for transformation. Now become aware of your sitting posture, and try to fully engage with the present moment. This meditation is split into four stages:

1. We breathe in and out, and then count "one" silently to ourselves. Breathe in and out, and count "two" silently to ourselves. Breathe in and out, and count "three" silently to ourselves. We keep going in this way until we reach "ten," and then we go back to the beginning, breathing in and out, counting "one," and all the way up to "ten" again. We repeat this counting sequence over and over again for five or ten minutes. (If you are dyslexic or numbers seem daunting, you can do this first stage by saying silently to yourself as you breathe in: "Breathing in, I'm breathing in." And as you breathe out you say: "Breathing out, I'm breathing out." And you repeat these phrases, coming back to the breath every time you have wandered.)

2. Next we tag the breath before breathing in. We count "one" silently to ourselves, and then breathe in and out. We count "two" silently to ourselves, and then breathe in and out. We count "three" silently to ourselves, and then breathe in and out. We keep going in this way until we reach "ten," and then we go back to the beginning, counting "one," breathing in and out, and all the way up to "ten" again. We repeat this counting sequence over and over again for five or ten minutes. (In this stage, if numbers are an issue, you can say silently to yourself as you breathe in: "Lifting," and as you breathe out: "Falling." You repeat this over and over again, and if the mind wanders you bring it back to the breath.)

3. In this stage we let go of the counting, and become aware of the breath, giving continuous attention to the flow of the breath going in and out of the body, without altering its natural flow. We become aware of how the breath may fill our lungs, chest, or abdomen; we become aware of the whole breath. If we stray

into internal dialogue, or wandering thoughts, we try not to engage, but gently bring ourselves back to the breath. We follow the breath for five or ten minutes.

4. In this final stage we work at becoming more aware of the subtleties of the breath, becoming aware of its sensation, and especially the sensations of the breath entering the body through the nostrils, the sensations on the upper lip or in the throat. We try to be receptive to the cool or warm brushing sensation of the breath as it enters the body. Sensation on the upper lip or inside the nostrils can be tickling, itchiness, sharp pain, pulsing, or heat. If you feel something, then this is sensation. We put our whole attention onto the area of the upper lip and nostrils and focus as much as we can for five or ten minutes. We are working with full attention to try to refine our concentration.

In the first two stages, if we find ourselves counting beyond ten, then we just gently bring ourselves back to one, without getting hooked into why or how we got distracted. Being aware of our counting beyond ten is part of becoming more focused. Also, if we lose count and don't know which number we are on, we just notice that has happened and start again at one. Mindfulness of Breathing is noticing that our mind has become distracted, noticing that we have counted beyond ten, noticing we have not got beyond three, and bringing ourselves back to the breath. Similarly, in the last two stages, if we find our mind wandering, caught up in thinking, we just notice and let go of the thinking and come back to the breath. If we keep on noticing how distracted we are and keep on bringing ourselves back to the breath throughout all four stages, we are practicing Mindfulness of Breathing.

Through focusing on the breath continuously, we will eventually become one with the breath. The Mindfulness of Breathing is a practice of concentration, which is an important component of recovery. However, concentration is only one aspect of mindfulness meditation. In mindfulness-based approaches for depression, addiction, and relapse prevention, the emphasis is on awareness. We notice where the mind has gone off to, so that we start to be able to recognize our habits. Then we learn to turn toward them, so that we are more able to contain our difficult emotions.

If we are continually being distracted, then it is very difficult to recognize our stumbling blocks. Therefore, coming back to the breath every time we are distracted begins to break the seductive habit of distraction. The Mindfulness of Breathing is also a practice of compassion. We must be kind and gentle with ourselves when we notice we have become distracted. When this happens, we gently bring ourselves back to the breath. This is the same in recovery: when we notice we have lapsed or relapsed, we gently bring ourselves back to our focus of recovery without beating ourselves up.

Loving-kindness meditation: the Metta Bhavana

> "To reteach a thing its loveliness" is the nature of metta.
> Through lovingkindness, everyone and everything can
> flower again from within. When we recover knowledge
> of our own loveliness and that of others, self-blessing
> happens naturally and beautifully.[2]

"Metta" is a Pali word for unconditional loving-kindness. It is the first of the four attitudes necessary for our well-being and inner peace. The other three attitudes – compassion, sympathetic joy, and equanimity – grow out of a strong practice of metta. These four attitudes help to support the basic needs of the heart, which are attention, affection, appreciation, and acceptance. The practice of metta is about focusing upon our heart. It is the loving-kindness that a good parent has toward their child, even to the extent of risking their own life while protecting their child. When we have cultivated metta, there is an absence of attitudes like resentment, jealousy, anger, hatred, and ill will.

Metta Bhavana is also sometimes known as the meditation of unlimited friendliness, sometimes called the Maitri Bhavana. Friendliness is an antidote for ill will. If we have a mind full of hate and anger for the world, it will only make us restless, irritable, and negative, and our view of the world will be quite narrow and limited. By cultivating metta we can begin to cultivate healthier states of mind whenever we wish, helping us to cultivate abstinence and sobriety in our lives. There are many people who don't love themselves, and enter a relationship so that someone will love them. If we want to be loved by another person healthily and well, we must first learn to love ourselves. If we want to love others well, we must also learn to love ourselves. People who don't love themselves will love others back from their place of craving, neediness, and attachment, which will inevitably lead to some form of suffering.

Metta is the practice of unconditional love. It has the capacity to open up the heart area, and has no expectations of reciprocity or rewards. In loving we expect nothing back, we are in total harmony with ourselves, not craving for affirmation, approval, or love. This is why it is important to learn to love ourselves. A lack of well-being toward ourselves can have two disastrous consequences. First, it means that our "inner critic" is particularly severe – a persistent and belittling voice that spells out all the reasons why we cannot do what we are trying to do. Second, it makes us overly dependent upon the opinion of others: we want others to praise (or, sometimes more perversely, condemn) us in a way that we are unable to do ourselves. Loving-kindness is something we can feel on a visceral level. We can think loving-kindness, we can feel it pulsating in our hearts, we can feel it vibrating in our bodies; we can radiate loving-kindness to others too. If you practice metta it will transform your life. Of course, don't take our word for this. Try practicing metta and be your own judge.

There are many ways to experience this meditation. We offer this way as a suggestion. If you are inspired by the ideal of unconditional loving-kindness and find our suggestions are not working, there are many alternatives available on the Internet and in books. What is important is that we come into awareness with the relationship that we have with ourselves, which in turn can inspire us to begin to learn to love ourselves more, and have an impact on all the other relationships we have in our lives.

There are five stages in this meditation. Before meditating, it is helpful to do a brief preparation. We suggest that you take five minutes to cultivate a response to the basic needs of the heart – attention, affection, appreciation, acceptance. Pay attention to yourself, give yourself some affection, appreciate yourself for opening up to the practice of metta, and accept yourself right now in this moment. Then just sit with the strong wish for yourself not to suffer. In this practice we are cultivating so much loving-kindness that we can radiate it out to our friends, people we don't know, our enemies, and the whole world. We have the strong wish for absolutely no one to suffer in this world. Each stage of this meditation is an aspect of ourselves. There is an aspect of ourselves that we like, otherwise we wouldn't be reading this book. There is also an aspect of ourselves we don't even know, and a part of ourselves we don't like very much. When we dedicate time to doing this practice of loving-kindness, we begin to accept all aspects of ourselves and others. So let's begin. We settle ourselves in a chair or on our meditation cushions and start to respond to the four basic needs of the heart in ourselves, with the strong wish not to suffer.

1. Once we are settled, we try to visualize ourselves as we are now, or as a baby. We try to see a photograph of ourselves that we like. If this is too hard, an image of a flower opening or a positive symbol that represents us is fine. We begin to focus on the image of ourselves, or a symbol that resonates for us. Then we say to ourselves from time to time: "May I be happy, may I be well, may I be free from all suffering." We have the strong wish for ourselves not to suffer. We allow the phrases to resonate in our being, seeing if we can feel the subtle vibrations of the phrases. If this feels difficult, or even scary, we allow ourselves to become aware of the difficulty and pain, but try not to feed it or engage with it, allowing the painful or negative thoughts to arise and burst like bubbles. Eventually, through patience, we will break through and begin to feel genuine thoughts of loving-kindness to ourselves. This may take a long while. Be patient. As long as you have the intention of loving yourself, this will be

enough, and one day you will feel loving-kindness radiating toward yourself. Self-hatred can become an intoxicant. Beware of this poison of the mind, and practice metta to quell the subtle embers of hatred that can burst into flame at unexpected times. We advise you to work with this first stage for a few weeks, unless of course you are familiar with this meditation. If you are new to this meditation, perhaps just do this first stage daily for a couple of weeks before moving on to the next stages. Give yourself five to ten minutes of metta every day.

2. Once this base of metta has been built up for ourselves, it is hoped that we can begin to give loving-kindness to another human being from a much healthier place in the heart. With the metta that we have cultivated, we begin to think of a good friend, preferably someone who is alive, and someone we don't have sexual desires for when we first begin this practice. We imagine our friend, visualize them somewhere beautiful, and similarly wish them well: "May they be happy, may they be well, may they be free from all suffering." We have the strong wish for them not to suffer. We repeat these phrases from time to time while focusing on our friend. If you notice you are able to experience a feeling of metta toward your friend, when you begin the practice next time, see if you can love yourself as much as you loved your friend.

3. By the third stage, a strong basis of well-being for ourselves and another has been temporarily cultivated, and on this basis of loving-kindness we try to imagine a neutral person. This person could be the postman, the shopkeeper, the bus driver, the person who lives four doors away from you that you have never said hello to. Somebody we see from time to time during our regular routine, but whom we never really acknowledge or have any strong feelings of like or dislike toward. In this stage we try to visualize them, and become aware that this person is a human being

like us, who doesn't want to suffer. We imagine our neutral person, visualize them somewhere beautiful, and similarly wish them well: "May they be happy, may they be well, may they be free from all suffering." We have the strong wish for them not to suffer. We repeat these phrases from time to time while focusing on our neutral person. This stage may feel difficult and awkward too. If you can, consider that once upon a time all the people we know were neutral. We didn't know them, but something made us open our hearts to them. In this case, we are using unconditional loving-kindness to open up our hearts. When we radiate loving-kindness to people we don't know, we are seeing that we are connected to the rest of the world and not separate from it.

4. In this next stage, we choose somebody we are in conflict with. To begin with, we could think of a person who just seems to irritate us for no apparent reason. Or perhaps a friend who has upset us or annoyed us. Once we are experienced with the practice of the Metta Bhavana, we can explore using somebody we have shut out of our lives, or someone we have really difficult issues with, or someone we strongly dislike. We imagine our person of conflict, visualize them somewhere beautiful, and similarly wish them well: "May they be happy, may they be well, may they be free from all suffering." We have the strong wish for them not to suffer. We repeat these phrases from time to time while focusing on the person of conflict. This stage can also be challenging. We try to visualize the person, and get in touch with the fact that they are a human being who does not want to suffer. Although we may be in conflict with them or perhaps dislike them, we remind ourselves that there are people out there in the world who love them and care about them. With this thought, we may be able to break through and begin to feel genuine thoughts of loving-kindness. If strong negative dialogue or thoughts surface, just let

them arise, don't engage with them, just acknowledge them and let them pass like clouds. Eventually they will pass and a glimmer of genuine feeling will arise. Having the intention to cultivate loving-kindness toward an enemy may be all we can do right now – and that is OK. Our hearts may close in this stage – notice this and trust in the process of intention. In fact all four stages are aspects of ourselves. There are parts of ourselves we don't like, parts we do like, and aspects of ourselves we don't even know. And of course our friends can end up in all the stages too. We make people in our lives enemies of the mind, and so we can also make people friends of the mind. Remember our enemies are our gifts: they help us develop and grow. Make friends with your enemies.

5. In this final stage of the practice, we bring ourselves, our friend, neutral person, and person of conflict all together in our imagination and try to equally wish each and every one happiness and freedom from all suffering. This metta is then spread out toward the people who are physically present in our immediate environment, into our neighborhood, into the town we live in, and then we send metta out into the whole wide world, toward all sentient beings. If we have more time to practice, we can alternatively shift our focus to ourselves and, as we do this, imagine our biological lineage – wishing that all our biological family be free from all suffering, even the ones we have banished from our hearts. Then we shift our focus to our friends and wish all our family of friends freedom from all suffering, even the ones we don't speak to or see anymore. Then we shift our focus onto the neutral person and wish all the people in the world we don't know freedom from all suffering. Then we shift our focus onto the difficult person and wish all our enemies to be free from all suffering. Finally we shift our focus back to ourselves and sit quietly absorbing the practice.

Mindfulness and metta will help to cultivate integration and positive emotion, which is what we all need if we are to begin working with our addictions and/or compulsive behaviors.

We can use the practice of metta to help make amends with people before we do it face to face. We can put the people who have been impacted by our addiction in our meditation and begin to wish that they be well and free from suffering.

The benefits of both practices are far-reaching. We recommend you find a teacher to guide you. You can also contact us at eightstepsrecovery@gmail.com or via our website, or follow us: @8StepRecovery.

You can also contact us via our website (http://thebuddhist centre.com/eightsteps) for information on the Mindfulness-Based Relapse Prevention course we speak about in this book. Since writing we have decided to rename this course Mindfulness-Based Addiction Recovery (MBAR), because some professionals and clients have said that calling it Relapse Prevention is setting people up for relapse rather than for recovery. We offer training for the trainer to deliver this course, and the eight-week course for people in recovery.

What next?

Contact your local Buddhist center to learn more about meditation and have the chance to practice with other people. You can find information about our Buddhist centers around the world at http://thebuddhistcentre.com/text/triratna-around-world. But our centers are not the only ones. If you search online for meditation or Buddhist centers, you will find an abundance of places to go to.

Appendix 1

....

Mentorship: The tool of asking for help (We do not have to do it alone)

The book lends itself to people being mentored through the Eight Step Recovery. You do not have to be a Buddhist or have knowledge of Buddhism to mentor someone through the program. We have put together some suggested questions for each step. It's a road map, and sometimes you will stray from the road map, because together you will notice something you want to pursue. However, always come back to the road, otherwise you will get lost. If you remember to come back to every exercise and reflection in the book you will not get lost. We suggest that if you want to mentor someone through the book that you first read the book and work through every exercise and reflection on your own or in a book study. If you take on a mentee, then it would be expected that you take the mentee through every exercise and reflection, and discuss the answers. We suggest that all mentees practice the twenty-one meditations for recovery, which are free and available on our website: https://thebuddhistcentre.com/eightsteps. We recommend requesting that they practice one every day for three weeks.

We also suggest that mentees attend meetings. Meetings can include Eight Step Recovery, twelve-step meetings, or SMART (Self-Management and Recovery Training), Refuge Recovery Meetings, and any other meeting that supports recovery. Additional activities can include attending a Buddhist center weekly – but not as an alternative to working the steps. Same-gender mentoring is often helpful, although note that there are

....

many different shades of gender beyond a rigid binary of just male and female.

Here are some questions for mentees to answer before beginning the step work to establish the agreement between you and the mentee – this is important before you begin the mentorship process:

The Agreement

- Are you prepared to go to any lengths to get your recovery? If someone asks "What do you mean by this?" then you can say: "Are you prepared to do every exercise and reflection in the book?"
- Are you prepared to give what I may suggest serious effort (as long it does not cause you physical, mental, or emotional harm)?
- Are you prepared to attend one or more recovery meetings – which could include going along to a twelve-step meeting, or a Refuge Recovery Meeting, or a Buddhist Recovery Meeting, or an Eight Step Recovery Meeting, or attend a therapy group or one-to-one session?
- What kind of support are you receiving? We ask all of this because we know from experience that support is a big part of recovery. Few people have cleaned up on their own. Some of your mentoring may come from the Twelve Step tradition and, if you state that someone needs to do forty meetings in forty days, then we suggest it's a combination of the above as well as perhaps online meetings. Bring your experience of what has worked for you when you were sponsored or coached. Please find a meeting or meetings that work for you so you can commit to attending regularly. They are one of the most important tools of your recovery.
- Are you prepared to listen to the twenty-one meditations for recovery, once a day? These meditations are available on www. buddhistcentre.com/eightsteps and https://www.insighttimer. com/vimalasara. They are only fifteen minutes long. If the mentee already has a meditation practice this is additional and not instead of their usual practice. This gives the mentee fifteen minutes a day of practice for the first twenty-one days of you working together. You can send them one a day – or give them

the link to the meditations. We suggest this so you can have day-to-day contact for the first three weeks, and it's not a deal breaker: you don't need to force the mentee to do the meditations, although we have found they have helped.

Once your mentee has said yes to all of this, then the mentorship process is ready to begin. Make sure your mentee is attending meetings, which can include online meetings if there are no meetings nearby, or has some other support. Meetings and/or support are an important part of help with recovery.

Once you have this agreement, we suggest that for all addictions you ask all mentees to do the following:

Record and send in daily everything they are eating and drinking; any pharmaceuticals; and what time they are eating, going to bed, and waking up. This is required for three weeks, so you as the mentor can talk over what has been happening with your mentee. You will notice if there is a lack of food and sleep (which could cause a relapse). Again, this is a suggestion and not a deal breaker. You may like to ask your mentee what they think they need to focus on in terms of personal care hygiene. However, when working with food addictions, sending in the food record daily for several months is part of the required mentorship process.

Together you are looking out for Hunger, Anger, Loneliness, Tiredness, and Stress (HALTS).
Together you are looking out for Don't Even Notice I Am Lying (DENIAL).
Together you are looking out for Fearing Events Again Repeating (FEAR) , False Evidence Appearing Real (FEAR), and helping your mentee with fear, by Facing Everything And Recovering (FEAR).

You will notice patterns that can support someone's recovery. If the person is a food addict of some degree, including anorexia, bulimia, compulsive overeating, then sending in a record of their food daily will be part of their long-term program.

During the first three weeks, while mentees are daily sharing their food and sleep health and listening to meditations, please ask them to reflect on the following questions:

What is your self-view?

Are you willing to let go of self-view to get your recovery?

(Self-view is all the identities people have been attached to for years, including "I'm no good, a piece of crap, a loser," and all the stories people keep on telling themselves. Self-view also includes all the different rights and rituals, and the overwhelming doubt that debilitates people and hinders a person's recovery.)

You can ask the two questions above face to face or via email. It is important you set up a regular time to meet. It can be face to face or on a social media platform. However, if you are working with someone with sex addiction or Internet addiction then it's advisable to meet face to face as social media platforms can be one of their triggers.

Then ask your mentee to read the foreword and the introduction and then answer the following questions:

- What does addiction look like in your life today?
- What does recovery mean to you?
- Share your personal story of addiction. What are the early conditions in your childhood that you perhaps have struggled with? What are the events that have marked your addiction?

Discuss the answers – and then begin work on the steps.

If you are a Buddhist practitioner and have a good understanding of the Dharma then the following way to mentor is appropriate.

Ask the mentee to read a step, and then discuss with you what resonated for them, what came up for them. What buttons is it pushing? Just listen without judgment.

Then go back to the beginning, and work through each exercise and each reflection one at a time. Always discuss the reflection and the exercises. Ask your mentee to email answers to the reflections so you can discuss when you meet face to face or on Skype. Be careful of doing all the work: your mentee needs to be doing more of the work. Be patient, as working these steps can take more than a year to complete, especially if you allow spaciousness and kindness. There is no need to rush. Life can also get in the way so, even if there has been a break, just get back on track and pick up from where you left off. If you complete all the steps, great, and if you don't complete all the steps, great. If you are finding it difficult to commit to working all the steps then you may need to consider working another program.

Once the step work has been completed, you may want to ask them if they would like to consider doing a set of twelve steps specific to their addiction. It is not a prerequisite but it can be useful if people are open to it. Or the mentee may ask to work the steps all over again. Once your mentee has completed Step Four and has abstinence, they can begin mentoring someone through the program.

When working with people who are compulsive eaters, or have bulimia, you will need to ask them to identify which are their binge foods. And then there will need to be an agreement about being abstinent from these foods.

When working with sex addicts you may need to ask what apps and websites they are going to abstain from, and if they are prepared to have a security lock placed on certain sites that they have visited in the past.

If you are stuck, you can always post a question on our website where we have a sobriety hangout: www.thebuddhistcentre. com/eightsteps.

If you are new to Buddhist principles and are not a Buddhist and are inspired to mentor people through the eight steps we encourage you to do so. Just make sure you have read the book, and have worked the steps, and follow the script of questions while mentoring. You too can be of service and great help.

Always begin with the agreement, and with the introductory questions and reflection on self-view. Then take your mentee through each question and exercise and reflection one by one. Ask them to reflect on each question before answering. You can explore one question at a time face to face. Or one question at a time via email. If you notice something in a response, you can ask your mentee to explain, or ask how they are feeling before moving onto the next question. Please let all your mentees know that it's okay to use images and/or symbols to answer questions, and it's also okay to send in a recording of their answers too.

Step One: Accepting that this human life will bring suffering

There is suffering – what does that look like in your life today? (Please read pp.25–6)

> What physical suffering do you experience? (Please read pp.26–7)
> What psychological suffering do you experience? (Please read pp.27–8)
> What existential suffering do you experience?
> Which one of these sufferings triggers your addiction and why?

Please do the *Face your pain with the breath* exercise (p.30) over a period of a week. Keep a daily journal or if that is too much, find a time to write about how this exercise has been for you.)

Read pp.30–2.

> What are your addictive behaviors?
> How has your physical body been affected by your habitual behaviors?

How has your emotional health been affected by your
    habitual behaviors?
What has changed in your life that you have resented?
What is the truth of your addiction?
What is the truth of your suffering?

Please do the *Reflection: Counting the costs of addiction* exercise
(p.33), at least three times over a period of a week, answering
the same questions.
    Are you the only one in your life who is struggling, if not,
who else is struggling with depression, obsessive compulsive
behaviors, addictions, and who else is not happy?

Please take a week to reflect on the *Four reminders reflection*
exercise (p.37) and answer the questions.
    Ask yourself: What are the limitations of your addictive
behaviors?
    Practicing Step One may be challenging for you; remember
the Buddha's last words: "With vigilance strive to succeed."

What vigilance do you need to take to begin working this
    step?
How helpful is the three-minute breathing space?
If the three-minute breathing space is too long sometimes,
    shorten it – and practice just stopping and taking one
    full breath.

Why is Step One positive?
What have you learned about yourself in Step One?
What's one thing you are prepared to let go of that has
    created your self-view?

Give the Mindfulness of Breathing exercise (p.40) a go.
Meditation may be hard, and it may be easy. Just try it. If it
doesn't work for you that is fine. We just ask that you practice
the AGE (three-minute breathing space) daily while you are
working the steps with a mentor.

Step Two: Seeing how we create extra suffering in our lives

How do you create extra suffering in your life?

Read pp.43–4.

> What do you crave for in your life?
> What do you have aversion toward in your life?

Read pp.44–5.

> When you are hungry, angry, lonely, tired, stressed (HALTS), and/or triggered, how do you avoid this experience?
> When you are HALTS and/or triggered, who do you blame?
> When you are HALTS and/or triggered, how do you distract yourself?
> What addictive behaviors do you turn to while distracting yourself from the HALTS or trigger?
> What does self-pity look like in your life when HALTS and/or a trigger arises?

Now look at the diagram on p.45 and read pp.46–7, and then recall a recent time you relapsed, lapsed, or turned toward one of your addictive behaviors.

> What was the trigger?
> What were the feelings? (Was it pleasant/unpleasant/ vague/neutral/uncomfortable?)
> What thoughts did you have?
> What were my actions?
> What did I gain from picking up my distraction of choice?
> What did it cost me picking up my distraction of choice?
> How does this vicious cycle play out in your life?

Read pp.50–6.

> What does craving for sensual pleasure look like in my life?
> What does craving for existence look like in my life?
> What does craving for non-existence look like in my life?

Please do the *Noticing your triggers* exercise (p.54) and list and name as much as you can. You may surprise yourself.

> What is it like to be in the Hungry Ghost Realm?
> Why is it difficult to be with HALTS, triggers, and/
>   or painful experiences?

Read Bruce's story on pp.60–1. Can you think of a personal story when you were able to stay with discomfort and unpleasant experiences and not pick up your distractions? Please write it down. And then re-read it and underline all the things you were able to do which helped you stay with your experience.

If you did not turn away from your direct experience unfolding in the moment what could happen differently?

Read the example on p.63 and then see if you can write your own example.

Take your time doing the *Which of these thoughts have you made fact?* exercise (pp.64–5). Perhaps even do it together with your mentor. However, it is okay to do it on your own.

Remember to take a breathing space when you have completed it.

Read Darren's story on p.66. What small or big shifts have you noticed in your behavior since you have been working the steps?

Please try the *Mindfulness of Breathing – ten minute meditation on turning toward difficulties* (p.68) at least once. If you like it take it on daily for a week. If it is a challenge then continue with AGE.

How could you begin to slow down in your life?

Choose one of the examples in *Slowing down* (p.72) to help you slow down and see what happens.

Becoming aware of the suffering we create in our lives (p.74) is a good exercise to do with your mentor, but again you can do it on your own too. Perhaps ask yourself why you are choosing to do all the exercises on your own (if that is what you are doing). Part of recovery is asking for help. You could ask a friend or partner to do the exercise with you. And then talk about it.

How is Step Two positive?
What have you learned about yourself in Step Two?
What's one thing you are prepared to let go of that has created your self-view?

Now do the *Responding to the four basic needs of the heart* exercise (p.76).

AGE – how is this three-minute breathing space becoming part of your life?

Step Three: Embracing impermanence to show us that our suffering can end

Do you believe that your suffering can end?

> If no, why?
> If yes, how?

If you don't believe your suffering can end, try to imagine the freedom and happiness you would have if your suffering did end and write what that would be like for you.

Read pp.81–3.

> What do you need to do to change?
> What would your life be like if you changed?

Read Pete's story – and then reflect on your own journey of addiction and when you had moments of insights and waking up to your reality.

Read Jackie's story, and then reflect on turning points in your own journey. Try and recall as many as possible. It doesn't matter if they were a long time ago.

Now do the *Noticing change* exercise (p.86). Allow yourself to reflect on this exercise for a week, and then record what you noticed.

Now do the *Mirror-like wisdom* exercise (p.87). This exercise could trip you up. Some people may not be able to find pictures of themselves when they were young. If this is the case, watch yourself moving away from this sad and challenging moment with avoidance, blame, distraction, or self-pity. If you can't find a picture of yourself when you are young, do an AGE. Pick the youngest photo you have of yourself, and use this for the exercise.

Read Mohammed's story, then ask yourself:

> What changes do you have to accept in your life?
> What changes are you not accepting?

From the day your addictive behaviors began up to today, what are some of the many changes that have happened in your life?

Practice the *Bringing kindness to craving* exercise (p.89) daily for a week, and write down your experiences of reciting this phrase daily.

Read pp.90–1.

What are your thoughts about mantra?

Now do the *Chanting mantras* exercise (p.92).

If chanting a mantra seems strange, that is perfectly okay. You may have a mantra of your own. If mantras are an issue then say silently to yourself for the next five minutes, "I can change." Then complete the rest of the exercise by answering all the questions.

How is Step Three positive?
What have you learned about yourself in Step Three?
What's one thing you are prepared to let go of that has created your self-view?

AGE – how is this three-minute breathing space becoming part of your life?

Step Four: Being willing to step onto the path of recovery and discover freedom

We are asking you now: Are you willing to step onto the path of recovery and discover freedom?

If no, why?
If yes, why?

Whatever you answer we invite you to continue working through the steps.

Read p.95.

What hopes do you have for the future?

Read p.96.
We ask you to be really honest with yourself. What is your life like today? (If you are still using, relapsing, please write about that.) Get really clear about what is currently happening in your life.

What do you want more, your recovery or your addiction?
If your recovery, why?
If your addiction, why?
If you really want your recovery, how aware are you that every time you pick up your distraction of choice you are choosing your addiction over your recovery in that moment?
What really matters to you?
Are you choosing what matters or something else?

Read p.97.

What does your path of recovery look like?
Are you attending recovery meetings? Do you have a recovery coach? Are you in a rehab or detox unit, are you seeing a counselor? Or are you doing it on your own? (Write down exactly what your recovery plan looks like.)
If your life was heading in the direction of recovery, describe what that looks like for you – be imaginative

and metaphorical. Use the first two paragraphs of p.97 to inspire you.

What do you need to make the decision to choose recovery? (Be as detailed as you can. Then look at the list and ask yourself how you can begin to make this happen.) What could you begin doing now?

What does kindness look like in my life today?
How am I kind to myself?
How could I be kinder to myself?

Read Tania's story (p.98), then ask yourself: What has been my approach to my recovery?

Allow yourself to do the *Kindness reflection* (p.99) daily for a few days.

Read pp.99–100.

How can I be more warm, sympathetic, and caring toward myself?
What thoughts of kindness could I have about myself?
How could I be more helpful toward myself?
If I was a better friend toward myself what could I be doing?

Read Angela and Bill's and Doris and Eve's stories, then ask yourself what acts of kindness you need to begin doing.

Now do the *Creating a safe and kind space* reflection (p.102).

Read pp.103–6 and then do the *Weighing up the benefits and costs of our addiction* exercise (p.105).

Read Molly's story (p.106), then list some of the positive and helpful things that you do in your life. That could be getting up in the morning, or taking care of someone who has overdosed, or feeding yourself. Be creative.

Now do the *Compassion toward the costs of our addiction* reflection (p.107).

Read pp.107–9, then do the *Loving-kindness meditation*.

Read pp.111–12, then find a quiet place to sit, and have the strong wish to be free of suffering. Experience this wish on a visceral level. Write down what comes up for you.

Compassion is action. Self-compassion is not wishing to harm yourself. So if you were not harming yourself, what things would you begin to stop doing?

Read Giles's story (p.112), then ask yourself the following:

What friends do I have in my life who can help support me in my recovery?
What things in the past which I used to do, could be supportive if I began doing them again?
What is the meaning of my life?

Now do the *Benefits and costs of recovery* exercise (p.113). What do you notice about your answers?

Read pp.113–15.

What do I have gratitude for today?
What do I appreciate about my life today?
How can I cultivate more gratitude and appreciation in my life?

Now do the *Making changes* exercise (p.114) – please answer all the questions.

How ready am I to step onto the path of recovery and discover freedom?
How is Step Four positive?
What have you learned about yourself in Step Four?
What's one thing you are prepared to let go of that has created your self-view?

AGE – how is this three-minute breathing space becoming part of your life?

Step Five: Transforming our speech, actions, and livelihood

This step focuses on your moral inventory. It is important that you have someone to support you in this: a sponsor, a mentor, a therapist, or a friend who is in recovery. It's important that you have self-kindness and compassion while doing this step. Remember to at least do AGE and perhaps the four basic needs of the heart or the kindness practice.

In relationship to your addictions, compulsive obsessive behaviors, and habitual patterns, please answer the following questions:

> What thoughts have you had that have become spoken words?
> What words have you had that have become actions?
> What actions do you have that have become habits?
> What habits have you had that have become your character?
> How has your character become your destiny?

Read p.118.

> What have been the consequences of your addictive behaviors?

Read James's story.

> What subtle thoughts have you had in the past and how have they facilitated your addiction?

Read Transforming speech (pp.120–1).

> What false speech have I made that has supported my addiction?
> What harsh speech have I made that has been a result of my addiction?
> What unhelpful speech have I made that has impacted others?
> How has my speech caused disharmony in my life and in others?

Practice this refrain for a week.

Before speaking ask yourself these questions posed by blogger Jim McBeath, who points out that this guideline has been around for a long time (as far back as Socrates):

Is it true? Is it kind? Is it necessary? Is it helpful?

Notice and report back (to a mentor or therapist) how it has impacted your speech.

Read Mumtaz's story.

How have you been like Mumtaz, and which part of her story resonates with yours?

Read Transforming actions (pp.122–4).

What memories still trouble you from your addictive past?
What are you still finding hard to speak about in your past?
What habitual behaviors are you choosing to do that distract you from actions in the past that you do not want to face?
What could you do to help clean up your life?
What actions do you still need to take to transform your life?
What ways could you act that would bring your life more in line with how you would really like it to be?

Read Transforming livelihood (pp.124–6).

How is your lifestyle supporting your addictive behaviors?
Do you need to change your livelihood?
Are you getting enough sleep?
Have you organized your lifestyle so that you don't have to get up early in the mornings?
How regularly are you eating?
What impact do your addictive behaviors have on your sleep and eating patterns?
What impact has Jennifer's story had on you?
What are you doing to pay your bills?

If you are unable to pay your bills, how much of that is
   because of your addiction?
How are you earning your money? (Is it legal?)
How willing are you to commit your life to recovery?

Read Training principles to guide our actions toward sobriety
and abstinence (pp.126–30).

We suggest, like Valerie, that you take this up as a practice
and recite them daily, as part of your recovery program. Learn
them off by heart. At least recite them for one week.

Devise a training principle specific to your addictive
behaviors. Just choose one. When you no longer need that
principle, you can devise another principle to recite. And
remember to include the action plan that will help you.

You can also think of an action plan for the five training
principles that we introduce to you in the book. This will help
you become more aware of them.

Make a list of all people you have harmed – and then
   radiate kindness toward yourself and to the list of
   people.

Make a list of all people, companies, and organizations from
   which you have taken the not-given – and then radiate
   kindness toward yourself and to the list of people.

Make a list of all people with whom you have
   committed sexual misconduct (this includes sexual
   fantasies about people you were not in relationship
   with, talking about people inappropriately sexually,
   touching someone or making someone touch you
   without their consent, non-consensual affairs,
   including those affairs where you may not have
   consummated it sexually but you were in a romantic
   relationship) – and then radiate kindness toward
   yourself and to the list of people.

Make a list of all people you have communicated false,
   harsh, useless, and/or slanderous speech to – and
   then radiate kindness toward yourself and to the list
   of people.

Make a list of all people you have harmed through taking intoxicants, including intoxicating thoughts that could harm other beings, too – and then radiate kindness toward yourself and to the list of people.

Now do the *Reflecting on the five training principles* exercise (p.130).

Read Coming to terms with past and ongoing unhelpful actions (and acknowledgment and regret) (pp.131–3).

What regret do you have regarding your addictions? (Please remember that regrets are unhelpful actions for which you are willing to fully accept the consequences without berating or criticizing yourself.)

What things have you done in your life that you consider to be unforgivable? If you have named some things, then please say: "I forgive myself" after each thing you have named. For your own recovery, you need to find a way to forgive yourself, and that could actually mean you walk into a police station with a friend and confess. It may mean you that you have to sit down and tell your partner or your family the truth, and then have to face the consequences of their actions.

Read Making amends and A promise and a plan (pp.133–7).

Sometimes making amends may cause more harm than good. So, before you decide to make amends it is important to discuss this with your sponsor, mentor, coach, or therapist. This is called self-care. Making amends is an important part of your recovery, and we have to realize that the amends must be unconditional. Do not think just because you have made amends or an apology everything will be okay. Some people will be upset, others may choose not to hear your apology or accept your amends, and others may appreciate it. Whatever the response we can still purify ourselves. Making amends is a type of purification – it helps to lighten our emotional and mental load.

The first part of the amends is acknowledging unskillful actions.

Write down unskillful actions, and beside the action name whom you have harmed, always including yourself. Beside the names, state if you are able to make amends to these people. Then check it out with a confidante.

Amends and apologies can also be anonymous. For example, if you ripped somebody or a company off, you could send money in the post anonymously. There may be some things that you have done that have had a huge impact on a community of people, which involves the police. Only you can decide what is best to do. Only you can know what will lighten the emotional load. We have known people who have turned themselves over to the police, done their prison sentence, and come out of the whole process much happier and calmer. This is your process, and it is important to listen to your heart's whisper.

Now do the *Making a promise* exercise (p.135).

Read Ritual approaches to coming to terms with our past (pp.136–40).

We ask that you do all the things at least twice, even if it feels odd.

You can do the ritual on your own, in a special place for you. We ask that you find someone to witness your ritual, like a Buddhist chaplain, a Christian minister, a Muslim guru, a Hindu guru, or any other spiritual teacher or confidante. It is important to admit to another human being the exact nature of our actions and give ourselves forgiveness.

First write your version of the prayer admitting your faults with compassion.

Then choose one of the mantras to recite. If this seems strange then you could repeat the phrase: "May I be forgiven" or "May I be purified."

Read p.141.

List all the times you have had Great Indicators For Throwing Stuff out (GIFTS).

Read your list and see if any of these indicators are relevant today. In the midst of your day, is there an opportunity to do something different?

How is Step Five positive?

What have you learned about yourself in Step Five?

What's one thing you are prepared to let go of that has created your self-view?

AGE – how is this three-minute breathing space becoming part of your life?

Step Six: Placing positive values at the center of our lives

List all the things you spend most of your time thinking about.
How many of these things are connected to your addictive behaviors?

Read pp.143–4.

What is your spiritual tradition?
If you don't have one, what do you believe in?
What are your values?

Now do the *Connecting to our values* exercise (p.144).

Now do the *Imagining a party at the end of your life* exercise (p.145).

Read pp.145–7, then do the *Placing what you value at the center of your life* exercise.

How does Janet and Bob's story (p.148) resonate with your own life?

Read pp.149–55.

If you are able to place some of the qualities of the Buddha at the center of your thoughts, what does this inspire in you?
If you are unable to place any of the qualities of the Buddha at the center of your thoughts, who else could you think of to go to for refuge? Choose someone, perhaps, who is not living, that you are inspired by.
If you are able to place the Dharma at the center of your thoughts, what does this inspire in you?
If you are unable to place the Dharma at the center of your thoughts, what other teachings or values could you think of to go to for refuge?
If you are able to place the sangha at the center of your thoughts, what does this inspire in you?

If you are unable to place the sangha at the center of your
thoughts, what other spiritual or social communities
or like-minded people could you think of to go to for
refuge?

Read Paramabandhu's story (p.153).

What assumptions do you have?
What expectations have you had?
When have you listened to your assumptions and been
wrong?
How often do you expect things to be a certain way?

Read Sandra's and Elaine's stories (p.158).

How connected are you to the people in your recovery
groups?
How often do you put yourself on the edge of social
gatherings because of the assumptions: "I'm the only
working-class person, I'm the only person of color,
I'm the only woman, man, trans person. I'm the only
queer or straight person. I'm the only person with a
particular political, environmental, ecological view."

Now do the *Becoming aware of what inspires us* exercise (p.161)

How is Step Six positive?
What have you learned about yourself in Step Six?
What's one thing you are prepared to let go of that has
created your self-view?

AGE – how is this three-minute breathing space becoming part
of your life?

Step Seven: Making every effort to stay on the path of recovery

What effort is needed in your life to continue to stay on the path of recovery?

> List all the things you can do to keep continuing your effort.
> What are some of the things that have taken you off the path of recovery?
> List all those things.
> Do you want to stay on the path of recovery?
> If yes, what do you need to do?
> If no, what makes you continue to stay in this mentorship process or personal inquiry with yourself?
> Can you admit that a part of you does want to stay on the path of recovery?
> List those parts of yourself that want to.

Read Liam's story – ask yourself what this makes you feel and think.

You may or may not have a friend who died as a result of addiction, but you may have someone you know of who is struggling with addiction.

If you can believe the best thing to help your friend or family member is your own commitment to staying on the path of recovery, what do you need to do right now?

Now do the *Breathing space, AGE, after a slip* exercise (p.165).

Please do this exercise regardless of whether you have had a slip or not. If you have not had a slip, you can do this exercise after you have had a bout of stinking thinking.

> What has it cost you if you have tried to get recovery on your own?
> What has it cost you if you have avoided going to recovery meetings?
> What has it cost you if you keep on relapsing?

Now do the *Being kind to ourselves by asking for help* reflection (p.166).

Read pp.167–74.

> How can we prevent unhelpful situations that may trigger us to pick up our addiction and relapse?

Read Liam's story – how can this story inspire you to do something different next time you realize you are in an unhelpful situation or are being triggered?

> What types of thoughts do you have in your mental chatter?
> What types of rationalizations do you make?
> What hindrances do you need to watch out for if you want to eradicate unhelpful states of mind?
> What impact does sensual desire have on your actions?
> What impact does ill will have on your actions?
> What impact do restlessness and anxiety have on your actions?
> What impact do sloth and torpor have on your actions?
> What impact does doubt have on your actions?
> When one of these hindrances arises, what can we do to help ourselves?

Read Veronica's story – how does her story resonate with your own?

Now do *The hindrances* exercise (p.174).

> What can you do to cultivate more helpful states of mind?

Now do *The four sublime abodes directed toward ourselves* exercise (p.175).

> What can you do to maintain helpful states of mind?

Read Tracey's story (p.176) – what can you learn from this story?

How willing are you to do what it takes to stay on the path of recovery?

How is Step Seven positive?
What have you learned about yourself in Step Seven?
What's one thing you are prepared to let go of that has created your self-view?

AGE – how is this three-minute breathing space becoming part of your life?

Step Eight: Helping others by sharing the benefits we have gained

Since you have been working these eight steps how have you been helping yourself?

How has your recovery changed from when you began working these steps?

Read pp.179–83.

Who has been the fourth sight in your recovery?
What qualities and values did this person have?
What was it that inspired them?
How can you be a fourth sight for someone else in the throes of addiction?
What qualities and values could you radiate without telling someone what to do?
How would you be living your life?
What actions could we do to help others in their recovery without being co-dependent or an authority?
When you have helped someone, what has that left you feeling? (If you think you were manipulated or used, then the helping was conditional and you had expectations. If you experience a positive impact on your own recovery, and you manage to stay sober and abstinent then the helping has come from the unconditional.)

What do you remember about the suffering of your addiction if you have had more than six months' abstinence?
If you have not had more than six months' abstinence what do you remember about the suffering of some of your past and recent relapses?
What help have you been given to support your recovery?
What were some of the qualities these people had who supported you?

What are some of the benefits you have gained in your
recovery process?
How can you share some of these benefits with others?

Read pp.183–9.

What were you preoccupied with the past?
What is your sense of purpose?

Read Justin's story – how is this story inspiring?

Since working the steps what has changed in your life?
Before you began working these steps we asked: Were
you willing to let go of self-view to get recovery?
Where do you stand today with this question?
How have you built a self-view?
How have your feelings become part of self-view?
How have rights and trials created your self-view?
How has doubt created your self-view?
How has your mind become part of self-view?
How have your thoughts become part of self-view?
How have your perceptions become part of self-view?
If the self is not fixed what is it doing?
What does that mean about your addictive behaviors?

Read Valerie's story (pp.185–6) – and then write your own
story about realizing that there is no fixed self, and how you
understand that the self you have created is an illusion.

What do you think is me, mine, and I?
How have you been trying to control and direct your life?
When you have reached out for help, has that dismantled
your self-view in any way?
What does wisdom look like in your life?
What does compassion look like in your life?

Read pp.188–9.

Now do the *Helping others* exercise (p.189).

Whose life have you been exploring while working
through these steps?

What are you dependent on?

What do you turn to when things get tough?

Does Winsome's story (p.190) ring a bell? If yes, that is
okay, and the steps can begin right now. Ask yourself
who needs help. If the answer is you, that's okay –
you may want to go back to Step One.

If Winsome's story does not ring a bell with you, that is okay too.
With regard to helping others, please read Paige's and Marianne's
stories (pp.192–3) and then answer the questions on p.192.

Read pp.194–9.

What has your journey of recovery been like? (Be
imaginative, use metaphor, images; you may want
to draw your journey and then share it with your
sponsor, mentor, coach, therapist, or confidante.)

What does faith look like in your life today?

What has been your journey of faith in this recovery
process?

How much energy have you needed to keep on the path
of recovery?

When you have lapsed or relapsed how much energy
have you needed to get back on track?

What can you do to harness your energy within?

List several things that will help tap into your energy.
(This could include having more sleep, eating less
sugar, and eating more regularly.)

What does mindfulness look like in your life today?

How could you be more mindful?

List several things you could do to be more mindful.

How much concentration have you needed to work with
your craving, boredom, and negative mental states?

What more could you do to help narrow your focus in
your recovery?

Are you working at keeping abstinent and sober as if
your hair is on fire?

If yes, how?

If no, why not?

What wisdom have you experienced in:

Step One

Step Two

Step Three

Step Four

Step Five

Step Six

Step Seven?

How are you accepting the challenges on your recovery journey?

Have you done every exercise, answered every question, and shared with another person?

If yes (to earlier question), are you still using?

If yes, then don't give up. It doesn't mean you haven't learned anything. It may mean you need to ask yourself again: "What do I want more, my recovery or my addiction?"

If it's the latter, acknowledge that and move on. If it's your recovery, ask yourself what you need to do next.

If you haven't completed all the exercises, answered every question, and shared with another person, ask yourself why not. If you are still using, still relapsing, it may mean you need to stop reading books, stop listening to what we say, and just try for yourself. You can do that by working the steps and finding out for yourself.

How is Step Eight positive?

What have you learned about yourself in Step Eight?

What's one thing you are prepared to let go of that has created your self-view?

AGE – how is this three-minute breathing space becoming part of your life?

Now look at the Tools for recovery section (pp. 201–2) and decide which ones you will continue to use.

May you be blessed on your path of recovery.
May you find kindness on your path of recovery.
May you find forgiveness on your path of recovery.
May you find self-compassion on your path of recovery.
May you be liberated from the hell realm of addiction.

You can follow us on:
twitter @8StepRecovery
instagram eightsteprecovery
www.eightstepsrecovery.com
email: eightstepsrecovery@gmail.com

Appendix 2

....

Mindfulness-Based Addiction Recovery (MBAR) Course

Acknowledgments

We are grateful to Zindel Segal, Mark Williams, and John Teasdale for their seminal work, *Mindfulness-Based Cognitive Therapy for Depression*, which was the inspiration for developing the MBAR course.[1] Thanks too to Leap Confronting Conflict for some of the interactive games.

Introduction to MBAR

One of the starting points for the development of Eight Step Recovery was the MBAR course (originally called MBRP, Mindfulness-Based Relapse Prevention). It is a secular course, and does not expect you to take on any Buddhist rituals and or practices. Mindfulness is central to Steps One and Two, and in fact supports the remaining six steps. The MBAR course is a great way to develop skills in mindfulness to support your recovery. The course can be done as a foundation before pursuing the Eight Steps or as a way of deepening your practice of mindfulness while practicing or after going through the Eight Steps. Many people ask what to do next after attending an eight-week mindfulness for addiction course, and we suggest exploring the Eight Step Approach, especially if they are open to having a deeper understanding of Buddhism.

We have usually taught the MBAR course in a group format. It works fine to follow it on your own, but, for those doing it in a group, you will find some group exercises indicated by this icon:[2]

We have also included some pointers for running a group (e.g., to discuss something in pairs, then in the whole group) and themes to draw out. We suggest that if you are running a group you have two facilitators and approximately eight people in the group. The group needs to be large enough to encourage a group experience, and small enough so that people have time to individually share. It can also work with a larger group if you have helpers, such as people who are graduates from the course, who can facilitate small-group discussions. The interactive group exercises and pair work are for people running groups.

The games are a fun way of bringing the material of the course to life and can help deepen learning. They can be adapted if we have differently abled people in the group, so please be creative. You may find that you know of some different games that help bring out the learning. Sometimes facilitators are worried if someone is triggered. Turn toward the person who has been triggered, as this is a learning and teaching opportunity. Guide the participant to use some of the tools like the three-minute breathing space – get the whole group to join in the AGE so the person is not under the spotlight. And then, when you are ready, gently and kindly be curious and inquire what is going on for them in the moment.

We recommend that if you do decide to run this program you have your own daily mindfulness practice as well as some training and/or experience in one of the mindfulness courses for depression, stress, or pain. We have also developed a two- to five-day professional training for the trainer of this course, depending on the needs of your organization or employees working with people with addictions.

If you want to do the MBAR course for yourself:

- We suggest that you work through the exercises one by one.
- We encourage you to find someone to share your experience with.
- You could also do the course with a friend and share your responses with each other.
- We run the six-week course online for people, and you can find our contact email on p.212.

You can download our meditations and all the handouts attached to the course for free. Go to our Facebook page, https://www.facebook.com/eightsteprecovery/, or join our community, https://thebuddhistcentre.com/eightsteps/ eight-step-recovery-sobriety-hangout?display=latest, and you can find us on insight timer https://www.insighttimer.com/ vimalasara.

General pointers for the MBAR course:

- It can be done in six or eight sessions; we run the sessions weekly.
- There is a core of six sessions, with an optional introductory session and an additional final session.
- We generally run each session for two and a half hours with a break, although you could have two breaks, depending on the needs of your group, or run through without a break.

If you are running MBAR as a course, these are the group expectations that we suggest you introduce at the start of the course:

- Be on time.
- One person speaking at a time.
- Phones on silent.
- Challenge the statement, not the person.
- What's said in the room stays in the room.
- Be kind.

In the following course material you will find cross-references in brackets to led meditations and other material from the main body of the book.

At the end of each session there is a Practice Record Form to further deepen your learning.

Following the optional Welcome Session, there is a sample questionnaire for professionals or facilitators who are running the course. It can also be helpful for anyone, including someone using these resources on their own.

Optional Session: Welcome

Content for Optional Session: Welcome

Introduction to the course
Learning outcomes
Group expectations
Gathering
Three-minute breathing space
Mindfulness game 1: 1–20

Break

Four basic needs of the heart
Mindfulness game 2: Sun shines on
Home practice
Closing

Introduction to the course

MBAR is based on three principles, an ABC, which build cumulatively over the six or eight sessions. A is for developing *Awareness* of our thoughts, emotions, and body sensations. B is learning to *Be* with difficult experiences as they arise, rather than pushing then away or blotting them out with addictive behavior. C is making wise *Choices*. Developing awareness forms the ground of MBAR. Through becoming more aware of our experience, especially the subtle aspects that we easily overlook, we can learn to pick out triggers to addictive behavior before they get too strong, as well as give ourselves a fuller, richer life. When difficulties arise, our tendency is to want to get rid of them, which can result in becoming angry, pretending that it's not happening (often getting tense as we do so), or resorting to our addiction. The key to success in MBAR is not to do any of these, but counterintuitively to turn toward our experience with an attitude of acceptance and curiosity. If we are able to notice more fully what is going on and are able to stay with our experience, especially when it is difficult, we are then in a much better position to decide what to do next – to make wise choices.

Learning outcomes

The chief aims of the MBAR course are for you to:

- Learn to pause.
- Learn to meditate.
- Develop new skills to help with recovery.
- Become more conscious of what is going on in your mind, heart, body.
- Be confident to make some new choices.

Group expectations

See the sample Questionnaire at the end of this session for questions to elicit experience and expectations of participants.

 Gathering

Each person gives their name and says something they do to support their recovery.

 Introduce the Three-minute breathing space, AGE (p.23)

Mindfulness game 1: 1–20

The aim of this game is to count in chronological order from one to twenty as a group. Anyone starts by saying out loud "one." Then someone else says "two," and so on up to twenty. When two people say a number at the same time, we go back to one. If you call out a number, you can't say the next one. No one is allowed to direct the game – if someone starts to do this, we go back to one. The aim is to be aware of each other, but with a playful spirit.

Afterwards debrief, perhaps using the following questions: What was it like playing? How aware did you need to be? What did awareness feel like? How easy was it to stay aware in the game? What distracted your awareness? The learning here is that awareness does not mean you have to do things in slow motion. Awareness is seeing how your responses have an impact on other people, noticing that we are all interconnected and it's not just about what we do as an individual.

 Responding to the four basic needs of the heart (p.76)

 Mindfulness game 2: Sun shines on

Everyone sits on a chair in a circle, except for one person who stands in the center.

Round 1: The person in the center chooses a visible attribute such as the color of a piece of clothing and says, for example, "The sun shines on everyone who is wearing a blue jumper." Then everyone with a blue jumper has to get up and find a new chair. The one in the center also tries to take a place on a chair. Whoever is left without a chair stands in the center and gives the next call, for example, "The sun shines on everyone who has gray hair." Again, everyone with this attribute moves, and we continue a few times before moving onto the next round.

Round 2: This time the person in the center picks an invisible attribute, for example, "The sun shines on everyone who has a sister," or "The sun shines on everyone who likes cheesecake." After a few times, we move onto round three.

Round 3: This time the person in the center picks an attribute to do with addiction, for example, "The sun shines on everyone who has tried to give up cigarettes," or "The sun shines on everyone who has struggled with overeating."

Debriefing icebreakers and games are important, because they can help with some learning.

What was it like being in the middle?
What was it like being the only person who moved?
Who moved because everyone else moved?
What was it like when all of you moved?
Anything else that you noticed while playing?

Draw out when we are the only one and feel vulnerable as it could be a trigger to pick up. Peer pressure can be another trigger – all our friends are doing it and we want to join in. Playing games where we can laugh and relax can open us up, and participants notice things they were perhaps closed to.

Home practice

Home practice is an important part of MBAR. Like any skill, mindfulness develops through regular practice. Daily practice is what really makes it possible to learn mindfulness skills and embed them in our lives so that we can easily use them, especially when things are difficult. Getting into the routine of regular practice can be hard, so we need to find a balanced approach, neither browbeating ourselves into practice, nor letting ourselves off the hook too easily or being harshly critical of ourselves if we don't practice. It can take time to build up a regular practice, and, if we find that this is tricky, we can bring an attitude of curiosity to what happens to prevent us from practicing.

The home practice for this introductory week is relatively light:

- The three-minute breathing space (AGE) once a day – you could spend some time in pairs working out when you will do this. It's likely to be easier to remember if you pick the same time each day, or you could set a timer to go off on your watch or phone.
- Complete the Practice Record Form.
- Once during the week do the four basic needs of the heart meditation.

 Closing

Go round in turn, each person saying:

1. Why you chose to come on the course (write on flip chart and keep).
2. Why you may not want to be on the course.
3. Something about your addiction journey.

Sample Questionnaire

How did you hear about the course?

What would you like to get from the course?

How long have you been in recovery for?

What other support do you have for your recovery?

Practice Record Form – Welcome Session

Record on the Practice Record Form each time you practice. Also, make a note of anything that comes up in the practice, so that we can talk about it at the next meeting.

Day/date	Practice (circle)	Comments
	Yes / No	
	Yes / No	
	Yes / No	
	Yes / No	
	Yes / No	
	Yes / No	
	Yes / No	

Session 1: Becoming Aware

Content for Session 1: Becoming Aware

Opening gathering
or if this is the first week of the course
Introductions to each other and to the course

Brief meditation exercise
Principles of awareness
A mindful drink of water
Triggers to addictive behavior
Body scan meditation

Break

Review of body scan
Game: prisoner/jailer
Home practice
Just sitting for two minutes

 Opening gathering

Invite people to respond to the question "When sadness arises, what do you normally do?"

Brief meditation exercise

Take three deep breaths (together).

 Principles of awareness

1. Discuss in groups of three: "What is awareness?"
2. Receive comments.
3. Ask whole group: "What are you aware of in your experience *right now*?"
4. Receive responses and continue to ask "What else are you aware of right now?" until there are no more answers (different aspects of self, other people, and the environment).

5. Lead a guided awareness using material they offered in exercises 3 and 4.
6. Ask group: "What is the difference between *talking about* awareness (exercise 1) and *being aware* (exercises 3, 4, and 5)?"
7. Mindfulness is about *direct experience. Talking about* awareness is different from *being aware*. With mindfulness we know what's happening as it is happening, rather than being on automatic pilot. Automatic pilot is when we are not really aware of what we are doing. We might notice this, for example, if we find ourselves having gone into another room and come to, realizing that we have forgotten why we went into the room, or if we intended to stop off at the supermarket on the way home and find that we have missed the turning because we were automatically following our usual route home.
8. Draw out the differences between being on automatic pilot and being aware.

A mindful drink of water

An alternative exercise is to ask people "What is it like to drink some water?" Then hand out a glass of water to each participant and invite them to notice each stage of drinking a mouthful of water: the look and the feel of the glass in the hand, the weight of the glass of water, the anticipation of drinking the water, the movements of the arm lifting the glass to the mouth, the sensations of the water in the mouth (taste and texture), the sensations of swallowing, and anything else that they notice. Now compare the difference between talking about drinking water and actually drinking it, as well as the difference between how they usually drink water and taking a mindful mouthful. In particular, draw out the difference between drinking on automatic pilot and mindful drinking.

Triggers to addictive behavior

Reflect on what your triggers are that can lead to addictive behavior. Include both external events (e.g., being offered a drink, conflict with partner), and internal ones (e.g., feeling angry). For the external events explore what the mediating mental events are (e.g., feeling too shy to say no, thoughts of "deserving a drink"). Make a note and keep for the next session.

Research suggests there are three main types of high-risk situations: negative mental states (downers), interpersonal conflict (rows), and peer pressure (joining the club). However, the last two will be mediated by thoughts and emotions (usually negative mental states – although also positive ones, as in feeling happy and wanting to celebrate when something good happens).

Reflect: If you are running on automatic pilot, is it more or less likely that you would drink (or use drugs, etc.) when a trigger arises compared to if you are aware?

By developing mindfulness we can learn to step out of being on autopilot and so are less vulnerable to triggers. In particular, there is more chance of catching difficult thoughts, emotions, and cravings early before they get too big to work with. We are also more fully alive, and can enjoy the richness of life.

 ### Body scan meditation

The body is an excellent foundation for mindfulness. Noticing where the mind has gone when you are distracted enables you to get to know your mental habits. Returning your attention to the body is a way of stepping out of being caught up in habitual thinking / automatic pilot.

 ### Review of body scan

Discuss in pairs and then discuss in the whole group and take questions. If you are doing this for your own personal development write down what you experienced in your journal.

Draw out how easy or not it was to be aware. How much were people on automatic pilot / caught up in thinking? Emphasize that each time you noticed you had gone off, you have stepped out of automatic pilot and are back into awareness.

 Game: prisoner / jailer

This game can be used to reflect on triggers. With everyone sitting in a circle, go round and name people alternately: prisoner, jailer, prisoner, jailer. Then ask all the jailers to stand up and push their chairs to the edge of the room and ask all the prisoners to create a circle. Jailers stand an arm's length away, with arms by their sides, behind the seated prisoners. There also needs to be one empty chair. As the facilitator, you stand behind this chair.

You play by first describing your empty prison and how you need some power, so you need a prisoner. You get your prisoner by winking at someone sitting in the seat. Do a trial run. Ask all prisoners to sit in their chairs properly and look at you. You wink or blink at someone, and the prisoner tries to run to your seat. The jailer prevents them from escaping by tapping them on the shoulders ONLY. Make sure you say no tapping on the head. The one who now has the empty chair winks or blinks at someone to try to get someone in their "prison." Invite the jailer to ask permission to tap the prisoner on the shoulder. If somebody says no, be affirming and just swap. Make sure you keep to just this game – that is, not another one – and that nobody has tapped somebody hard or inappropriately.

In the debrief ask who enjoyed being a jailer more and why? Who enjoyed being a prisoner more and why? What was the trigger? When the prisoner was triggered, where did the prisoner keep on ending up? The answer you want is in prison or the same place. How can this be like life? The answer you want is how we can keep on ending up in the same place or in a relapse, or using or in the addiction.

Quote: "If you keep on doing what you have always done, you'll always get what you have always got." Reflect, how can this be different? What could the prisoner have done differently when they were winked or blinked at? The answer you want is to stop playing the game, physically step out of the game. The learning in this game is that when we are triggered we have to learn to do something different. And that may mean physically taking yourself out of a triggering situation.

Home practice

1. Body scan.
2. Complete the Practice Record Form.
3. One mindful activity (e.g., washing up, showering, walking to bus, etc.).
4. Eat at least one meal mindfully.

 In order to help plan the home practice, invite people to discuss in pairs (or small groups):

- which routine activity they will do;
- when they will listen to body scan download;
- obstacles to practice and to how to overcome them.

Just sitting for two minutes

Just sit quietly following the breath.

Practice Record Form – Session 1: Becoming Aware

Record on the Practice Record Form each time you practice. Also, make a note of anything that comes up in the practice, so that we can talk about it at the next meeting.

Day/date	Routine mindful activity (circle)	Body scan practice (circle)	Comments
	Yes / No	Yes / No	
	Yes / No	Yes / No	
	Yes / No	Yes / No	
	Yes / No	Yes / No	
	Yes / No	Yes / No	
	Yes / No	Yes / No	
	Yes / No	Yes / No	

Session 2: Triggers (Vicious Cycle)

Content for Session 2: Triggers (Vicious Cycle)

Introduction to the theme
Mindfulness of Breathing
Review of current practice and home practice

Break

Chain of events
(Optional extra exercise) Thoughts and feelings exercise
Vicious cycle
Awareness of feeling tone
Home practice
Just sitting

Introduction to the theme

In the last session we looked at the difference between being aware and being on automatic pilot, and how being on automatic pilot leads to being more vulnerable to triggers. This session we will use our developing awareness (or mindfulness) to delve more deeply into the processes that led to being in a high-risk situation and ended up in addictive behavior.

There are a number of intermediary processes in the mind that it can be helpful to be mindful of. These include *automatic judgments*, and the *feeling tone* of our experience, which is sometimes called our internal barometer.

Focusing on the body in meditation reveals more clearly the chatter of the mind and especially its automatic judgments. These can (1) be habitual, (2) grip and convince the mind, and (3) mean that we don't necessarily see what is actually happening. We can start to notice how these judgments control our reactions to everyday events.

Mindfulness of Breathing (pp.40–1)

We can think of meditation as practicing shifting from doing mode to being mode. Doing mode is where we are caught up in planning and getting things done (which has its place). Being mode is an appreciative, non-striving space that can create a different sort of relationship to our experience, which is more open. It is associated with "slow mind" that solves problems differently (e.g., having things on the back burner or "Eureka!" in the bath).

In this session's meditation, in particular, notice automatic judgments and try to let them go.

 Review of current practice and home practice

Chain of events

Review some of the high-risk situations that were noted in the last session. Try to track back to what led you into this situation. What was the chain of mental events? How did it start? How did it build up?

Draw out the negative spiral of unpleasant feeling tones leading to negative judgments leading to more unpleasant feelings. All experience (physical sensations, emotions, and thoughts) is colored by being pleasant, unpleasant, or neutral (feeling tone or hedonic tone). It is sometimes referred to as our internal barometer, the instrument that reads our internal weather. It tells us if things are generally pleasant or unpleasant. We are often powerfully affected by this feeling tone, and it can trigger rumination or the mind to wander, especially with automatic judgments of our experience and how it should be. It is important to become aware of these pivotal moments. *If necessary, do the following exercise:*

(Optional extra exercise) Thoughts and feelings exercise

Set up as if for meditation, then notice responses (body sensations, thoughts, feelings, images) to the following scenario:

> "You are getting out of a crowded train. You see someone on the platform smiling and waving. You smile and wave back, then you realize that you don't know the person."

Notice thoughts, feelings, images, and body sensations.
Points to draw out:

1. A (triggering event) → B (feeling tone) → C (thoughts) → D (emotions); however often we don't notice B and C – A happens and we end up with D. The more we can be aware of the feeling tone and our (automatic) thoughts, the less we will be carried away on the cascade of emotions.
2. The internal barometer can act as an early warning system. Often, we don't notice it because we (1) distract ourselves from it, (2) use alcohol or other substances, or (3) zone / numb out. These elements can reinforce each other (in this example, the addictive behavior is drinking).

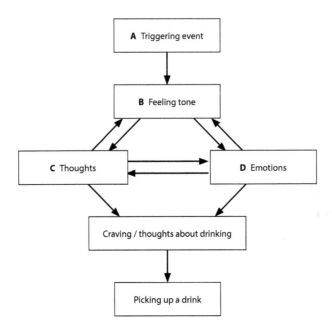

Fig. 3: Triggers

3. How we *interpret* the event will affect how we feel. Our interpretation reflects what we bring to the situation as much as its objective content. Also, how we interpret the event will be affected by how we are feeling (i.e., what thoughts would you be most likely to have if you were in a bad mood?). That interpretations of the same situation vary over time or between people indicates that *thoughts are not facts.*

Vicious cycle (pp.44–47)

Identify the different elements of the vicious cycle using an example from someone in the group (or start with one of your own, then that of someone from the group). First ask someone to give a trigger for their addiction, then ask the following:

> What were you feeling? Where did you feel it in the body? On a scale of one to ten, how big is the feeling?
> What were you thinking?
> What emotions are stirred?
> What action did you take (especially the addictive behavior)?
> What is gained?
> What are the costs?

Or another way in is mapping the vicious cycle on the floor. Have six pieces of paper and on each one write one of these phrases: Trigger, Body, Feeling Tone, Thought, Emotion, Action, Gain, Cost. Place the papers in a circle.

You can bring it to life more by writing each element on a piece of flip chart paper – trigger, feeling, thought, action, gain, cost, mapping it as a circle on the floor and walking through it.

Here is an example, with the situation of a friend not turning up to go out for the evening.

As the facilitator walks the cycle, saying out aloud as you step onto each element:

> First step onto Trigger: "Friend didn't turn up."
> Step onto Feeling Tone: "Unpleasant."
> Step onto Body: "I feel it in the abdomen, and hands. It's a number seven."
> Step onto Thought: "My friend has found something better to do."
> Step onto Emotion: "I'm upset."
> Step onto Action: "I begin thinking about a drink."
> Step onto Gain: "I stop thinking about my friend letting me down."
> Step onto Cost: "Feel low."

And then point out that the trigger is irrelevant, so step onto Feeling: "Unpleasant and uncomfortable."

> Step onto Body: "I feel it in my body, and in my jaw. Now I'm number eight."
> Step onto Thought: "I want a drink."
> Step onto Emotion: "I'm angry."
> Step onto Action: "I drink."
> Step onto Gain: "I feel better for a moment."
> Step onto Cost: "I'm drinking."

As you go round the cycle, pick the pace up.

> Step onto Feeling Tone: "Very unpleasant."
> Step onto Body: "All over. At ten with my emotions of rage."
> Step onto Thought: "Don't care anymore."
> Step onto Emotion: "Rage."
> Step onto Action: "Carry on drinking."
> Step onto Gain: "Don't care."
> Step onto Cost: "Relapse."

The facilitator can ask a participant to share their example. You first write all the answers on the paper and then invite the participant to step onto their cycle. You, as the facilitator, stand outside of the circle with the participant opposite standing on each piece of paper, as you guide them around the cycle.

It's important to explore where the participant could get off this cycle, for example, changing your thoughts or staying with the unpleasant feeling tone without responding with anger or ill will. You don't tell the participant if they are stuck; invite an answer from the rest of the group. If the participant suggests emotions, step off, and then ask what they will do with their emotions. See if you can point them in the direction of stepping off at feelings. The feelings may overwhelm, so take them through the three-minute breathing space. Hold them kindly and maybe move them onto thoughts and see if they can choose a helpful thought rather than a facilitative thought.

The learning here is to slow the process down so that people can see what is happening. This exercise also helps people to see that feeling tone in the body is unpleasant, pleasant, neutral, and all of them can be uncomfortable. And the emotions are often anger and rage. The idea is to point people to see that when feelings are uncomfortable we move away from the discomfort with thoughts, and these are often stoked into actions and strong emotions that lead to a relapse.

Awareness of feeling tone

These are some of the benefits of becoming more aware of the feeling tone of our experience:

- Bringing mindfulness to pleasant events can be a way of experiencing them without adding any extra thoughts (e.g., wishing it to go on forever, wondering why it doesn't happen more often).
- Help us to notice what (even slightly) positive things may (already) be occurring, which we tend not to notice especially if depressed / in a bad mood.
- Bringing mindfulness to unpleasant events can help to alert us to triggers that, left unchecked, might lead to unhelpful behavior.
- Just noting "unpleasant" can be helpful when we are unsure exactly what we are feeling.
- Help us to link awareness of the body to awareness of the body's reactions and responses to everyday events (i.e., chains of events).

Home practice

1. Notice one pleasant event each day, and complete the Pleasant Events Diary. This week just focus on pleasant events (life enhancement) to start to notice the feeling tone of our experiences.
2. Mindfulness of Breathing each day.

Just sitting

Two minutes' sitting meditation (or longer if time permits), with an emphasis on body sensation and feeling tone.

Practice Record Form – Session 2: Triggers

Record on the Practice Record Form each time you practice the meditation. Also, make a note of anything that comes up in the practice, so that we can talk about it at the next meeting.

Day/date	Mindfulness of Breathing (circle)	Comments
	Yes / No	
	Yes / No	
	Yes / No	
	Yes / No	
	Yes / No	
	Yes / No	
	Yes / No	

Pleasant Events Diary

Be aware each day of one pleasant event at the time it is happening. Use the following question to focus your awareness on the details of the experience as it is happening. Write it down later.

What was the experience?	Were you aware of the feelings while the event was happening?	How did your body feel, in detail, during this experience?
☺ Example: *Going out to buy a pint of milk – stopping, noticing the blue sky.*	Yes	*Hands releasing, breathing slowing, shoulders dropping, uplift of corners of mouth.*
Monday date: ☺		
Tuesday date: ☺		
Wednesday date: ☺		

What moods, feelings, judgments, and (other) thoughts accompanied this event?	What thoughts are in your mind now as you write this down?
A quiet joy, happiness – "How lovely to see some blue sky again!" "The sky is so vast," "It's great to be outside."	*Just seeing the blue sky gives me some perspective on my life.*

What was the experience?	Were you aware of the feelings while the event was happening?	How did your body feel, in detail, during this experience?
Thursday date: ☺		
Friday date: ☺		
Saturday date: ☺		
Sunday date: ☺		

What moods, feelings, judgments, and (other) thoughts accompanied this event?	What thoughts are in your mind now as you write this down?

Session 3: Accepting Experience

Content for Session 3: Accepting Experience

Introduction to the theme
Mindfulness of Breathing – turning toward difficulties
Review of meditation and home practice

Break

More on feeling tone
Optional group discussion: Why we use avoidance
Mindful exercises and Mindfulness of Breathing
Three-minute breathing space, AGE – introduction
    or reminder if Welcome Session was done
Home practice
Three-minute breathing space, AGE

Introduction to the theme

This session we move onto the second phase of the course: learning to "be with" our experience and to find acceptance. In particular, we will be focusing on being with our emotions, especially difficult mental states such as anxiety, anger, and depression (since these can be triggers to addictive behavior). Next session we will explore being with thoughts.

When any emotion arises, we have some kind of response to it. There are three main habitual strategies that people often use in response to difficult mental states: blame, self-pity, and distraction (pp.44–50).

Acceptance is not the same as resignation, which implies passivity and a sense of helplessness. Acceptance is about letting things be, finding out what's happening before rushing in to try and fix things. The advantages of acceptance are:

1. Paying attention intentionally, we prevent our attention being hijacked by passing thoughts and moods.

2. Changing our basic stance from "not wanting" to "opening," we help to break the chain of habitual reactions that leads toward more painful states that can lead to addiction (e.g., "I am stupid to think this," "I should be able to cope with this").
3. It provides an opportunity to check the accuracy of our thoughts (e.g., "If this goes on any longer, I shall scream").

 Mindfulness of Breathing – turning toward difficulties (p.68)

 Review of meditation and home practice

More on feeling tone

At first it can be difficult to learn to read our internal barometer because we just notice a fused whole of unpleasant feeling tone with the downstream aversion and related thoughts. So we might:

1. At first notice just the fused ensemble, perhaps as a somewhat unpleasant contraction.
2. Then recognize this fused ensemble more clearly.
3. With increased awareness to the body (especially the forehead, jaw, shoulders, lower back, and belly), notice how unpleasant feeling tone triggers aversion.
4. With more awareness, distinguish two distinct events: unpleasant feeling tone then aversion (e.g., "get me out of here").

Optional group discussion: Why we use avoidance

Reasons include:

- Avoiding people/things in the outside world can work (unlike mental states that just arise).
- The adverts tell us that happiness/success is the absence of any painful feeling.
- As children we may have been told, "Don't cry," which gives the message that we can get rid of unpleasant emotions, and that those giants (the adults) appeared to be in control of their emotions.
- Avoidance can work in the short term (as in distraction).

Mindful exercises and Mindfulness of Breathing

The exercises are another way to become aware of body sensations and feeling tone, and to practice acceptance / "being with" sensations. Any exercises can be done with mindfulness, such as simple stretches, yoga, or qigong. Below is a suggested sequence. Following the mindful exercises, go straight into a period of Mindfulness of Breathing, turning toward difficulties.

1. With knees slightly bent, feet hip width apart, rotate the body from side to side allowing the arms to swing.
2. Standing on one leg, rotate the foot in turn, clockwise and then anti-clockwise. Repeat with other foot.
3. Hold legs just above the knees, and with both knees together rotate knees in one direction, then the other.
4. Standing on one leg, draw a circle with the kneecap, clockwise and then anti-clockwise. Repeat with other leg.
5. With hands on hips, rotate hips, clockwise and then anti-clockwise.
6. Draw three circles forward and then backward with the whole of each arm in turn.
7. Rotate shoulders, forward and then backward.

8. Rotate head carefully, clockwise and then anti-clockwise.
9. Slowly reach up with each hand in turn, as if grasping a fruit high up on a tree.
10. Hold arms out in front of you as if holding a big beach ball. As in exercise 1, rotate the body from side to side. Gradually make the movements less, until you come to a standstill, facing forward with arms still up. Hold the position for fifteen seconds, or longer if you wish, then gradually allow the arms to float back down to the sides.
11. Close eyes and stand still.

 Take feedback and questions from the whole group on the meditation.

 Three-minute breathing space, AGE – introduction or reminder if Welcome Session was done (p.23)

Introduce people if this was not already done in the Welcome Session, or remind people of the stages, then do the breathing space.

 Discuss, in pairs, how and when people will do the three-minute breathing space three times each day.

Home practice

1. Mindful exercises plus Mindfulness of Breathing – turning toward difficulties.
2. Pleasant and Unpleasant Events Diary.
3. Three-minute breathing space, AGE, three times each day.

 Three-minute breathing space, AGE (p.23)

Practice Record Form – Session 3: Accepting Experience

Record on the Practice Record Form each time you practice. Also, make a note of anything that comes up in the practice, so that we can talk about it at the next meeting.

Day/date	Mindful exercises (circle)	Mindfulness of Breathing (circle)	Comments
	Yes / No	Yes / No	
	Yes / No	Yes / No	
	Yes / No	Yes / No	
	Yes / No	Yes / No	
	Yes / No	Yes / No	
	Yes / No	Yes / No	
	Yes / No	Yes / No	

Continue your notes on this page.

Pleasant and Unpleasant Events Diary

Be aware each day of one pleasant and one unpleasant event at the time it is happening. Use the following questions to focus your awareness on the details of the experience as it is happening. Write it down later.

What was the experience?	Were you aware of the feelings while the event was happening?	How did your body feel, in detail, during this experience?
☺ Example: *Going out to buy a pint of milk – stopping, noticing the blue sky.*	*Yes*	*Hands releasing, breathing slowing, shoulders dropping, uplift of corners of mouth.*
☹ Example: *Standing in a queue at the supermarket and realizing that I am running late for an important meeting.*	*Yes*	*Churning in the stomach, tension in my shoulders, hands are sweating.*
Monday date: ☺		
☹		

What moods, feelings, judgments, and (other) thoughts accompanied this event?	What thoughts are in your mind now as you write this down?
A quiet joy, happiness – "How lovely to see some blue sky again!" "The sky is so vast," "It's great to be outside."	*Just seeing the blue sky gives me some perspective on my life.*
Angry, helpless – "Why do I always pick the wrong queue?" "They should have more checkouts at this time of day," "I really didn't want to miss this meeting."	*I must try not to squeeze so many things into one day.*

What was the experience?	Were you aware of the feelings while the event was happening?	How did your body feel, in detail, during this experience?
Tuesday date: ☺		
☺		
Wednesday date: ☺		
☺		

What moods, feelings, judgments, and (other) thoughts accompanied this event?	What thoughts are in your mind now as you write this down?

What was the experience?	Were you aware of the feelings while the event was happening?	How did your body feel, in detail, during this experience?
Thursday date: ☺		
☺		
Friday date: ☺		
☺		

What moods, feelings, judgments, and (other) thoughts accompanied this event?	What thoughts are in your mind now as you write this down?

What was the experience?	Were you aware of the feelings while the event was happening?	How did your body feel, in detail, during this experience?
Saturday date: ☺		
☹		
Sunday date: ☺		
☹		

What moods, feelings, judgments, and (other) thoughts accompanied this event?	What thoughts are in your mind now as you write this down?

Session 4: Changing Our Relationship to Thoughts
Content for Session 4: Changing Our Relationship to Thoughts

Gathering
Interpretation exercise 1: Head in hands
Interpretation exercise 2: Sentences
Mindfulness of Breathing – turning toward difficulties
Review of meditation and home practice

Break

"Favorite" thoughts questionnaire
Coping breathing space, AGE
Mindful walking
Home practice
Just sitting

 Gathering

Invite participants to bring to mind and share the following: "A time I blamed someone and I was wrong."

 Interpretation exercise 1: Head in hands

For this exercise a volunteer sits in a chair with their head in their hands. Ask participants what is happening, with the aim of getting a variety of responses. Then explore which of the responses given are fact and which are interpretation. Usually most of the responses are interpretation, and the facts – things that can be proved without a doubt – are few.

 Interpretation exercise 2: Sentences

Invite participants to notice what goes through their mind when you say the following sentences:

Taylor had fallen and broken a leg during a soccer game.
She was worried that she would miss her summer
  holidays.
She was new in her job and was concerned about the sick
  leave she would need to take.

Her mother scolded her and said it was time she grew up and behaved like an adult.

Ask for feedback. Most people find that they have revised who they thought Taylor was as the sentences proceeded. We interpret bare information all the time. When thoughts pop into our mind (as we discover, in meditation, they continually do), we tend to take them at face value and believe them. "If I've thought it, it must be true!" rather than try to evaluate the thought.

There are two broad categories of unhelpful thoughts: negative thoughts and facilitative thoughts. Negative thoughts are those that make a negative interpretation about the world, ourselves, or other people. How we interpret the world will affect how we feel. If we habitually fall into negative thinking, we are more likely to suffer, and then use an addictive behavior as a solution.

Facilitative thoughts are like rationalizations that lead to addictive behavior, for example, "I deserve a drink," or "I have had one chocolate, so I might as well finish the box."

In MBAR we are learning to change our relationship to thoughts. Instead of relating *from* the thoughts (being completely identified with them), we relate *to* the thoughts as objects of awareness. With trivial thoughts, just bringing them into awareness can lead to them disappearing. However, when thoughts mesh with one's prevailing mood, they can become more compelling, for example, "I feel so anxious, I really need a drink to steady my nerves." In these circumstances, we can still practice seeing these thoughts as just thoughts, noting them and letting them go (as best as we can), and it can be helpful to spend time turning toward the experience more fully, especially attending to the body sensations.

 Mindfulness of Breathing – turning toward difficulties (p.68)

 Review of meditation and home practice

"Favorite" thoughts questionnaire (pp.64–65).

Coping breathing space, AGE

When difficulties arise, we can modify the breathing space by turning toward the difficulties in the third stage, in which we expand our attention. For this stage, allow your attention to expand to the whole of the body, especially to any difficult sensations. We can breathe with them, softening and opening with the outbreath. If we find it helpful, we can say to ourselves, "It's okay. Whatever it is, it's okay. It's already here. Let me feel it."

Mindful walking

Walking is a great opportunity to practice becoming mindful, especially of the body sensations. We can bring awareness to our body when we are walking to the bus stop or the local shop. We can also practice in a more meditative way, in which we slow down the walking, perhaps walking up and down ten to twenty paces. This can be good to do in a park or garden, or in our own home if we have enough room.

Home practice

1. Mindfulness of Breathing – turning toward difficulties.
2. Regular and coping breathing space.
3. About ten minutes of mindful walking.

Just sitting

Two minutes' sitting meditation (or longer if time permits), with an emphasis on noticing thoughts coming and going.

Practice Record Form – Session 4: Changing Our Relationship to Thoughts

Record on the Practice Record Form each time you practice. Also, make a note of anything that comes up in the practice, so that we can talk about it at the next meeting.

Day/date	Mindfulness of Breathing (circle)	Mindful walking (circle)	Comments
	Yes / No	Yes / No	
	Yes / No	Yes / No	
	Yes / No	Yes / No	
	Yes / No	Yes / No	
	Yes / No	Yes / No	
	Yes / No	Yes / No	
	Yes / No	Yes / No	

Session 5: Taking Care of Myself

Content for Session 5: Taking Care of Myself

Gathering
Introduction to the theme
Responding to the four needs of the basic heart
    meditation
Mindfulness of Breathing – turning toward difficulties
Review of meditation and home practice

Break

Lifestyle balance
Early warning system
Emergency action plan
Home practice
Three-minute breathing space, AGE

 Gathering

Invite participants to reflect on and share the following: "Something I do to take care of myself."

Introduction to the theme

The three steps of MBAR are developing awareness, being with our experience, and making skillful choices. This session we move onto the third step – making skillful choices. Once we have brought awareness to our experience, we know what is going on, and we can then choose how best to respond to the situation. Intentionally choosing to do something is different from fleeing from our experience in a habitual way, which may only exacerbate the difficulties. In the second half of the session, we shall look at the sort of activities that can help prevent relapsing into addiction.

Responding to the four needs of the basic heart meditation (p.76)

 Mindfulness of Breathing – turning toward difficulties (pp.59–69)

 Review of meditation and home practice

Lifestyle balance

So far we have been looking at becoming aware of thoughts and emotions, and learning to be with them. We also need to make skillful choices about our life. It is worth examining our lives to see how we can minimize the stress we experience that can make us more vulnerable to relapse.

Exercise

For a typical working day, write down the activities you do. Of these note which ones lift your mood, nourish you, increase your energy (uplifts), and which ones lower your mood, make you anxious, dampen your spirits, drain your energy (hassles)?

Reflect or discuss how you could do more of what *uplifts* you or could be more aware of these activities (look for spaces even amid the busyness) and do fewer of the activities that are *hassles* (or do them less frequently). The aim is to create more of a balanced lifestyle.

If we are struggling there are two types of activities that can help lift our mood: activities that bring pleasure (P) and activities that give us a sense of accomplishment or mastery (M). Now go back to the list of your activities and mark the list with either a P or an M. How could you make some changes in your life to bring more pleasure or mastery?

Early warning system

Reflect on or discuss what the warning signals are of an
impending relapse.

Reflect on what in the past has prevented you from
noticing and attending to signs of a relapse. How can
you include others in an early warning system? What
stops you from asking for help?

Fill in the Early Warning System sheet on (p.296).

Emergency action plan

Reflect on what practical steps you can take when
things are getting difficult or you recognize the early
warning signs that could lead to a relapse.

Fill in the Emergency Action Plan sheet on (p.297).

Home practice

1. Select your own practice.
2. Breathing space (regular and coping).
3. Continue to work on early warning system and
   emergency action plan.

 Three-minute breathing space, AGE (p.23)

Practice Record Form – Session 5: Taking Care of Myself

Record on the Practice Record Form each time you practice. Also, make a note of anything that comes up in the practice, so that we can talk about it at the next meeting.

Day/date	Practice (circle)	Comments
	Yes / No	
	Yes / No	
	Yes / No	
	Yes / No	
	Yes / No	
	Yes / No	
	Yes / No	

Early Warning System

What are the signs that you may be building up to a relapse?

1. _____

2. _____

3. _____

4. _____

Who could you share this with to help you notice the early warning signs, and to respond rather than to react to them?

1. _____

2. _____

3. _____

4. _____

Emergency Action Plan

If you find yourself in a high-risk situation or craving:

1. Take a breathing space (AGE).
2. Remind yourself of the reasons you want to stay in recovery

   _____

   _____

3. Do something from the course (e.g., listen to one of the meditations) and/or do something that may give you a sense of accomplishment or pleasure.

   a. _____

   b. _____

   c. _____

   d. _____

   e. _____

4. Phone a sober support.

   a. _____ 📱_____

   b. _____ 📱_____

   c. _____ 📱_____

Session 6: Tools You Can Begin to Use in Your Daily Life

Content for Session 6: Tools You Can Begin to Use in Your Daily Life

Gathering
Introduction to the theme
Review of the relapse process
Mindfulness of Breathing – turning toward difficulties
Review of meditation and home practice, including
relapse prevention emergency action plans

Break

Review of the course
Home practice/future practice
Responding to the four basic needs of the heart
meditation

 Gathering

Invite participants to contribute "Something I've not shared with the group."

Introduction to the theme

The essence of this course has been to find skillful ways of responding to relapse-associated automatic thought patterns. Often the skillful response is to do nothing. This does not mean ignoring or pushing away unpleasant experience, which paradoxically often can lead to maintaining the difficulties. Instead we hold it in awareness, which:

- prevents automatic unhelpful habits coming into operation
- allows "wise mind" to come into operation, and clarify our experience.

On the basis of this we may then find the appropriate action to take (if any).

Review of the relapse process

One way of understanding the relapse process is illustrated below (with the example of drinking):

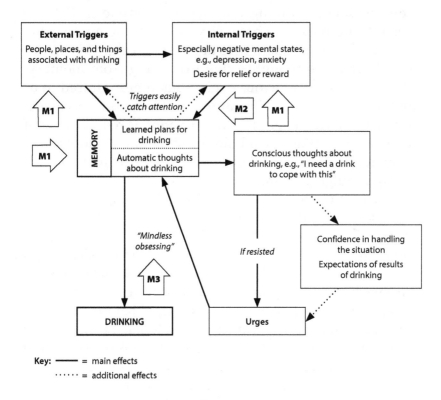

Fig. 4: Relapse process

In this model, there are two main routes to relapse. The first is pre-conscious or automatic. An external trigger (such as someone offering you a drink) or an internal trigger (such as feeling anxious) activates automatic planning and thinking from memory. In the same way that, once you have learned how to drive a car, you can do it without thinking much about it (learned behavior), your body and mind "know" how to pick up a drink and go into action automatically. For example, you feel anxious when you are out, and you find yourself being drawn toward going down a street that has a favorite pub in it (which will then be hard to pass without going in for a drink ...).

The second route to relapse is more conscious or non-automatic. In this case a trigger stimulates thoughts from memory about drinking that become conscious. If these thoughts are resisted – because you are trying not to drink – you are likely to experiences urges or craving. This in turn stimulates more thoughts about drinking from memory, which can create a vicious cycle, sometimes referred to as "mindless obsessing." The urges are likely to be greater if your confidence in handling the situation is reduced, and if you believe drinking will help the situation. Paradoxically, trying to ignore the urges makes it more likely that you will end up indulging them.

During the course we have been learning to develop awareness, so that we can become more familiar with these patterns, and be less likely to be hijacked by them. Increased mindfulness of our habitual patterns (M1 on the model) makes it less likely that you will go down the automatic relapse route. We have been learning to stay with and to accept difficulties, rather than to block them out – a strategy that may make us more likely to return to drinking as a solution. Learning to be with difficult emotions can help to break the link between those emotions and thoughts about drinking (M2). Learning to be with urges and to step out of compulsive thinking can help to reduce the likelihood of relapse through "mindless obsessing" (M3).

This map can also be placed on the floor. The facilitator can use an example and be creative in showing what can happen.

Mindfulness of Breathing – turning toward difficulties (p.68)

 Review of meditation and home practice, including relapse prevention emergency action plans

Review of the course

Reflect on what you have learned from the course, what's been helpful, what was difficult, and what you could take forward into the future.

Home practice / future practice

If this is the final session, decide which will be your main meditation practice over the next few weeks. If there is one more session, choose to practice daily a meditation of your choice until the final session.

 Responding to the four basic needs of the heart meditation (p.76)

Practice Record Form – Session 6:
Tools You Can Begin to Use in Your Daily Life

Record on the Practice Record Form each time you practice. Also, make a note of anything that comes up in the practice, so that we can talk about it at the next meeting.

Day/date	Practice (circle)	Comments
	Yes / No	
	Yes / No	
	Yes / No	
	Yes / No	
	Yes / No	
	Yes / No	
	Yes / No	

Optional Session: Closing

This optional closing session can be done in a number of ways:

Option 1: As the eighth week of an eight-week course, the focus can be on inviting participants to lead short practices, to gain more confidence in the practices.

Option 2: As a booster, for example, some weeks after the completion of the course. The emphasis is on reviewing how things have been and reconnecting with the material.

Option 1 Content	Option 2 Content
Gathering	Gathering
Mindfulness of Breathing – turning toward difficulties	Mindfulness of Breathing – turning toward difficulties
Review of meditation and home practice	Review of meditation and past few weeks
Three-minute breathing space (AGE)	*Break*
Break	Walking meditation
Responding to the four basic needs of the heart meditation	Responding to the four basic needs of the heart meditation
Looking to the future	Looking to the future
Just sitting	Just sitting

Option 1

 Gathering

Invite participants to reflect on and share "Something that I am apprehensive about."

 Mindfulness of Breathing – turning toward difficulties (p.68)

 Review of meditation and home practice

 Three-minute breathing space, AGE (p.23)

Invite participants to lead AGE. The group walks around and one of the participants says, "Stop," then leads the three-minute breathing space. Remind participants that this is something they can do in their daily life silently to themselves.

 Responding to the four basic needs of the heart meditation (p.76)

Invite a participant to lead the four basic needs of the heart meditation.

Looking to the future

Reflect on what you will take from the course and incorporate into your life, and how you will do that.

Just sitting

Two minutes' sitting meditation.

Option 2

 Gathering

Invite participants to reflect on and share "Something that has gone well over the last few weeks."

 Mindfulness of Breathing – turning toward difficulties (p.68)

 Review of meditation and past few weeks

Walking meditation

Responding to the four basic needs of the heart meditation (p.76)

Looking to the future

Reflect on what you will take from the course and incorporate into your life, and how you will do that.

Just sitting

Two minutes' sitting meditation.

....
Notes and references

Preface to the second printing

1 Kevin Griffin, *One Breath at a Time: Buddhism and the Twelve Steps*, Rodale Press, Emmaus, PA 2014; Kevin Griffin, *A Burning Desire: Dharma God and the Path of Recovery*, Hay House, London 2010; Noah Levine, *Refuge Recovery: A Buddhist Path to Recovering from Addiction*, HarperOne, New York 2014; Valerie Mason-John, *Detox Your Heart: Meditations on Emotional Trauma*, Wisdom Publications, Somerville, MA 2017.

Foreword by Gabor Maté

1 *The Long Discourses of the Buddha: A Translation of the Digha Nikaya*, trans. Maurice Walsh, Wisdom Publications, Boston 1995, p.70.
2 Sogyal Rinpoche, *The Tibetan Book of Living and Dying*, HarperSanFrancisco, San Francisco 1996, p.316.

Introduction

1 Paramabandhu Groves and Roger Farmer, "Buddhism and Addictions," *Addiction Research & Theory*, 2:2 (1994), pp.183–94.
2 Zindel V. Segal, J. Mark G. Williams, and John D. Teasdale, *Mindfulness-Based Cognitive Therapy for Depression: A New Approach to Preventing Relapse*, Guilford Press, New York 2002.
3 *Dhammacakkappavattana Sutta: Setting in Motion the Wheel of Truth*, trans. Piyadassi Thera, available at http://www.accesstoinsight.org/tipitaka/sn/sn56/sn56.011.piya.html, accessed on September 6, 2013.

Step One: accepting that this human life will bring suffering

1 M. Scott Peck, *The Road Less Travelled: A New Psychology of Love, Traditional Values and Spiritual Growth*, Rider, London 2003, p.3.
2 Pema Chödrön, *The Places that Scare You: A Guide to Fearlessness in Difficult Times*, Shambhala, Boston 2001, p.75.

....

Step Two: seeing how we create extra suffering in our lives

1 Shinzen Young, "Break through Pain: Practical Steps for Transforming Physical Pain into Spiritual Growth," available at http://www.shinzen.org/Articles/artPain.htm, accessed on September 6, 2013.
2 See Dr. Gabor Maté's best-selling book *In the Realm of Hungry Ghosts: Close Encounters with Addiction*, Knopf Canada, Toronto 2008.
3 Jon Kabat-Zinn, *Full Catastrophe Living*, Delta, New York 1990.
4 MESS: Acronym first coined by Abe Brown, president of the Certified Coaches Federation.

Step Three: embracing impermanence to show us that our suffering can end

1 Mark Williams and Danny Penman, *Mindfulness: A Practical Guide to Finding Peace in a Frantic World*, Piatkus, London 2011.

Step Five: transforming our speech, actions, and livelihood

1 This quote has variously been attributed to the Chinese philosopher Lao Tzu, the late president of BI-LO stores Frank Outlaw, and American essayist Ralph Waldo Emerson.
2 Interview with Anita Roddick (founder of the international franchise The Body Shop, which produces natural and ethical body products), available at http://www.shareguide.com/Roddick.html, accessed on September 6, 2013.
3 "On the Meaning of OM MANI PADME HUM: The Jewel Is in the Lotus or Praise to the Jewel in the Lotus," available at http://enlight.lib.ntu.edu.tw/FULLTEXT/JR-AN/an141056.pdf, accessed on September 6, 2013.

Step Eight: helping others by sharing the benefits we have gained

1 *Dhammapada: The Way of Truth*, trans. Sangharakshita, Windhorse Publications, Birmingham 2001, p.13.
2 *The Maranasati Sutta*, in *The Numerical Discourses of the Buddha: A Translation of the Anguttara Nikaya*, trans. Bhikkhu Bodhi, Wisdom Publications, Boston 2012, VI, 20.
3 *The Kalama Sutta*, in *In the Buddha's Words: An Anthology of Discourses from the Pali Canon*, ed. by Bhikkhu Bodhi, Wisdom Publications, Boston 2005, pp.89–90.

Tools for recovery

1 Buddhaghosa, *Visuddhimagga: The Path of Purification* (traditional commentary, fifth century AD), trans. Bhikkhu Nanamoli, available at http://www.accesstoinsight.org/lib/authors/nanamoli/PathofPurification2011.pdf, p.272, accessed on September 16, 2013.
2 Sharon Salzberg, *Loving Kindness*, Shambhala, Boston 1995, p.18.

Appendix 2: Mindfulness-Based Addiction Recovery (MBAR) Course

1 Zindel V. Segal, J. Mark G. Williams, and John D. Teasdale, *Mindfulness-Based Cognitive Therapy for Depression: A New Approach to Preventing Relapse*, Guilford Press, New York 2002.
2 Icon made by Freepik from www.flaticon.com.

Index

WINDHORSE PUBLICATIONS

Windhorse Publications is a Buddhist charitable company based in the UK. Our books, which are distributed internationally, champion Buddhism, meditation, and mindfulness. They offer fresh interpretations of Buddhist teachings and their application to contemporary life, with subject matter and authors from across the Buddhist tradition, catering for a broad range of interest and experience. In addition to publishing titles exploring classic texts for modern audiences, we aspire to publish books that offer a Buddhist perspective on today's challenges, including social inequality, the environment and climate, gender, mental health, and more. Established in the 1970s to publish the writing of Urgyen Sangharakshita (1925–2018), the founder of the Triratna Buddhist Order, Windhorse Publications continues to be dedicated to preserving and keeping in print his impressive and influential body of work, making it accessible for future generations. As well as high quality print and eBooks, Windhorse Publications produces accompanying audio, podcast, video, and teaching resources.

Windhorse Publications
38 Newmarket Road
Cambridge CB5 8DT
info@windhorsepublications.com

North America Distributors:
Consortium Book Sales & Distribution
210 American Drive
Jackson TN 38301
USA
www.cbsd.com

Australia and New Zealand Distributors:
Windhorse Books
PO Box 574
Newtown NSW 2042
Australia
windhorse.com.au/books.html

THE TRIRATNA BUDDHIST COMMUNITY

Windhorse Publications is a part of the Triratna Buddhist Community, an international movement with centres in Europe, India, North and South America, and Australasia. At these centres, members of the Triratna Buddhist Order offer classes in meditation and Buddhism. Activities of the Triratna Community also include retreat centres, residential spiritual communities, ethical Right Livelihood businesses, and the Karuna Trust, a UK fundraising charity that supports social welfare projects in the slums and villages of India.

Through these and other activities, Triratna is developing a unique approach to Buddhism, not simply as a philosophy and a set of techniques, but as a creatively directed way of life for all people living in the conditions of the modern world.

If you would like more information about Triratna please visit thebuddhistcentre.com or write to:

London Buddhist Centre
51 Roman Road
London E2 0HU
UK
contact@lbc.org.uk

Aryaloka
14 Heartwood Circle
Newmarket NH 03857
USA
info@aryaloka.org

Sydney Buddhist Centre
24 Enmore Road
Sydney NSW 2042
Australia
info@sydneybuddhistcentre.org.au

Entertaining Cancer
The Buddhist Way

Devamitra

You're diagnosed with an aggressive cancer – what do you do?

Devamitra – English actor and Buddhist teacher – describes the discomforts and indignities of being treated for prostate cancer. He draws on the deep well of his Buddhist practice to work with his mind and meet fear, uncertainty and frailty with resolve.

Devamitra has written a compelling book about his cancer journey that straddles a wide range of emotions: gruelling, funny, poignant and uplifting. You are drawn into his world as he undergoes particularly challenging treatment, whilst always maintaining a uniquely wry, even amused, perspective on life and death. – Vidyamala Burch, co-founder of Breathworks, author of *Living Well with Pain and Illness* and *Mindfulness for Health*

This is a remarkable book – honest, lucid, unflinching, funny and radical in its willingness to confront the facts of life and death. Devamitra tells the story of prostate cancer, and how his Buddhist practice met the challenges of diagnosis and treatment, even how cancer led to the deepening of his practice and his love of life. – Maitreyabandhu, author of *Life with Full Attention* and *The Journey and the Guide*

Quite often stories about cancer are framed in terms of a battle. This isn't always helpful, as it implies that disease progression means defeat or failure. Devamitra frames his account with interweaving themes of struggle, victory and setback, but also of calm and insight. We hear this story flavoured with his deep engagement with Buddhist teachings and practice, and his devotion to his teacher. – William Stones, Professor of Obstetrics and Gynaecology and researcher in global health

Who would have thought that having cancer could be so instructive, and at times so amusing? Devamitra writes of his experiences with a style unique to him: beautifully crafted, engaging, witty, poignant, reflective and always disarmingly honest. Devamitra faces his test as a Buddhist, but he wears his Buddhism lightly, even though it is Buddhism that guides him through it. – Subhuti, author of *Mind in Harmony*

ISBN 978 1 911407 88 1
224 pages

The Burning House
A Buddhist Response to the Climate and Ecological Emergency

Shantigarbha

We are living in an age of climate and ecological emergency. Buddhist teacher and Nonviolent Communication trainer Shantigarbha suggests practical ways to make a difference. With personal stories, examples and guided reflections you will learn to work with doubt, overwhelm, grief and anger; engage with the science of the climate debates; free yourself to align with life; and act with courage, humour and generosity.

One thing is certain: no meaningful systemic change in response to the ecological and climate emergency faced by all planetary life will be possible without a shift in human consciousness. This beautifully crafted, accessible book skilfully weaves Buddhist teachings, the author's personal journey and a passionate political and ethical commitment to an empathic path of transformation. – Anna Grear, founder of the Global Network for the Study of Human Rights and the Environment (GNHRE); Editor in Chief *Journal of Human Rights and the Environment*

How can Buddhism help us understand and respond to the greatest challenge that humanity has ever faced? Shantigarbha provides a welcome and very accessible introduction to the relevant teachings and how to embody them in our practice and activism. – David Loy, author of *Ecodharma: Buddhist Teachings for the Ecological Crisis*

The ecological crisis is nothing if not a spiritual crisis, a crisis of meaning and direction for our civilisation. The Burning House *is approachably written, and abides by the precautionary principle: moving as we are in a fog, it behoves us to slow down. Take a pause, and read this book.* – Professor Rupert Read, author of *This Civilisation Is Finished*, and former student of Thich That Hanh and Joanna Macy

For so many years now, we have heard the alarm of the climate and ecological emergency sounding, telling us that the house is on fire. If, like so many of us, you are uncertain what a Buddhist response to the climate emergency would look like, you will find Shantigarbha's book very helpful indeed. – Vajrashura, Dharma teacher in the Triratna Buddhist Community

ISBN 978 1 911407 75 1
272 pages

Life with Full Attention
A Practical Course in Mindfulness

Maitreyabandhu

In this eight-week course on mindfulness, Maitreyabandhu teaches you how to pay closer attention to experience. Each week he introduces a different aspect of mindfulness – such as awareness of the body, feelings, thoughts and the environment – and recommends a number of easy practices; from trying out a simple meditation to reading a poem. Featuring personal stories, examples and suggestions, Life with Full Attention is a valuable aid to mindfulness both as a starting point and for the more experienced.

ISBN 9781 899579 98 3
328 pages

Buddhism
Tools for Living Your Life

Vajragupta

In this guide for all those seeking a meaningful spiritual path, Vajragupta provides clear explanations of the main Buddhist teachings, as well as a variety of exercises designed to help readers develop or deepen their practice.

Appealing, readable, and practical, blending accessible teachings, practices, and personal stories . . . as directly relevant to modern life as it is comprehensive and rigorous. – Tricycle: The Buddhist Review, 2007

I'm very pleased that someone has finally written this book! At last, a real 'toolkit' for living a Buddhist life, his practical suggestions are hard to resist! – Saddhanandi, Chair of Taraloka Retreat Centre

ISBN 9781 899579 74 7
192 pages

Introducing Mindfulness
Buddhist Background and Practical Exercises

Bhikkhu Anālayo

Buddhist meditator and scholar Bhikkhu Anālayo introduces the Buddhist background to mindfulness practice, from mindful eating to its formal cultivation as *satipaṭṭhāna* (the foundations of mindfulness). As well as providing an accessible guide, Bhikkhu Anālayo gives a succinct historical survey of the development of mindfulness in Buddhism, and practical exercises on how to develop it.

A wise and helpful presentation of essential elements of the Buddha's teaching . . . it will be of great value for those who wish to put these teachings into practice. A wonderful Dharma gift. – Joseph Goldstein, author of *Mindfulness: A Practical Guide to Awakening*

A gold mine for anyone who is working in the broad field of mindfulness-based programs for addressing health and wellbeing in the face of suffering – in any or all of its guises. – Jon Kabat-Zinn, author of *Meditation Is Not What You Think: Mindfulness and Why It Is So Important*

Bhikkhu Anālayo offers simple skilled mindfulness practices for each of the dimensions of this book. Open-minded practices of embodied mindfulness are described, beginning with eating and health, and continuing with mindfulness examining mind and body, our relation to death, and the nature of the mind itself. Significantly, by highlighting the earliest teachings on internal and external mindfulness, Bhikkhu Anālayo shows how, individually and collectively, we can use mindfulness to bring a liberating understanding to ourselves and to the pressing problems of our global, social, modern world. We need this more than ever. – Jack Kornfield, from the Foreword

ISBN 978 1 911407 57 7
176 pages

Not About Being Good
A Practical Guide to Buddhist Ethics

Subhadramati

While there are numerous books on Buddhist meditation and philosophy, there are few books that are entirely devoted to the practice of Buddhist ethics. Subhadramati communicates clearly both their founding principles and the practical methods to embody them.

Buddhist ethics are not about conforming to a set of conventions, not about 'being good' in order to gain rewards. Instead, living ethically springs from the awareness that other people are no different from yourself. You can actively develop this awareness, through cultivating love, clarity and contentment. Helping you to come into greater harmony with all that lives, this is ultimately your guidebook to a more satisfactory life.

In touch with the wonder of being alive, Subhadramati is a realistic and sympathetic guide to ethics in the twenty-first century. – Vidyamala Burch, author of *Mindfulness for Health*

Writing with passion, humour and delicacy, gloriously free from moralism, her aim is to help us live a richer and fuller life. – Maitreyabandhu, author of *Life with Full Attention*

Places ethics and meditation at the heart of Buddhist practice, and shows how they work together in transforming ordinary human beings into Buddhas. – Professor Damien Keown, author of *The Nature of Buddhist Ethics*

ISBN 9781 909314 01 6
176 pages